Making the most of
Cheese & Wine

ROBERT CARRIER'S KITCHEN

Making the most of Cheese & Wine

Editor	Roz Fishel
Editorial Staff	Caroline Macy
	Kate Toner
	Jill Wiley
	Fiona Wilson
Designer	Alan White
Series Editor	Pepita Aris
Production Executive	Robert Paulley
Production Controller	Steve Roberts

Photography
Bryce Attwell: 10, 35, 103
Theo Bergstrom: 83, 92
Paul Bussell: 16, 19, 29, 36, 40, 54, 82, 88, 99
Alan Duns: 50, 52
Laurie Evans: 31, 69, 77, 86, 87, 96
Edmund Goldspink: 66
Melvin Grey: 44
Tony Hurley: 2, 64, 72
James Jackson: 13, 46, 47, 75, 107, 110
Chris Knaggs: 11, 14, 78, 94
Don Last: 17
David Levin: 26, 68
Vernon Morgan: 28
Peter Myers: 8, 14, 15, 42, 67, 70, 71, 74, 81, 84, 97, 100, 105
Roger Phillips: 18, 60, 62, 101
Paul Williams: 30, 53, 80, 91, 109
Cover picture: **Tony Hurley**

Weights and measures
Both metric and imperial measurements are given. As these are not exact equivalents, please work from one set of figures or the other. Use graded measuring spoons levelled across.

Time symbols
The time needed to prepare the dish is given on each recipe. The symbols are as follows:

  simple to prepare and cook

  straightforward but requires more skill or attention

  time-consuming to prepare or requires extra skill

  must be started 1 day or more ahead

On the cover: A selection of cheeses and wines

New wine guide, page 63, courtesy the Wine Development Board, London EC4V 3BH

This edition published 1986
© Marshall Cavendish Limited 1986

Printed in Italy by L.E.G.O. S.p.A. Vicenza

Typeset by Quadraset Limited, Midsomer Norton, Bath, Avon

Published by Marshall Cavendish House
58 Old Compton Street London W1V 5PA
ISBN 0 86307 264 X (series)   ISBN 0 86307 415 4 (this volume)

Contents

If you tend to think of using only Cheddar cheese in your cooking, then read the first section of this volume *Making the most of Cheese & Wine* which includes four chapters on cheese — Hard cheeses, European soft cheeses, Semi-hard and semi-soft cheeses, and Blue cheeses. The hard cheese chapter does include Cheddar but also Cheshire, Lancashire and a good selection of other British and foreign cheeses, some more well-known and popular than others. From Buck rarebit (Welsh rarebit with an egg on top), Spaghetti loaf, Apple and cheese pie, Broccoli cheese with almonds to Scalloped haddock, the recipes are all tasty and interesting. Be adventurous and try the Camembert soup from the European soft cheese section — it was originally made with champagne, but if that seems a little extravagant, then it is just as good made with a dry white wine.

The semi-hard and semi-soft cheese chapter gives you first some information about the methods of making the different cheeses and then pages of delicious recipes, including Cheese in vine leaves, Dutch savoury truffles and two different fondues. Blue cheeses are the aristocrats of the cheeseboard, but instead of only using them to round off a meal, try a starter of Pears with Roquefort and watercress dressing; or use Gorgonzola or Dolcelatte to stuff grapes and gooseberries for spectacular cocktail snacks. Any left-over fragments of Stilton can be put to good use in the 200-year-old recipe for Potted Stilton.

Are you intimidated by a wine list? Do you feel that you do not know enough about wines to choose which ones go with different courses, meals or occasions? Well, my Wine section should help you. I give you essential information for buying, storing and serving wine and I describe wines from most of Europe's wine-producing countries, not just France, Italy, Spain and Germany but also Hungary, Romania and England. With each chapter I have included recipes, either using wine in the dish or suggesting the appropriate wine to serve with the recipe. However, if you are prepared to be patient and want to try making your own wines, then there are four recipes specially to start you off.

Happy cooking and bon appétit!

Robert Carrier

Cheese

HARD CHEESES

Nearly all hard cheeses have their place on the cheeseboard but they are also the ones most often used in cooking. Here I show you how to use their well-flavoured nourishment in a large range of exciting dishes.

Hard cheeses, used to give their distinctive flavour to a host of basic ingredients, will turn the recipes into something sensational. Buck rarebit (see page 11) is probably the simplest yet most classic example of how the full flavour of mature Cheddar cheese may be used to spice-up a plain slice of bread. Topped with a fried or poached egg you have created a tasty snack that is full of goodness.

Cheddar is probably the best known of the hard cheeses, and the method of cheese-making called 'cheddaring' was developed before Tudor times on West Country farms. Parmesan, the pungent Italian grating cheese, has been famous for centuries as the finest cheese for seasoning. It is often used together with other cheeses to enchance the flavour of the dish, as in my Gruyère soufflé (see page 14). Swiss Emmental and Gruyère are particularly prized for their keeping and unrivalled melting qualities, and my Cheese fondue recipe (see page 15) uses both cheeses, for this typical Swiss dish, to full advantage.

Although all these, and a good many more, are described as 'hard' cheeses, they are all different in texture, made under different conditions and by different methods.

Characteristics of hard cheeses

All hard cheeses share four important features, set out below, which distinguish them from the soft, semi-hard and blue cheeses.

Pressing: all hard cheeses are dry and compact because they are pressed. Some liquid whey is allowed to drip out, as in making any cheese, but the process is continued under increasing pressure, for a varying time, to dry out and condense the cheese further before it is cured and ripened. Hard cheeses are pressed for longer than soft or blue cheeses, and unlike the blues, are not aerated before pressing — the holes found in Emmental and Gruyère are not air pockets, they are made by acid gases.

Maturing: because pressure and fairly long ripening make most hard cheeses comparatively dry, they do not turn rancid quickly. As a result they can mature slowly, taking time to reach their peak flavour. They can also become harder and stronger-flavoured with age. Some, like the grainy Italian cheeses, take a long time to reach their best and are by then very hard and strong-flavoured indeed. Moisture content and degree of protection from the air determine how long a hard cheese stays at its best when mature. A traditional, bandaged Farmhouse English Cheddar or rinded Emmental profits by being matured for nine months or more. Moister, softer Lancashire is at its best 2–3 months after being made.

Storing qualities: hard cheeses store better than any other kind of cheese when cut. Even if a piece of Cheddar or Double Gloucester grows a surface mould, you can scrape it off and use the cheese underneath. Crumbly cheeses keep less well in the refrigerator, but Cheddar and Swiss-style cheeses can be refrigerated for up to two weeks without deteriorating, if properly wrapped. Wrap the cheese closely in foil — not cling film in which the cheese is unable to breathe — keep it in the refrigerator, and remove it two hours before using.

To freeze hard cheese in a block, double wrap it, first in foil, then in cling film. Freeze grated cheese in a well-sealed plastic bag; take out as much as you need at a time, then reseal and refreeze the remainder. Always thaw frozen cheese before you use it for cooking — its texture tends to change and become crumbly after freezing, so it is better used for this purpose, although it can still be eaten at the table.

Cooking qualities: hard cheeses are the great cooking cheeses. Their matured flavour and aroma change pleasantly when heated, and they grate and melt quickly and easily.

When any cheese is heated, its casein (protein) molecules coagulate and trap the globules of fat surrounding them. If the cheese is heated too quickly or to an unduly high temperature, the globules of fat melt and separate from the casein; then the casein shrinks and toughens, and the cheese becomes stringy. Therefore, always melt cheese as slowly and gently—but also as briefly—as you can. Grated cheese melts much more easily than sliced or block cheese.

Fish, egg and vegetable dishes made with bechamel sauce flavoured with Parmesan and Gruyère cheese, for instance, are described as 'mornay'; those with a crisp topping made of

cheese and breadcrumbs as 'gratin'. If you want to toast or bake a dish with a grated or sliced cheese 'gratin' topping, using a high heat cover the cheese with foil at first while heating it; or mix the cheese with a little white sauce, or mix grated Parmesan with breadcrumbs, a little flour or extra butter, to be sure of getting a pliable, tasty coating.

English hard cheeses

Below I describe eight of the best-known English hard cheeses.

Cheddar has developed over the centuries from the West Somerset farms where the 'cheddaring' method of handling cheese is used. Cheddar-type cheeses are now made throughout the world by this process. However, none is quite the same as the real Farmhouse English Cheddar, which is still made on about 30 West Country farms.

First, the newly separated, fluffy curd is gently and slowly heated, then drip-drained.

Next, it is cut into 10–15 cm /4–6 in slabs to drain out more whey; when firm enough not to squash, the slabs are piled on top of each other and turned frequently to squeeze out the remaining moisture. Only after this are the curds milled to release the last of the whey, then they are salted, put into moulds and pressed. Traditionally-made Cheddar is dipped in hot water to give it a tough, thin, protective rind, which is salted, rubbed with fat and bandaged before the cheese is cured in a warm place and then matured in cooler storage rooms.

Farmhouse English Cheddar varies slightly in flavour, depending on which farm it comes from, but it is always nutty, richly full-flavoured and strong, though not bitter. It has a close, buttery texture and should not flake when cut. Do not confuse cheeses labelled 'mature' with Farmhouse which will be so labelled. Mature Cheddar is strong in flavour but is creamery-made in bulk, so lacks the full roundness that long-ripening

gives to the traditional Farmhouse cheeses.

Some creamery-made Cheddars made in other countries are as strong or stronger than mature English Cheddar, while some English Cheddars can be very mild. A good shop will let you taste a little of the cheese sold unwrapped from a large block or drum. Packaged Cheddar is consistent in its flavour according to the manufacturer, so try a selection to find the one you prefer.

Flavoured Cheddars include Windsor Red, which is a deep-pink, marbled mature cheese, once made with claret, but now made with elderberry wine. Rutland is flavoured with beer, garlic and parsley. Smoked Cheddar has recently become extremely popular.

Cheshire is the oldest English cheese. It is only made in Cheshire where certain salts in the soil impregnate the milk and give the cheese a subtle, salty flavour. So creamery Cheshire, which is usually medium-ripened, is more reliable in quality than the creamery Cheddar. However, the Farmhouse English Cheshire, made on only a few farms, is unmatched for its full, rich flavour — it may be slow ripened for as long as nine months — and for its crumbly texture. North Country people like their Cheshire white, but for elsewhere, Cheshire is dyed a pale apricot colour (called 'red') with anatto, a flavourless plant dye.

Lancashire is the only other English cheese of this type made on farms for public sale, but its short shelf life of 2–3 months makes it difficult to sell outside its local area. It is very smooth and white; even at three months old it should be spreadable like butter, and it melts to a custardy consistency when heated. Its flavour makes it excellent for cooking, and the best quality Farmhouse English Lancashire used to be called the 'Leigh Toaster' after the area where it was made and the way it was most often used.

Wensleydale is usually sold before being fully ripened, when it is still mild and tastes of buttermilk. It is a cheese that spreads easily and is especially good to eat with apples.

Derby was originally a honey-coloured cheese, but green Sage Derby, flavoured with the herb, is now very popular. It is sometimes made with a broad green band running through it, or it may be speckled or streaked throughout with green.

Leicester has a bright red colour and is

1 Jarlsberg; 2 Windsor Red; 3 Emmental;
4 Sage Derby; 5 White Cheshire; 6 Samsø;
7 Double Gloucester; 8 Rutland; 9 Parmesan;
10 Havarti; 11 Pecorino; 12 Sherwood;
13 Smoked Cheddar; 14 Leicester;
15 Farmhouse Cheddar; 16 Gruyère

quick-melting. It is moister than Cheddar and therefore has a shorter shelf life, reaching it peak at about six months old.

Double Gloucester has increased its reputation in recent years. Although made from thinner milk than formerly, it is still a rich cheese, especially if made from mid-summer milk and matured for nine months or more. At this point it has a close, satiny texture and a rich, gold colour. Cotswold, which is flavoured with chopped onion and chives, and Sherwood, which is flavoured with sweet-and-sour mixed pickles, are variations.

Caerphilly, formerly Welsh, now ranks as an English cheese because these days most is made in Somerset and Wiltshire. It is pressed much more lightly than the other hard cheeses and so is pale and springy; it is also slightly acid in taste since it is eaten very young, within 2–3 weeks of making.

Cheddar types

Cheddar has been imitated more than any other cheese. Some of the copies, however, notably the North American ones, have turned out so different and so good that they rank as first-class cheeses in their own right and have acquired distinctively different names. Canada has remained faithful to the name of Cheddar and makes the strongest of the Cheddars exported, as well as a smoked one. The U.S. makes a whole family of Cheddar-type cheeses grouped together as 'American cheese'. There are wheels, cylinders and blocks, white, yellow and orange, ranging in flavour from very mild to strong (called 'sharp' in the U.S.). Coon, Pineapple, Barrel, Daisy and Longhorn are among the best-known names. Colby and Monterey Jack are perhaps the best-known

U.S. cheeses; although similar to Cheddars, they are in fact hard cheeses with the rind washed in brine. Monterey Jack is copied from an old Spanish cheese introduced into Mexico in the 17th century.

Other countries also make Cheddar-type cheeses using the name Cheddar. New Zealand cheese production is mostly mild Cheddar. Australian Cheddar is made exactly as in Britain. A mild Cheddar-Edam type called Cheedam is also made. A few other nations make distinctive hard cheeses. The French Cantal is not unlike Cheddar to eat. A near relative of Cheshire cheese, called Chester, is also made in France.

Hard-grating cheeses

The hard-grating cheeses have rather grainy textures. In Italy they are known as *formaggi di grana*.

Parmesan is the world's most renowned hard-grating cheese and also one of the oldest, originating about the 12th century. It comes from an area containing five cities — Parma, Reggio Emilia, Modena, Bologna and part of Mantua — and was given its official name, Parmigiano-Reggiano, because Reggio Emilia complained it was only named after Parma.

True Parmesan is made by being 'cooked' in steam and then pressed and salted. It is cured for six months while being oiled and cleaned and given a protective coating. It is then matured for 2–3 years, during which time it develops an iron-hard rind.

Try to buy Parmesan in a piece and grate it for yourself. It has an incomparably fresh flavour, entirely different from the taste of the ready-grated Parmesan in packets. A well-aged block of Parmesan is pale yellow with

some spore-like grain marks. As it bruises white where the knife cuts it, it will have whitish streaks here and there. If it has a lot of these or a great many spore-marks, it is over-aged and has dried out.

You can eat well-aged Parmesan at the table if you cut it from the centre, away from the rind. However, a younger piece, whiter and slightly more moist, crumbly and easy to cut, will give the superb flavour of Parmesan without the 'edge' it acquires with age.

Grana Padano is another cheese that is very good for grating. It is made the year round, all over Italy; it is not as reliable in quality as Parmesan since it is not aged for so long. Paler and flakier when cut, with a sharp taste, it is often sold grated.

Other Italian grating cheeses: Grana Lodigiano and Grana Lombardo are made from low-fat cow's milk, while Pecorino Romano, from Rome, and Sardo, from Sardinia, are made from matured sheep's milk and have a very distinctive, acid taste.

Sbrinz (sometimes called Spalen) is made in central Switzerland and considered so good as a grating cheese that it is even exported to Italy. It is aromatic and sharp-flavoured but not bitter and it can be eaten as a table cheese, although it is used more for cooking. Cheese which is sufficiently hard for grating is also produced in other countries, for example the Greek Kefalotyli.

Swiss-style cheeses

Firm cheeses with holes are always associated with Switzerland, and rightly, because a great Swiss Emmental or Gruyère is unique, the result of centuries of training in producing cheeses which are notoriously difficult to make. However, unless the cheese has 'Switzerland' stamped on the rind it may be one of the great number of copies made in many different countries. Though some are very good, in my opinion, there is still a fragrance and texture in a real Swiss cheese which escapes even the best imitators.

Emmental is a long-lasting, superb cooking cheese, as smooth and clean to cut as butter, and pale yellow or ivory in colour. Its holes are round, about the size of cherries. Its flavour is slightly sweet, rather like mellow hazelnuts, without any bite. Four months' maturing time is the minimum required by Swiss law, but most Emmental is ripened for longer — sometimes up to ten months. It is also sold smoked, in a 'sausage'.

Gruyère is similar to Emmental in colour and texture, and is also excellent for cooking, but its holes are tiny slits or teardrop-shaped cracks, and it is pressed harder, salted more and has a slightly greasy rind. It is also matured longer, for a minimum of eight months, and therefore has a lower water content than Emmental.

Swiss types from other countries: France produces distinguished cheeses of the Gruyère type: Comté and Beaufort are both derived from Swiss Gruyère. From Norway there is Jarlsberg, which is a semi-hard cheese which becomes hard with time. The Danish Samsø is derived from Emmental and has a relatively firm paste. Another Danish cheese often hardened is Havarti.

Welsh rarebit

Buck rarebit

 10 minutes

Serves 4
4 eggs
30 g /1¼ oz butter, plus extra for spreading
salt and freshly ground black pepper
15 ml /1 tbls flour
45 ml /3 tbls milk
30 ml /2 tbls brown ale or beer
5 ml /1 tsp mild Dijon mustard
2–3 drops Worcestershire sauce
150 g /5 oz mature Cheddar cheese, grated
4 thick slices of white bread

1 Heat enough water in an egg poacher to poach the eggs. Grease 4 cups of the poacher with a little of the butter. Break an egg into each cup and season them lightly with salt and pepper. Cover and leave the eggs to poach gently (about 4 minutes).
2 Meanwhile, melt the remaining butter in a saucepan. Stir in the flour and cook gently, stirring for 2 minutes, without letting the flour colour. Gradually stir in the milk. Now, very thoroughly mix in the ale or beer, mustard and Worcestershire sauce.
3 Remove the pan from the heat and very gradually stir the grated cheese into the mixture, until the cheese is melted. Season.
4 Toast and butter the bread. Turn the grill to medium heat. Spread the rarebit mixture evenly over the buttered sides of the toast. Lay the slices on the grill rack, cheese side up, and grill for 2 minutes.
5 Slip an egg on top of each and serve.

● This dish can be served without the egg and is then called Welsh rarebit.

Tomato and cheese slices

 40 minutes, plus
1 hour 20 minutes rising

Makes 32
a pinch of sugar
15 g /½ oz fresh yeast or 6 g /¼ oz dried yeast
50 g /2 oz butter, plus extra for greasing
450 g /1 lb flour, plus extra for dusting
5 ml /1 tsp salt
1 medium-sized egg, beaten
For the topping
350 g /12 oz matured Cheddar cheese, grated
900 g /2 lb tomatoes
salt and freshly ground black pepper
10 ml /2 tsp fresh basil

1 To make the base, measure 200 ml /7 fl oz of warm water into a jug, add the sugar and sprinkle on the yeast. Stir and leave the mixture to stand for 10–15 minutes, until frothy. Next, grease two shallow 33 × 23 cm / 13 × 9 in tins.
2 Sieve the flour and salt into a bowl and rub in the butter. Make a well in the centre and add the egg and the yeast mixture. Pull the dry ingredients into the liquid and work them together to form a soft dough.

Cotswold scones

3 On a floured board, knead the dough until it is smooth, then place it in a floured bowl and cover it with a cloth. Set it to rise in a warm place until the dough has doubled in size (about 40–50 minutes).
4 Knock back the dough and knead it briefly. Divide it into two and place a piece in each of the tins. Flatten each piece of dough in turn with your hands, pressing and pushing it evenly over the tin and into the corners. The dough will form quite a thin layer. Thicken the edges into a rim.
5 Sprinkle the cheese over each dough base. Slice the tomatoes and spread them over the surface of the cheese on both bases.
6 Heat the oven to 220C /425F /gas 7. Season the tomatoes with salt and pepper and basil. Set the tins in a warm place for about 15 minutes.
7 Bake for 15 minutes. Slice each piece into 16 and serve the slices hot.

Cotswold scones

 25 minutes

Makes 12 scones
275 g /10 oz self-raising flour
2.5 ml /½ tsp salt
a pinch of ground white pepper
2.5 ml /½ tsp mustard powder
50 g /2 oz butter, diced small
25 g /1 oz raw minced beef
25 g /1 oz button mushrooms, finely chopped
5 ml /1 tsp grated onion
75 g /3 oz Cotswold or Double Gloucester cheese, grated
50–75 ml /2–3 fl oz milk

1 Heat the oven to 230C /450F /gas 8. In a mixing bowl, mix the flour, salt, pepper and mustard. Rub in the butter with your fingertips until the mixture resembles crumbs.
2 Stir the mince, mushrooms, onion and

50 g /2 oz of the cheese into the mixture in the bowl. Bind the ingredients with enough milk to make a soft, but not sticky, dough.
3 On a lightly floured board, pat out the dough into a rectangle about 20 mm /¾ in thick. (Patting rather than rolling the dough makes the scones rise better.) Evenly sprinkle the dough with the remaining grated cheese, pressing it in lightly. Now cut the dough into 12 rectangles.
4 Bake for 10–15 minutes. Eat hot or cold.

● The scones are excellent served with cheese, pickles and salad.

Cheese beignets

 30 minutes

Serves 4
3 medium-sized eggs, separated
1.5 ml /¼ tsp salt
50 g /2 oz butter
90 ml /6 tbls flour
oil, for deep frying
175 g /6 oz Gruyère cheese, grated
25 g /1 oz Parmesan or Sbrinz cheese, grated

1 Beat the yolks until frothy. Separately, whisk the whites and salt until stiff.
2 Melt the butter in a small saucepan. Stir in the flour. Stirring continuously, add 225 ml /8 fl oz water. Continue stirring until the mixture boils, thickens and becomes smooth. Remove the pan from the heat.
3 Heat the oil in a deep-fat frier to 180C / 350F; at this temperature a bread cube will brown in 60 seconds.
4 Beating continuously, add the egg yolks, a little at a time, and the Gruyère cheese to the hot sauce. Now fold in the egg whites.
5 Fry 15 ml /1 tbls batter, a few at a time, turning them once with a slotted spoon. When golden, remove and leave to drain on absorbent paper. Sprinkle with Parmesan or Sbrinz cheese and serve.

Souffléed cheese boulettes

 30 minutes

Makes 15
oil, for deep frying
5 egg whites
175 g /6 oz Gruyère cheese, freshly grated
50 g /2 oz Parmesan cheese, freshly grated
1 egg yolk
a pinch of cayenne pepper
freshly ground black pepper
fresh white breadcrumbs

1   Heat the oil in a deep-fat frier to 170C / 340F.
2   Whisk the egg whites until stiff but not dry. Gently, but thoroughly, fold in the grated Gruyère and Parmesan cheeses.
3   Using a fork, beat the egg yolks lightly, adding the cayenne and freshly ground black pepper to taste. Fold the yolk lightly into the cheese and egg white mixture.
4   Spread the breadcrumbs in a shallow dish. Using 15 ml /1 tbls of the cheese and egg mixture at a time, form 15 balls and roll them in the breadcrumbs until coated.
5   Drop the boulettes in the hot oil, a few at a time, and deep fry for 3 minutes or until they are puffed and golden.
6   Remove them from the oil with a slotted spoon, drain on absorbent paper and serve the boulettes immediately.

Pot roast of lamb

 2 hours

Serves 4–6
1 kg /2¼ lb fillet end of leg of lamb, boned
salt
freshly ground black pepper
paprika
6 large slices of tongue
6 × 12.5 × 7.5 cm /5 × 3 in slices of Gruyère cheese
6 thick slices of streaky bacon, rinded
30 ml /2 tbls softened butter
30 ml /2 tbls vegetable oil
2 carrots, thinly sliced
2 onions, chopped
50 ml /2 fl oz rum
175 ml /6 fl oz dry cider
1 bay leaf
2.5 ml /½ tsp dried thyme
stock, home-made or from a cube, if required
250 g /8 oz button mushrooms
60–90 ml /4–6 tbls thin cream

1   To prepare the pot roast, make 5 evenly spaced slits in the joint, cutting across the grain of the meat but through only three-quarters of the depth. This will give 6 equal-sized slices of meat attached at the base like the leaves of a book. Season the lamb all over with plenty of salt, black pepper and paprika.
2   Trim the tongue and cheese slices to the same size as the 'leaves' of lamb. Place a tongue and a cheese slice in each slit, and cover the cut end of the joint with the last cheese and tongue slices.
3   Press the joint into its original shape. Cover with overlapping slices of bacon at right angles to the slits; tie the joint with string in the same direction as the bacon.
4   Heat the oven to 380F /180C /gas 4. Heat the butter and oil in a large, flameproof casserole over a moderate heat and in it brown the joint on all sides. Remove the joint and fry the carrots and onions gently in the casserole until the onions are light gold.
5   Place the meat on the vegetables in the casserole and baste it well with the fat. Pour the rum over the joint and then set it alight. When the flames die down, pour in the cider, and add the herbs.
6   Cover the joint and cook in the oven for 45 minutes. Now baste it with the pan juices and add a little stock if the dish is becoming dry. Return the casserole to the oven and cook for 30 minutes longer.
7   Add the mushrooms, and cook for a further 15 minutes or until the mushrooms are tender. Remove the joint and vegetables, using a slotted spoon, and keep warm while you make the sauce.
8   Strain the cooking liquid in the casserole and reserve 300 ml /10 fl oz. Skim off all the fat and pour the liquid into a saucepan. Stir in the cream and reheat without boiling. Adjust the seasoning if necessary.
9   Remove the string from the joint and serve the vegetables and the sauce.

Cheese gnocchi

 15 minutes, plus cooling, then 10 minutes

Serves 4
50 g /2 oz butter, melted
600 ml /1 pt milk
125 g /4 oz semolina
1.5 ml /¼ tsp grated nutmeg
salt
freshly ground white pepper
2 eggs
140 g /4½ oz Parmesan cheese, grated
300 ml /10 fl oz fresh tomato sauce (see note), to serve

1   Use 15 g /½ oz of the butter to grease a 32 × 23 cm /13 × 9 in Swiss roll tin.
2   Bring the milk gently to the boil, then remove it from the heat. Sprinkle in the semolina and nutmeg and season to taste with salt and pepper. Stir it over a very gentle heat until the mixture leaves the sides of the pan cleanly. Remove from the heat.
3   In a small bowl, lightly beat the eggs. Beat them into the semolina with 90 g / 3½ oz of the cheese. Mix very thoroughly.
4   Spread the mixture evenly over the prepared tin. Chill until quite cold.
5   Heat the oven to 200C /400F /gas 6. Cut the cold gnocchi mixture into 25 mm /1 in squares. Grease a shallow, flameproof baking dish with a little of the melted butter and arrange the gnocchi in a single layer in the dish. Brush with the remaining melted butter and sprinkle with the remaining cheese.
6   Bake in the oven for 6 minutes, or place under a moderate grill and heat until the cheese topping bubbles and browns. Serve straight from the dish, with the hot tomato sauce served separately.

● For fresh tomato sauce: skin, seed and dice 450 g /1 lb tomatoes. In 30 ml /2 tbls olive oil, sauté, until soft, ¼ large, finely chopped onion and 1 unpeeled garlic clove. Crumble in ¼ chicken stock cube and add the tomatoes, 30 ml /2 tbls tomato purée and 150 ml /5 fl oz water. Simmer for 5 minutes. Season to taste with salt, black and cayenne peppers and lemon juice. Stir in 30 ml /2 tbls of both chopped fresh parsley and olive oil. Remove the garlic clove and serve.

Swiss potato and cheese quiche

 1 hour 40 minutes, including chilling the pastry

Serves 4–6
300 g /10 oz potatoes, grated
50 g /2 oz Emmental cheese, grated
2 eggs
150 ml /5 fl oz thin cream
salt and freshly ground black pepper
grated nutmeg
15 ml /1 tbls grated Sbrinz or Parmesan cheese

For the shortcrust pastry
175 g /6 oz flour, plus extra for dusting
a pinch of salt
50 g /2 oz butter, diced small, plus extra for greasing
25 g /1 oz hard margarine, diced small

1   First make the pastry. Sift the flour and salt into a mixing bowl and add the butter and margarine.
2   Using your thumb and fingertips, press out the lumps of fat, keeping your hands high over the bowl so that the crumbs shower back. Continue until the mixture resembles coarse breadcrumbs.
3   Sprinkle 30 ml /2 tbls cold water over the surface and pull the dough together with a flat-bladed knife. Now use your fingers to continue the process.
4   Turn the dough out onto a lightly floured board and knead it lightly. Pat it into shape. Wrap it and chill it for 15 minutes if it seems soft.
5   Heat the oven to 200C /400F /gas 6. Roll out the pastry on a lightly floured board. Grease a 20 cm /8 in flan case and line it with the pastry. Line the pastry case with foil and beans and bake for 10 minutes. Reduce the oven heat to 180C /350F /gas 4 and bake for 5–10 minutes without the foil and beans.
6   Combine the grated potatoes and Emmental cheese. Beat the eggs with the cream and stir into the potato and cheese mixture. Season well with salt, pepper and nutmeg to taste. Pour the mixture into the prepared pastry case.
7   Sprinkle the top of the tart evenly with the grated Sbrinz or Parmesan cheese. Bake for 30–35 minutes, until the filling is set and golden brown. Serve hot.

Souffléed cheese boulettes

Glamorgan 'sausages'

🔪 30 minutes

Serves 3–4

150 g /5 oz mature Cheddar or Lancashire
   cheese, grated
250 g /8 oz 1 day-old breadcrumbs
5 ml /1 tsp mustard powder
2.5 ml /½ tsp dried thyme
2.5 ml /½ tsp dried rosemary, crushed
15 ml /1 tbls white leek, finely shredded
salt and freshly ground black pepper
2 medium-sized eggs, separated
flour, for coating
dried breadcrumbs, for coating
bacon fat or oil, for frying
To serve
tomato halves and apple rings, grilled
watercress sprigs

1   In a large bowl, mix together the cheese, soft breadcrumbs, mustard, herbs and leek. Season to taste with salt and pepper.
2   Put the egg whites in a soup plate. Add the yolks to the cheese mixture and knead by hand to make a paste which holds its shape.
3   Form the paste into 15 equal-sized small sausage shapes. Roll them in the flour.
4   Whisk the egg whites until they are frothy. Dip each 'sausage' in egg white, and roll them in dried crumbs, coating them well.
5   Heat about 20 mm /¾ in depth of bacon fat or oil in a frying-pan. Put in the 'sausages', in batches, and turn them in the fat until they are golden all over. Drain them and serve them arranged around the tomato-topped apple rings and the watercress sprigs.

● For milder 'sausages' that are firmer after frying, use Caerphilly cheese.

Baked egg surprise

🔪 20 minutes

Serves 4

4 eggs, separated, at room temperature
salt and freshly ground white pepper
butter, for greasing
60 ml /4 tbls thick cream
60 ml /4 tbls freshly grated Parmesan cheese

1   Heat the oven to 230C /450F /gas 8. Whisk the egg whites until they are very stiff. Using a metal spoon, gently fold in salt and white pepper to taste.
2   Butter 4 individual gratin dishes (each 10 cm /4 in diameter) and spoon one-quarter of the egg white into each. Make a depression in the centre of each with the back of the spoon. Place an egg yolk in each depression. Surround each yolk with 15 ml /1 tbls of the thick cream (do not pour it directly over the egg yolk or the white). Sprinkle the grated Parmesan cheese over the whites.
3   Bake in the oven for 8–10 minutes, until the whites are turning golden but the yolks are still runny. Serve immediately.

● For a herby flavour, add 5 ml /1 tsp snipped fresh chives or 5 ml /1 tsp finely chopped fresh tarragon to the cream before pouring it around the yolks.

Gruyère soufflé

🔪🔪 50 minutes

Serves 3–4

butter, stale breadcrumbs and grated
   Parmesan, for coating the dish
275 ml /10 fl oz milk
40 g /1½ oz butter
45 ml /3 tbls flour
6 eggs, separated
75 g /3 oz Gruyère cheese, freshly grated
50 g /2 oz Parmesan cheese, freshly grated
salt and freshly ground black pepper
freshly grated nutmeg
cayenne pepper

Glamorgan 'sausages'

14

Baked egg surprise

1 Heat the oven to 190C /375F /gas 5.
2 Generously grease a 1.1 L /2 pt soufflé dish with butter, paying particular attention to the inside of the rim, and dust it all over with a mixture of stale breadcrumbs and grated Parmesan cheese.
3 Put the milk in a saucepan and bring it to the boil.
4 Melt the butter in a heavy-based saucepan, blend in the flour and stir, over a low heat, for 2–3 minutes to make a pale roux.
5 Gradually add the boiled milk to the roux, stirring vigorously with a wire whisk to prevent lumps forming. Bring it to the boil and simmer, over a moderate heat, for about 5 minutes longer, stirring, until the sauce is thick and smooth.
6 Remove the pan from the heat and beat in 5 egg yolks, one at a time. (Reserve the spare egg yolk for another dish.) Pour the sauce into a large bowl, add the grated cheeses and season generously with salt, black pepper and a pinch each of freshly grated nutmeg and cayenne pepper.
7 In another large bowl, whisk all the egg whites with a pinch of salt until they are stiff but not dry.
8 Using a large metal spoon, fold the egg whites into the sauce, working as quickly and lightly as possible. Spoon the soufflé mixture into the prepared dish and level it off lightly with the back of a spoon.
9 Cook in the oven for 20 minutes, or until the soufflé is well puffed and golden brown. Serve immediately.

Cheese fondue

Do the preliminary cooking for the fondue in the kitchen, then keep it hot over a spirit stove or electric hot plate at the table.

15–20 minutes

Serves 4–6
1 garlic clove, cut in half
350 g /12 oz Gruyère cheese
350 g /12 oz Emmental cheese
10 ml /2 tsp cornflour
30 ml /2 tbls kirsch
about 425 ml /15 fl oz dry white wine
10 ml /2 tsp lemon juice
a pinch of freshly ground white pepper
a pinch of freshly grated nutmeg
*1 large loaf of crusty French bread, cut into
    25 mm /1 in cubes, to serve*
pickled onions, to serve
pickled gherkins, to serve

1 Rub the inside of the fondue pot with the cut clove of garlic. Discard the garlic. Grate the Gruyère and Emmental cheeses fairly coarsely. Blend the cornflour with the kirsch until it is smooth and set it to one side.

2 Heat 425 ml /15 fl oz wine and the lemon juice in the pot until just boiling, turn the heat to low and stir in the cheese, very slowly, with a wooden spoon. Now add the kirsch mixture, pepper and nutmeg, stirring continuously until it is thick. The cheese mixture should be smooth — stir in a little more warmed wine if it is necessary.
3 Carefully transfer the fondue pot to a spirit stove or electric hot plate at the table and keep it simmering. The cheese fondue is now ready. Remember to stir it frequently during the meal. Do not let it boil.
4 Serve with cubes of French bread to dip into the fondue, accompanied by pickled onions and pickled gherkins.
5 When nearly all the fondue is eaten there will be a thick crust on the bottom of the pot and this should be scraped out and divided among the guests.

● Use a proper cheese fondue pot made of earthenware or enamelled iron. Or, improvize with a flameproof ceramic casserole. Stainless steel or copper pots become too hot.
● Lay a fondue fork and a table fork for each guest, since the fondue fork can become extremely hot while it is in the pot and mouths may be badly burnt.
● If you are serving a dessert to follow the cheese fondue, choose a simple fruit salad or a bowl of fresh fruit.

Cheese fondue

Tuna and cheese flan

 1 hour

Serves 6
200 g /7 oz canned tuna, drained and flaked
125 g /4 oz mature Cheddar cheese, grated
2 eggs
150 ml /5 fl oz milk
salt and freshly ground black pepper
15 ml /1 tbls snipped fresh chives
For the pastry
200 g /7 oz flour, plus extra for dusting
a pinch of salt
50 g /2 oz margarine
40 g /1½ oz lard

1 Heat the oven to 190C /375F /gas 5.
2 Now make the pastry. Sift the flour and salt into a bowl and rub in the margarine and lard until the mixture resembles bread-crumbs. Add 35 ml /7 tsp water and mix the ingredients to a short dough.
3 Roll out the dough on a floured board and use it to line a 22 cm /8½ in flan tin. Line the pastry case with foil, fill it with beans and bake it blind for 15 minutes. Remove it from the oven, discard the foil and beans and return the flan case to the oven and bake for a further 5 minutes.
4 Spread the tuna in the bottom of the flan and spoon the grated cheese over the top.
5 Beat together the eggs and milk, season

Potatoes stuffed with almonds and bacon

the mixture lightly and pour it into the flan case. Next, sprinkle the chives over the top.
6 Return the flan to the oven and bake for 30 minutes, until the filling is set and the top is golden. Serve either hot or cold.

Cider cheese fondue

 15 minutes

Serves 4
1 garlic clove
425 ml /15 fl oz dry cider
10 ml /2 tsp lemon juice, plus extra for sprinkling
275 g /10 oz Cheddar cheese, coarsely grated
275 g /10 oz Gruyère cheese, coarsely grated
30 ml /2 tbls cornflour
45 ml /3 tbls calvados or brandy
a pinch of ground cinnamon
freshly ground black pepper
For dipping
1 day-old crusty loaf
peeled, cooked potatoes
dessert apples
small pickled onions or gherkins

1 Cut the bread into about 25 mm /1 in cubes, each with some of the crust attached. Cut the potatoes into 25 mm /1 in cubes. Core the apples; cut into chunks and sprinkle with lemon juice to prevent discoloration.
2 Halve the garlic clove and rub both halves around the fondue pot, then discard.
3 Put the cider and lemon juice in the

fondue pot and place the pot over the burner. Heat the liquid gently, until it has warmed.
4 Add the grated cheese to the warmed cider, stirring well all the time. Heat the fondue, stirring continuously until it begins to bubble. Blend the cornflour with the calvados or brandy. Pour it into the fondue, stirring all the time.
5 Season the fondue with the cinnamon and pepper to taste. Stirring, cook for 2–3 minutes or until the fondue is smooth and well blended. The fondue is now ready. To eat, everyone spears a piece of food with a fondue fork and dips it into the cheese mix-ture to coat well. Remember to stir the fondue frequently during the meal.

● See notes following Cheese fondue on the previous page for additional information.

Potatoes stuffed with almonds and bacon

 1 hour 25 minutes

Serves 4
4 large potatoes
15 g /½ oz butter
4 slices back bacon, coarsely chopped
60 ml /4 tbls flaked almonds
60 ml /4 tbls thick cream
salt and freshly ground black pepper
60 ml /4 tbls finely grated Gruyère cheese
30 ml /2 tbls finely grated Parmesan cheese
sprigs of parsley, to garnish

1 Heat the oven to 190C /375F /gas 5.
2 Scrub the potatoes with a stiff brush until they are absolutely clean. Pat them dry and prick them all over with a fork. Bake them in the oven for 1–1¼ hours, or until they feel soft if squeezed gently (use an oven cloth to protect your hands).
3 Meanwhile, melt the butter in a frying-pan and sauté the bacon for 3–5 minutes. Add the almonds and sauté until they are golden.
4 Heat the grill to high.
5 Cut a thin slice from the top of each cooked potato and scoop out the centre with a sharp spoon, into a bowl. Take great care not to break the skin, and leave a shell about 5 mm /¼ in thick. Set the shells to one side.
6 Sieve or mash the scooped-out potato to a purée. Add the sautéed bacon and flaked almonds and the thick cream, and season with salt and freshly ground black pepper to taste. Mix the ingredients thoroughly and pile the stuffing back into the potato shells.
7 Sprinkle the top of each potato with the grated Gruyère and Parmesan cheeses and put the potatoes under the hot grill until the topping is golden brown and bubbling. Garnish each with a sprig of parsley and serve at once.

Gratin dauphinois with nutmeg

 1¼ hours, including soaking the potatoes

Serves 4

500 g /1 lb large new potatoes
½ garlic clove
10 ml /2 tsp butter
150 ml /5 fl oz thick cream
50 g /2 oz Gruyère cheese, grated
60 ml /4 tbls freshly grated Parmesan cheese
salt and freshly ground black pepper
freshly grated nutmeg

1 Heat the oven to 170C /325F /gas 3.
2 Scrape or thinly peel the potatoes and slice them wafer-thin; each slice should be no more than 1.5 mm /¹/₁₆ in thick. Thoroughly rinse the potato slices under cold, running water, then leave them to soak in a bowl of cold water for 15 minutes.
3 Select a shallow, 23 × 13 cm /9 × 5 in ovenproof dish. Rub the inside of the dish with the cut garlic clove, discard it and then thickly grease the dish with the butter.
4 Drain the potato slices and dry them with a clean cloth or absorbent paper.
5 Arrange a quarter of the potato slices in overlapping rows in the base of the dish, pour over 30 ml /2 tbls of the cream, sprinkle with 30 ml /2 tbls of the grated Gruyère cheese and 15 ml /1 tbls of the grated Parmesan cheese, then season to taste with salt, freshly ground black pepper and nutmeg. Continue to layer the potato slices, cream and cheese in this way, seasoning each layer

in turn, until the ingredients are all used up. You will make a total of 4 sets of layers, ending with cheese and seasonings.
6 Bake the dish in the oven for about 45 minutes, until the top is golden and bubbling and the potatoes feel tender when pierced with a skewer. Check the dish towards the end of the cooking time and, if necessary, cover it loosely with foil to prevent the top over-browning.
7 When the potatoes are cooked, remove the dish from the oven and leave it to 'settle' for a few minutes before serving.

Scalloped haddock

 55 minutes

Serves 4

50 g /2 oz butter, plus extra for greasing
700 g /1½ lb haddock fillets, cut into pieces
salt and freshly ground black pepper
1 small onion, sliced
50 g /2 oz button mushrooms, finely chopped
25 g /1 oz flour
200 ml /7 fl oz milk
150 ml /5 fl oz single cream
50 g /2 oz fresh white breadcrumbs
50 g /2 oz Cheddar cheese, finely grated
flat-leaved parsley, to garnish

Scalloped haddock

1 Heat the oven to 190C /375F /gas 5. Grease a shallow ovenproof dish.
2 Dry the haddock pieces with absorbent paper and place the pieces in the prepared dish in a single layer. Season the fish generously with the salt and freshly ground black pepper.
3 Melt the butter in a small saucepan and add the onion slices. Sauté them over a medium heat, until the onion is softened. Add the chopped mushrooms and stir well. Continue to cook for 1 minute.
4 Add the flour to the pan and stir, over the heat, to make a pale roux.
5 Remove the saucepan from the heat and, stirring the roux continuously, add the milk a little at a time.
6 Return the pan to the heat and, continuing to stir, bring the mushroom and onion sauce to the boil. Continue to cook until the sauce is smooth and thickened.
7 Stir in the single cream, adjust the seasoning if necessary and pour the sauce over the fish. Combine the breadcrumbs and the grated cheese and sprinkle the mixture over the top.
8 Bake in the oven for 30 minutes or until the fish flakes easily and the topping is golden brown. Garnish the dish with a little flat-leaved parsley and serve.

Jerusalem artichoke gratin

 55 minutes

Serves 4

750 g /1½ lb Jerusalem artichokes
25 g /1 oz butter, plus extra for greasing
1 small onion, thinly sliced
5 ml /1 tsp mustard powder
30 ml /2 tbls flour
300 ml /11 fl oz milk
175 g /6 oz Cheddar cheese, grated
6 sage leaves, chopped
45 ml /3 tbls rolled oats
5 ml /1 tsp paprika

1 Heat the oven to 200C /400F /gas 6. Peel the artichokes and cut them into 25 mm /1 in slices. Steam them for 10 minutes.
2 Melt the butter in a saucepan, over a low heat. Add the onion slices and cook them until they are soft.
3 Stir in the mustard and flour and cook for

Macaroni cheese

30 seconds. Pour in the milk and bring to the boil, stirring. Simmer the sauce for 2 minutes. Take the pan from the heat and stir in two-thirds of the grated Cheddar cheese and all the chopped sage leaves.
4 Butter a pie dish and put in the steamed artichoke slices. Cover them with the sauce. Sprinkle the remaining grated cheese over the top, then the oats and the paprika.
5 Put the dish in the oven for 20 minutes, until the top becomes crisp. Serve hot.

Macaroni cheese

making the bechamel sauce, then 45 minutes

Serves 4

Bechamel sauce (1½ × ingredients, plus method, see page 33)
25 g /1 oz butter, plus extra for greasing
7.5 ml /1½ tsp salt
225 g /8 oz macaroni
2.5 ml /½ tsp made mustard
1.5 ml /¼ tsp white pepper
a large pinch of cayenne pepper
100 g /4 oz Cheddar cheese, grated
25 g /1 oz fine, dry breadcrumbs

1 Firstly, prepare the bechamel sauce.
2 In the meantime, heat the oven to 200C / 400F /gas 6 and lightly grease a medium-sized baking dish.
3 In a large saucepan, add 5 ml /1 tsp of the salt to 1.7 L /3 pt water and, over a high heat, bring it to the boil. Lower the heat to medium and put in the macaroni and cook it for 8–10 minutes or until it is *al dente*, or just tender. When it is cooked, drain the macaroni in a colander and set it to one side.
4 In a large mixing bowl, combine the bechamel sauce with the made mustard, remaining salt, white pepper, cayenne pepper and 50 g /2 oz of the cheese and mix the ingredients together well. Add the cooked macaroni and stir well to blend the mixture.
5 Pour the macaroni mixture into the greased baking dish. In a bowl, combine the remaining cheese and breadcrumbs and sprinkle it over the top of the macaroni cheese. Cut the butter into small pieces and dot them over the top.
6 Place the dish in the oven and bake for 15–20 minutes, or until the top is crisp and golden brown. Serve immediately.

● This macaroni cheese is delicious served with a tossed green salad and crusty bread.

Apple and cheese pie

1 hour

Serves 6

400 g /14 oz made-weight shortcrust pastry
(2 × ingredients, plus method, see page 12)
500 g /18 oz cooking apples, peeled, cored
*   and sliced*
5 ml /1 tsp cornflour
a pinch of ground cloves
75 g /3 oz caster sugar
75 g /3 oz Wensleydale or mature Cheddar
*   cheese, crumbled or grated*
milk, for brushing

1 Heat the oven to 220C /425F /gas 7. Roll out two-thirds of the pastry and use it to line a 20 cm /8 in pie plate.
2 Toss the apple slices in the cornflour, cloves and sugar and place half this mixture on the pastry base. Cover evenly with the cheese and then top it with the remaining apple mixture.
3 Roll out the rest of the pastry to make a lid, moisten the edges and seal together. Flute the pastry edge and cut a steam vent in the top crust. Make decorations from the pastry trimmings if wished. Dampen these, place them on the pie and brush all over the top with milk. Bake for 15 minutes.
4 Reduce the temperature to 180C /350F / gas 4 and continue cooking for a further 25–30 minutes, or until the pie is golden brown. Serve warm or cold.

Parmesan biscuits

30 minutes,
plus 1 hour chilling

Makes 24 biscuits

25 g /1 oz ground almonds
25 g /1 oz freshly grated Parmesan cheese
100 g /4 oz flour, plus extra for dusting
25 g /1 oz caster sugar
a pinch of salt
50 g /2 oz butter, diced, plus extra for greasing
15 ml /1 tbls honey
1 medium-sized egg yolk

1 Put the ground almonds, Parmesan cheese, flour, sugar and salt into a large bowl. Make a well in the middle of the dry mixture and add the butter, honey and egg yolk.
2 Rub in the mixture with the fingertips, mixing everything together well. Knead the pastry until smooth. Wrap it in cling film and refrigerate it for 1 hour.
3 Heat the oven to 190C /375F /gas 5. Flour a work surface and roll out the pastry to a thickness of 3 mm /⅛ in. Next, using a 25 mm /1 in round cutter, cut out 24 biscuits, re-rolling the pastry as necessary.
4 Grease a baking tray. Put the biscuits, not too close together, on the tray. Bake for 12–15 minutes, until they are golden on top.
5 Remove the biscuits from the oven, let them settle for 15 minutes, then transfer them to a plate to cool.

Apple and cheese pie

Noodles with cheese sauce and spinach

Serves 8
salt
900 g /2 lb ribbon noodles (tagliatelle or fettucine)
6 egg yolks
275 ml /10 fl oz thick cream
175 g /6 oz Gruyère cheese, freshly grated
100 g /4 oz butter
225 g /8 oz fresh spinach, trimmed, washed, drained and coarsely shredded
30 ml /2 tbls olive oil
freshly ground black pepper
90 ml /6 tbls freshly grated Parmesan cheese, plus extra to serve

1   Bring a very large saucepan of salted water to the boil. Add the ribbon noodles and cook until *al dente*. This will take only 1–2 minutes with fresh noodles and up to 10 minutes with dried noodles. Rinse the cooked noodles under hot water and drain them thoroughly. Rinse the pan.
2   Meanwhile, in a bowl, combine the egg yolks and thick cream until well blended, then stir in the grated Gruyère cheese.
3   In a separate large saucepan, melt half the butter. Add the shredded spinach and toss it in the hot butter until it has wilted. Remove it from the heat and reserve.
4   Return the drained noodles to the rinsed saucepan. Add the olive oil and the remaining butter and heat gently, tossing constantly, until the noodles are well coated with butter. Season the noodles with freshly ground black pepper, and a little more salt if necessary.
5   Stir in the egg yolk, cream and cheese mixture and continue stirring over a gentle heat until the cheese has melted and the mixture forms a thick sauce over the noodles.
6   Add the buttered spinach to the noodles, and toss gently to mix.
7   Turn the noodles and spinach into a heated serving dish. Sprinkle with the grated Parmesan cheese. Serve with extra Parmesan cheese.

● If you are serving several courses, calculate how much pasta your guests will eat; 50 g /2 oz each may be plenty for a first course.

10–20 minutes

Little cheese and sardine fritters

Serves 4–6
500 g /1 lb fresh sardines, scaled and cleaned
150 g /5 oz Cheddar cheese, finely grated
½ garlic clove, finely chopped
a large pinch of cayenne pepper
2 eggs
juice of ½ lemon
75 g /3 oz flour
25 g /1 oz fine, dry breadcrumbs
2.5 ml /½ tsp salt
2.5 ml /½ tsp freshly ground black pepper
vegetable oil, for deep frying
2 lemons, quartered

1   Heat the grill to high. Wash the sardines under cold, running water and pat them dry with absorbent paper.
2   Place the sardines on the rack in the grill pan 7.5 cm /3 in from the heat. Grill for 3–4 minutes on each side.
3   Remove and discard the head, tail, spine and skin from each sardine. Place the flesh in a medium-sized mixing bowl. Add the Cheddar cheese, garlic, cayenne pepper, the lightly beaten yolk of 1 egg and the lemon juice. Blend the mixture well.
4   On a plate, combine the flour, dry breadcrumbs, salt and black pepper. Lightly beat the remaining whole egg and the egg white and pour it onto a second plate.
5   Roll 15 ml /1 tbls of the sardine mixture into a small ball to form a fritter. Dip the ball first in the beaten egg, then in the seasoned flour and breadcrumb mixture, shaking off any excess. Continue to make fritters in this way with the rest of the sardine mixture.
6   Fill a large deep-fat frier one-third full with vegetable oil. Set the pan over a moderate heat and heat the oil until it registers 190C / 375F on a deep-fat thermometer or until a 25 mm /1 in cube of stale bread dropped into the oil turns golden brown in 50 seconds. Place a few of the fritters in a deep-frying basket and fry them for 3–5 minutes, until they are golden brown. Remove the basket from the oil and transfer the fritters to absorbent paper to drain. Keep them warm while you fry and drain the rest.
7   Place the fritters on a heated serving dish, garnish with lemon quarters and serve immediately.

 40 minutes

Spaghetti loaf

Serves 4–6

softened butter, for greasing
salt
225 g /8 oz spaghetti
275 ml /10 fl oz milk
½ chicken stock cube
25 g /1 oz butter
3 eggs, beaten
150 g /5 oz Cheddar cheese, grated
1 green pepper, seeded and
   chopped

1 pimento, chopped
50 g /2 oz ham or cooked chicken,
   chopped
60 ml /4 tbls freshly chopped
   parsley
15 ml /1 tbls freshly snipped
   chives
freshly ground black pepper
For the garnish
3 tomatoes, cut into wedges
15 black olives

1 Heat the oven to 150C /300F /gas 2. Butter a 1.5 L /3 pt of loaf tin. Bring a large pan with at least 1.7 L /3 pt of salted water to the boil.
2 To cook the spaghetti, let the water boil briskly for a minute before adding the spaghetti. Do not break long spaghetti, let it soften and then curl it round into the pan until it is all submerged. Do not cover. Stir at the start of the cooking to prevent sticking.
3 Cook the spaghetti for about 10 minutes until *al dente* — tender but still firm. Do not overcook. Drain well in a large colander.
4 Meanwhile, heat the milk and dissolve the chicken stock cube in it. Then, in a large bowl, mix 25 g /1 oz butter with the beaten eggs. Stir in the flavoured milk, cheese, green pepper, pimento, ham or chicken, parsley and chives. Season generously.
5 Toss the spaghetti thoroughly with the cheese mixture, distributing the green pepper and pimento evenly. Pour into the loaf tin and cover tightly with a piece of lightly buttered foil. Bake in the oven for 1½–1¾ hours, until set and firm.
6 Turn the spaghetti loaf out onto a serving dish; if any butter runs out, wipe it away with absorbent paper.
7 Leave the turned-out loaf until it is cold. To garnish it, place the tomato wedges around the base and along the top of the loaf. Put the black olives in between the tomato wedges.

● When serving the spaghetti loaf cold, try accompanying it with a mustard-flavoured mayonnaise.
● The spaghetti loaf can be served hot, garnished with 50 g /2 oz small, open mushroom caps which have been softened for 10 minutes in 25 g /1 oz butter. Sprinkle with finely chopped fresh parsley.

 1¾ hours

Little cheese pancakes

Serves 6

75 g /3 oz flour
2.5 ml /½ tsp salt
2 medium-sized eggs
30 ml /2 tbls melted butter or oil,
   plus extra for greasing
150 ml /5 fl oz milk
For the filling
225 g /8 oz cottage cheese, drained
50 g /2 oz unsalted butter, softened
2 egg yolks

40 g /1½ oz Gruyère cheese, grated
60 ml /4 tbls freshly grated
   Parmesan cheese
10 ml /2 tsp lemon juice
freshly grated nutmeg
freshly ground black pepper
For the topping
25 g /1 oz Gruyère cheese, grated
paprika pepper
25 g /1 oz unsalted butter

1 Sift the flour and salt into a bowl. Beat the eggs and stir them into the flour with the melted butter or oil. Gradually add the milk and stir until smooth. Strain the batter through a fine sieve, then leave it to stand for 2 hours.
2 Heat a 12.5 cm /5 in crêpe pan and then grease it with a wad of absorbent paper smeared with oil. For each pancake spoon in 30 ml / 2 tbls batter. Tilt the pan so that the batter thinly coats the surface. Cook over a medium heat for 1 minute.
3 Flip the pancake over and cook it for 1 minute on the second side. Re-grease the pan as you make the pancakes and layer them up, covering each with foil. Make 12 pancakes. Leave them to cool.
4 Make the filling; rub the drained cottage cheese through a sieve into a bowl. Add the softened, unsalted butter and beat until it is smooth. Add the egg yolks, the Gruyère and Parmesan cheese, lemon juice, and grated nutmeg and freshly ground black pepper to taste. Beat the mixture until it is well blended.
5 Divide the cheese mixture among the prepared pancakes. Roll up each pancake and tuck under both ends of the roll to seal in the cheese filling.
6 Heat the grill to high. Lightly oil a rectangular flameproof dish and arrange the pancakes in the dish in a single layer, side by side, joins downwards. Sprinkle the grated Gruyère and paprika over the top and dot with the unsalted butter. Grill for 5–7 minutes, until the pancakes are warmed through and the top is golden and bubbling. Serve immediately.

1 hour 10 minutes,
plus resting and cooling

Broccoli cheese
with almonds

Serves 4–6
450–700 g /1–1½ lb fresh or frozen broccoli spears
For the garnish
50 g /2 oz slivered almonds
oil, for frying
salt and freshly ground black pepper
For the cheese sauce
75 g /3 oz butter
10 ml /2 tsp French mustard
75 g /3 oz flour
850 ml /1½ pts warm milk
225 g /8 oz Emmental cheese, grated
freshly ground white pepper

1 Prepare the garnish. In a heavy-based pan, fry the almonds in a little oil until they are golden, shaking the pan so that they brown evenly. Remove them from the pan with a slotted spoon and drain them well on absorbent paper. While they are still warm, sprinkle the almonds with salt and pepper to taste, then set them aside.
2 If using fresh broccoli, trim away the tough stalks and divide up any large heads. Cook the broccoli in boiling, salted water for about 10 minutes until it is tender. Cook frozen broccoli as directed on the packaging. Drain the cooked broccoli, arrange it in a heated serving dish and keep it warm.
3 Make the sauce. In a heavy-based saucepan, melt the butter over a low heat. Remove the pan from the heat and stir in the French mustard and the flour. Return the pan to a low heat and cook, stirring, for 1–2 minutes, until the roux is thick and smooth. Remove the pan from the heat and gradually blend in the warm milk. Return the saucepan to the heat and, continuing to stir, bring the sauce to the boil.
4 Boil the sauce for 2 minutes, then remove it from the heat and stir in the Emmental cheese. Season to taste with salt and white pepper, then return the sauce to the heat and, occasionally stirring, simmer it gently for about 1 minute until it is thick and smooth.
5 Pour the cheese sauce over the broccoli spears. Sprinkle with the seasoned almonds and serve.

30 minutes

Poached egg cheese
consommé

Serves 4
4 eggs
60 ml /4 tbls white wine vinegar
700 ml /1¼ pt well-flavoured beef stock, home-made or from a cube
12 thin slices French bread
60 ml /4 tbls freshly grated Parmesan cheese
30 ml /2 tbls freshly grated Gruyère cheese
salt and freshly ground black pepper
15 ml /1 tbls finely chopped fresh parsley
cayenne pepper

1 To poach the eggs, pour water to a depth of 7.5 cm /3 in into a large, wide saucepan. Add the vinegar and bring to the boil, then lower the heat to a simmer.
2 Break an egg into a cup, then slip it carefully into the pan. Repeat quickly with the remaining eggs, making a note of the order in which you put them into the water. Raise the heat to high until the water bubbles, then reduce the heat to a gentle simmer and poach the eggs for 3–4 minutes.
3 Meanwhile, in a separate saucepan, bring the stock to the boil, then reduce the heat and keep it simmering until ready to serve.
4 Place 3 slices of French bread into each of 4 heated soup plates or bowls. Sprinkle the Parmesan and Gruyère cheese over the bread.
5 Lift the cooked eggs from the pan with a slotted spoon. Rinse each one in hot, boiled water and drain well on absorbent paper.
6 Place one egg in the centre of each soup plate on top of the bread and cheese.
7 Season the simmering stock to taste with salt and freshly ground black pepper and divide it among the soup plates or bowls.
8 Sprinkle each serving with a little parsley and a pinch of cayenne pepper. Serve immediately.

25 minutes

Cheese and pimento potatoes

Serves 6
6 medium-sized cold, previously baked potatoes
120 ml /8 tbls thin cream
50 g /2 oz butter, softened
salt and freshly ground black pepper
100 g /4 oz Emmental cheese
2 pimentos, drained and very finely diced
watercress sprigs, to garnish

1 Heat the oven to 190C /375F /gas 5.
2 Cut a thin slice lengthways from each potato and reserve this to be used as a lid. Using a spoon, scoop out the flesh from each potato into a bowl, leaving a firm empty shell.
3 Mash the potato flesh with the cream and softened butter. Season it with salt and freshly ground black pepper to taste. Cut the Emmental into tiny dice and stir these, with the diced pimento, into the potato mixture.
4 Pile the potato mixture into the shells and then place the potatoes on a wire rack.
5 Bake for 25–30 minutes, or until the potatoes are hot. Serve with a reserved lid on each potato and garnished with watercress.

baking the potatoes and
cooling them, then 40 minutes

Baked cheese mash

Serves 4
450 g /1 lb floury potatoes
salt
60 ml /4 tbls thick cream
50 g /2 oz butter, plus extra for greasing
60 ml /4 tbls freshly grated Parmesan cheese
30 ml /2 tbls freshly grated Gruyère cheese
freshly ground white pepper
1 egg yolk, beaten

1 Heat the oven to 200C /400F /gas 6.
2 Peel the potatoes, cut them into even-sized pieces and cook them in a saucepan of boiling, salted water for 20 minutes or until they are tender. Push the potatoes through a vegetable mill into a large bowl, or press them through a sieve into a bowl, using the back of a wooden spoon. Keep them warm.
3 In a saucepan and over a low heat, stir together the thick cream, butter and Parmesan cheese. Continue stirring until the Parmesan cheese has melted.
4 Beat the cream mixture into the sieved potato with the Gruyère cheese. Season with salt and white pepper to taste.
5 Butter a 1.4 L /2½ pt ovenproof dish and spoon the potato mixture into the prepared dish, levelling the top with a palette knife. Brush the top with the beaten egg yolk and bake the mashed potato in the oven for 10–15 minutes or until it is golden brown. Serve as soon as possible.

45 minutes

Cod steaks in beer

Serves 4

850 ml /1½ pt lager	**For the sauce**
1 carrot, sliced	25 g /1 oz butter
1 Spanish onion, sliced	25 g /1 oz flour
1 celery stick, sliced	275 ml /10 fl oz milk
4 sprigs of parsley	60 ml /4 tbls freshly grated
8 black peppercorns	Parmesan
5 cloves	100 g /4 oz Gruyère cheese, diced
5 bay leaves	2 egg yolks, lightly beaten
4 cod steaks, weighing 225 g /	60 ml /4 tbls thick cream, whipped
8 oz each	salt and ground black pepper

1 Pour the lager into a saucepan that is large enough to take the cod steaks in a single layer. Add the carrot, onion, celery, parsley sprigs, peppercorns, cloves and 1 bay leaf. Bring to the boil, cover and simmer for 15 minutes.
2 Lay the cod steaks in the simmering liquid and cook them gently, turning with a fish slice, for 6 minutes on each side, or until the fish flakes easily with a fork. Remove the steaks from the pan and drain them on absorbent paper. Arrange them in a heated shallow serving dish. Keep them warm.
3 Boil the remaining cooking juices briskly until they are reduced to 300 ml /10 fl oz, then strain them through a fine sieve, lined with muslin. Reserve the juices.
4 Heat the grill to high. Meanwhile, to prepare the sauce, melt the butter in a heavy-based saucepan, blend in the flour with a wooden spoon and cook for 2 minutes until a pale roux forms. Gradually add the milk, stirring constantly to prevent lumps forming, and bring the sauce to the boil. Cook for a further 2 minutes until the sauce has thickened and no longer tastes of flour. Stir in the reduced fish stock and add the Parmesan, the Gruyère and the lightly beaten egg yolks. Cook the sauce over a very low heat, beating vigorously with a wooden spoon, until it is smooth and hot again. Do not let the sauce boil as the egg yolks may curdle. Stir in the whipped cream and season with salt and black pepper to taste.
5 Pour the sauce over the cod steaks and brown under the grill for 3–5 minutes, or until the top is golden brown and bubbling. Serve immediately, garnished with the remaining bay leaves.

 1 hour

Toasts au fromage

Serves 8

8 slices white toast, crusts removed
2 egg yolks
225 ml /8 fl oz thick cream
120 ml /8 tbls milk
450 g /1 lb Gruyère cheese, freshly grated
salt and freshly ground black pepper
freshly grated nutmeg
225 g /8 oz fresh white breadcrumbs
175 g /6 oz clarified butter (see note below)
sprigs of watercress, to garnish

1 Cut each slice of toast in half diagonally. Select a flat tray large enough to take the toast in a single layer and line it with cling film. Alternatively, use two smaller trays.
2 In a shallow dish, combine the egg yolks and thick cream, beating with a fork to blend. Dip the toast in the mixture to coat the toast on both sides, then lay the coated toast on the prepared tray or trays. Reserve the remaining mixture.
3 In a small, heavy-based saucepan, heat the milk until lukewarm. Stir in the Gruyère cheese and melt it over a low heat until the cheese becomes smooth, stirring constantly with a wooden spoon. Season the mixture to taste with salt and black pepper, and nutmeg.
4 With a palette knife or spatula, spread the cheese mixture evenly over both sides of each piece of toast. Dip the pieces in the remaining egg and cream mixture.
5 Sprinkle the fresh white breadcrumbs on a shallow dish and coat each piece of toast with the breadcrumbs, pressing them on firmly with the palms of your hands.
6 Line with fresh cling film another clean, flat tray large enough to take the toast in a single layer, or 2 smaller trays. Lay the coated toast on the prepared tray, or trays, and chill it for at least 2 hours.
7 When ready to serve, heat the clarified butter in a frying-pan. Over a low heat, cook the toasts for 2–3 minutes each side, or until golden, turning with a spatula. Transfer them to a heated serving dish or dishes and serve them immediately, garnished with watercress.

● To clarify butter, melt butter over a very low heat until it foams. The foam will then sink leaving the butter as clear as oil. Pour away the liquid butter, leaving the sediment behind.

 40 minutes, plus chilling,
then 10–15 minutes

Cheese soufflé pudding

Serves 4
6 slices white bread, crusts removed
125 g /4½ oz softened butter
275 ml /10 fl oz milk
45 ml /3 tbls flour
4 eggs, separated, plus 1 extra white
75 g /3 oz strong Cheddar cheese, freshly grated
salt and freshly ground black pepper
10 ml /2 tsp Dijon mustard

1 Heat the oven to 190C /375F /gas 5.
2 Reserving 40 g /1½ oz of the butter, use the rest to butter both sides of the slices of bread. Cut each slice into 2 triangles and arrange them around the sides of a 1.7 L /3 pt soufflé dish, with the points sticking above the rim.
3 Place the milk in a saucepan and bring it to the boil.
4 In a heavy-based saucepan, melt the remaining butter. With a wooden spoon, blend in the flour and stir it over a low heat for 2–3 minutes, to make a pale roux.
5 Gradually add the boiled milk to the roux, stirring vigorously with a wire whisk to prevent lumps forming. Bring the sauce to the boil, then reduce the heat and simmer it over a moderate heat for 5 minutes longer, stirring until it is thick and smooth.
6 Remove the pan from the heat and beat in the egg yolks, 1 at a time. Pour the sauce into a large bowl, then stir in the Cheddar cheese and season generously with salt and freshly ground black pepper, and the Dijon mustard.
7 Select another large bowl and make sure it is clean and dry. Put the 5 egg whites in it, add a pinch of salt and whisk until the whites are stiff but not dry.
8 Using a large metal spoon, fold the egg whites into the sauce, working as quickly and lightly as possible. Spoon the soufflé mixture into the prepared dish and then gently level off the top with the back of the spoon.
9 Cook in the oven for 30–35 minutes, or until the soufflé is well puffed and golden brown and the bread is also golden. Serve the soufflé immediately.

55 minutes

Baked anchovy eggs

Serves 4
butter, for greasing
4 eggs
salt and freshly ground black pepper
4 anchovy fillets
120 ml /8 tbls grated Gruyère or Emmental cheese
parsley sprigs, to garnish
For the anchovy butter
25 g /1 oz butter, softened
5 ml /1 tsp anchovy essence

1 To make the anchovy butter, cream the softened butter with the anchovy essence, mixing well, and then reserve. Heat the oven to 170C /325F /gas 3.
2 Butter 4 individual cocotte dishes. Break the eggs carefully into the dishes. Sprinkle them lightly with salt and freshly ground black pepper. (Bear in mind the saltiness of the anchovies).
3 With a sharp knife, halve the anchovy fillets lengthways and then widthways. Arrange 4 anchovy strips in a lattice on top of each egg. Cover each egg with 30 ml /2 tbls of the Gruyère or Emmental cheese and then divide the anchovy butter into 4 and dot a piece on each egg.
4 Bake for 12 minutes, or until the cheese has melted and the eggs are set but still creamy. Garnish the top of each with parsley sprigs and serve them immediately.

● Simple but delicious, this egg dish is equally suitable for serving as a snack or as an elegant party appetizer.

25 minutes

EUROPEAN SOFT CHEESES

Brie and Camembert spring quickly to mind as names of popular European soft cheeses but every European country makes a soft, creamy cheese. Try the recipes in this chapter to discover their many distinctive flavours.

Every European country has its own version of soft cheese. They can be made from rich milk, skimmed milk or whey; they can be sweet or salty; soft, creamy and buttery or dry and crumbly. Records of soft cheeses go back to ancient Sumer in 4000 BC. In the Bible, David was taking soft cheeses to King Saul when he was diverted to fight Goliath. In ancient Greece, little cheesecakes were given to children instead of sweets or buns and a cheesecake roasted with honey was the equivalent of our modern wedding cake.

Soft cheeses are made from milk solids (called curds) and when they are ready to eat they are still moist with whey (the thin fluid left when the curds have been removed). There are three main types of soft cheese and they are all highly perishable. They are: fresh cheeses, soft or quick-ripening cheeses and brine-washed, lightly ripened cheeses. Fresh cheeses are white and soft, not unlike thick cream to look at but less greasy. The best-known of the quick-ripening cheeses are sold in various shapes and are easily recognized by the white mould or *flor* on the outside — outstanding examples are Camembert and Brie. They ripen over differing periods of time and should not be eaten when they are under- or over-ripe.

The most distinctive and celebrated brine-washed cheeses have a golden or russet crust on the outside, such as Livarot.

Fresh cheeses

Fresh cheeses are not ripened and contain a considerable quantity of whey. These cheeses are soft, white and bland to the taste. They must be eaten quickly, as they become acid and go bad within a few days of being made.

Whey cheese: whey was originally a by-product of cheese-making, left over when the milk fats were removed. However, it can be used for making cheeses which are low in fat and these have traditionally been produced in countries where food is short. The whey is boiled up in order to curdle any remaining milk solids. In Italy this cheese is called ricotta, in Greece it is known as Myzithra. It can be used for sweet and savoury dishes, see Half-moon pizza, Rigatoni with ricotta and sage and Ricotta cheesecake.

Full-fat soft cheeses: full-fat soft cheese is both the name of a basic fresh cheese and the legal general name for all soft cheeses with a butterfat content not less than 20 per cent in the dry matter. Full-fat cheese can be up to 60 per cent water, the rest being varying proportions of fat protein and minerals. Cream cheese must have a butterfat content of at least 45 per cent and double cream cheese a butterfat content of 65 per cent in Britain.

Hundreds of subtly different full-fat soft cheeses are made, especially in France. Every French district, even every village, makes its own cheese and gives it a local name. These local cheeses are seldom exported; they must be eaten quickly because they contain no preservatives, and the richer a cheese the more quickly it goes off.

Only a few of the hundreds of different full-fat soft cheeses are sold commercially, but those that are available are in great demand. These are either vacuum packed or treated with preservatives.

The silver foil pack of American Philadelphia full-fat soft cheese is familiar on most supermarket shelves. It is now made with flavourings and is the classic cheese for cheesecakes (see Orange-apricot party cheesecake) because it is more stable when cooked than some other full-fat cheeses.

Modern Mozzarella is one of the few Italian fresh soft cheeses which is internationally exported. It is the correct cheese to use for pizzas and lasagne. Traditionally, it is made from water buffalo's milk but the cheeses which are exported are now made from cow's milk, and are sold preserved, in vacuum packs. A cheese like this has become a standard commercial type, which has been widely copied.

Medium-fat soft cheeses: curd cheese is what you get if you try cheese-making at home using whole milk. The curds, separated from the whey, are hung up in a bag to drain. When the cheese is dry enough, it is salted and eaten. Since it is so easy to produce, it is made in virtually every country. It is called curd cheese in Britain and pot or farmer's cheese in America, while the French call it *fromage maigre* (thin cheese) or *fromage*

Top row, left to right: Mozzarella, Pont L'Evêque, Carré de L'Est, heart-shaped Neufchâtel, quark. Middle shelf, left to right: Petit Reblochon, Danish nut and liqueur log, Margotin with peppercorns, soft cheese with walnuts. Cheese stand, clockwise: ricotta, Brie, Brie Suprême, Caprice des Dieux, Feta. Marble round, clockwise: goat's milk log, goat's milk parsley cheese, Margotin with herbs and Camembert. Foreground, left to right: Cottage cheese, Gervais and Philadelphia cream cheese

blanc. In Germany it is known as Quark. Demi-sel and Petit Suisse are both sold under the name of their producer, Gervais. Petit Suisse, in tiny 25 g /1 oz packs, is light, delicate and slightly sour to the taste. Use these cheeses for savoury and sweet dishes — see Chicken stuffed with herbs (Petit Suisse) and Coeurs à la crème (Demi-Sel). Look for Saint Marcellin or Margotin which both have herbs added. Also widely available are fresh Cantadou and double cream Boursin, flavoured with garlic and herbs or coated with black peppercorns.

Low-fat soft cheese: cottage cheese is a form of curd cheese. It has large, soft curds which are formed quickly when the milk is heated. Cottage cheese is very soft, as it contains a good deal of liquid whey. It can be produced at home, although commercial versions are available. It can be up to 80 per cent water.

Curd cheese can also be made from the partly skimmed milk left over from butter making. In this case it is a low-fat cheese, not a medium-fat one. It is very soft and despite draining contains a lot of liquid whey. Skimmed milk cheeses last several days before they become too acid to eat.

You may find assorted foreign, small creamy cheeses in vacuum packs or foil. They may be scented and flavoured with herb and spices or studded with nuts.

Soft or quick-ripening

Camembert and Brie are the most famous of these cheeses. Bacteria called *Penicillium candidum* are sprayed or sprinkled on the newly shaped cheeses. A light, soft rind with a white, floury surface mould is quickly formed. Because of this white, powdery rind they are sometimes called white mould cheeses or surface-ripening cheeses. There are many French cheeses of this type and several are made in other countries. These cheeses begin to ripen at the creamery where they are made. The rind and the cheese just under it ripen first.

The cheese goes on maturing steadily after it has been packaged until it is creamy all through, aromatic and delicious. Very soon after this stage it begins to drip like glue and to taste and smell bad.

Camembert accounts for two-thirds of all the soft cheese in France. It is said to have been invented in Normandy by Marie Harel in 1791, but its origins probably go back further. Marie Harel provided the conditions necessary for the mould-forming bacteria to work (and prevented other bacteria from acting). This made Camembert become the reliable, popular cheese it is today. It is a compact, small, round cheese made in tall moulds (the cheese settles into its familiar shape) from carefully stirred curds. It is matured for 7–12 days, before packaging, according to its destination. It is sold packaged, in whole or half rounds or in small, triangular portions.

Brie is made by ladling layers of curd into a shallow steel ring, using a slotted spoon to remove the whey. It is ripened for about four weeks before being distributed for sale. It is usually sold from a large, flat round or wheel, measuring 35 cm /14 in across, from which wedges are cut.

Other white moulded cheeses: best known French ones are Neufchâtel, often in a heart-shaped case; the small Carré de l'Est and the oval, double-cream Caprice des Dieux in a blue carton. There is also a very rich, double cream Brie-flavoured cheese — either called Brie or Suprême — which has flecks of green and red peppers, herbs or crushed black peppercorns either in the paste or covering it. Versions of most of these cheeses are made in other parts of Europe.

Brine-washed and lightly ripened

All soft cheeses, even bland fresh ones, have a little salt added to them. Sometimes salt is added to the curd before the cheeses are shaped. A whole Camembert may be dipped in a brine bath to salt it, and some cheeses are actually soaked in salted whey or water and are left to ripen in it for a short time. Feta, Greek sheep's or goat's milk cheese is one of these, and the vacuum-packed version which is exported can be very salty. Use them in such recipes as Spinach and cheese pie, Greek pepper salad and Greek cheese pastries.

Much subtler are the many French cheeses which are washed with brine while being ripened. These cheeses are deliciously aromatic and full-flavoured because the brine washing makes them stronger. They look splendid too — the brine turns their greyish, dry rind a peach-gold or russet colour. To many people these are the finest French cheeses of all. Look for the small, aromatic Pont L'Evêque, or you may be able to get a golden Maroilles or a russet Reblochon from a specialist supplier. Since these cheeses can weigh up to 800 g /1¾ lb, and are usually sold whole, it is worth trying the smaller versions of Maroilles called Mignon and Dauphin.

Buying and storing soft cheeses

Buy only the quantity you need of any fresh soft cheese. It will not keep long, even in the refrigerator, and may turn acid within a few hours in a warm room.

Buy Brie from a store where they cut slices from a wheel. This way you can see the condition of the cheese before you buy it. Any soft-ripening cheese should have a firm, creamy paste inside. If it has a chalky band through it, the outside will become over ripe and taste of ammonia before the chalky centre has time to mature. If the paste is runny, the cheese is already past its best.

If cheese is packaged, it should fill the wrappings, being neither swollen nor sunken, and the packaging should be clean and without any seepage.

It is best not to be over-enthusiastic at a specialist store and buy several of the brine-washed cheeses at one go. They ripen quickly and suddenly, especially when they have been cut open, and will not last for long. Serve one of these cheeses on its own, so that it can be finished at one meal.

If you have to store any of the soft cheeses temporarily, re-wrap it so no part is exposed to the air. If you have to store Brie, wrap it in uncreased foil and place it in the least cold part of the refrigerator for as short a time as possible. Remove it from the refrigerator about an hour before you intend using it.

Party ideas

Soft cheeses can be used for a wide range of party dishes as well as for nibbles. Try some of these ideas:

- for walnut pairs, sandwich walnut halves together with blue cheese spread (bleu de Bresse softened and creamed);
- for grape pairs, halve and seed the grapes, then sandwich them with cream cheese;
- flavour cream cheese with paprika, mustard powder or curry powder, pipe it onto biscuits; top with olives or gherkin fans;
- for stuffed tomatoes, scoop out the insides of tomatoes and fill them with a mixture of sieved cottage cheese and blue cheese;
- for slimmers' nibbles, mix sieved cottage cheese with pickle or chutney, pipe it down celery sticks, then cut them into small, bite-sized pieces to serve;
- for cheese-stuffed eggs, combine the yolks of hard boiled eggs with bleu de Bresse and refill the egg whites with the mixture;
- for cream cheese horns, fill the horns with a mixture of flavoured cream cheese or a cream cheese and blue cheese mixture;
- for Camembert canapés, toast bread on one side, place thin strips of Camembert on the untoasted side, grill the bread and cheese for 3 minutes under a medium grill, then cut into fingers to serve.

Canapés with Brie

30 minutes, plus chilling

Makes 10–12

300 g /10 oz creamy Brie cheese
30 ml /2 tbls finely snipped fresh chives
15 ml /1 tbls calvados
a pinch of paprika
cayenne pepper
2 garlic cloves
salt
50 g /2 oz butter
10–12 thin slices stale French bread
2 radishes, thinly sliced, to garnish
flat-leaved parsley, to garnish

1 Divide the Brie cheese into 10 pieces. Cut off the rind and discard it, then put the cheese in a bowl with the chives, calvados, a pinch of paprika and cayenne pepper to taste. Beat the mixture with a wooden spoon until it is creamy and smooth.

2 Mash 1½ garlic cloves with a pinch of salt and beat it into the Brie mixture until well blended. Cover with cling film and chill until required. Mash the remaining garlic.

3 In a frying-pan, melt 50 g /2 oz butter and add the remaining mashed garlic. When the butter is foaming, add the slices of French bread and fry them over a moderate heat on both sides, until golden and crisp. Remove the fried bread from the frying pan, drain it on absorbent paper to remove the excess fat, and leave it to get cold.

4 Spread some of the chilled Brie mixture on top of each croûte. Garnish them with 2 thin slices of radish and a little flat-leaved parsley. Transfer the canapés to a serving dish. Cover them with cling film and chill until ready to serve.

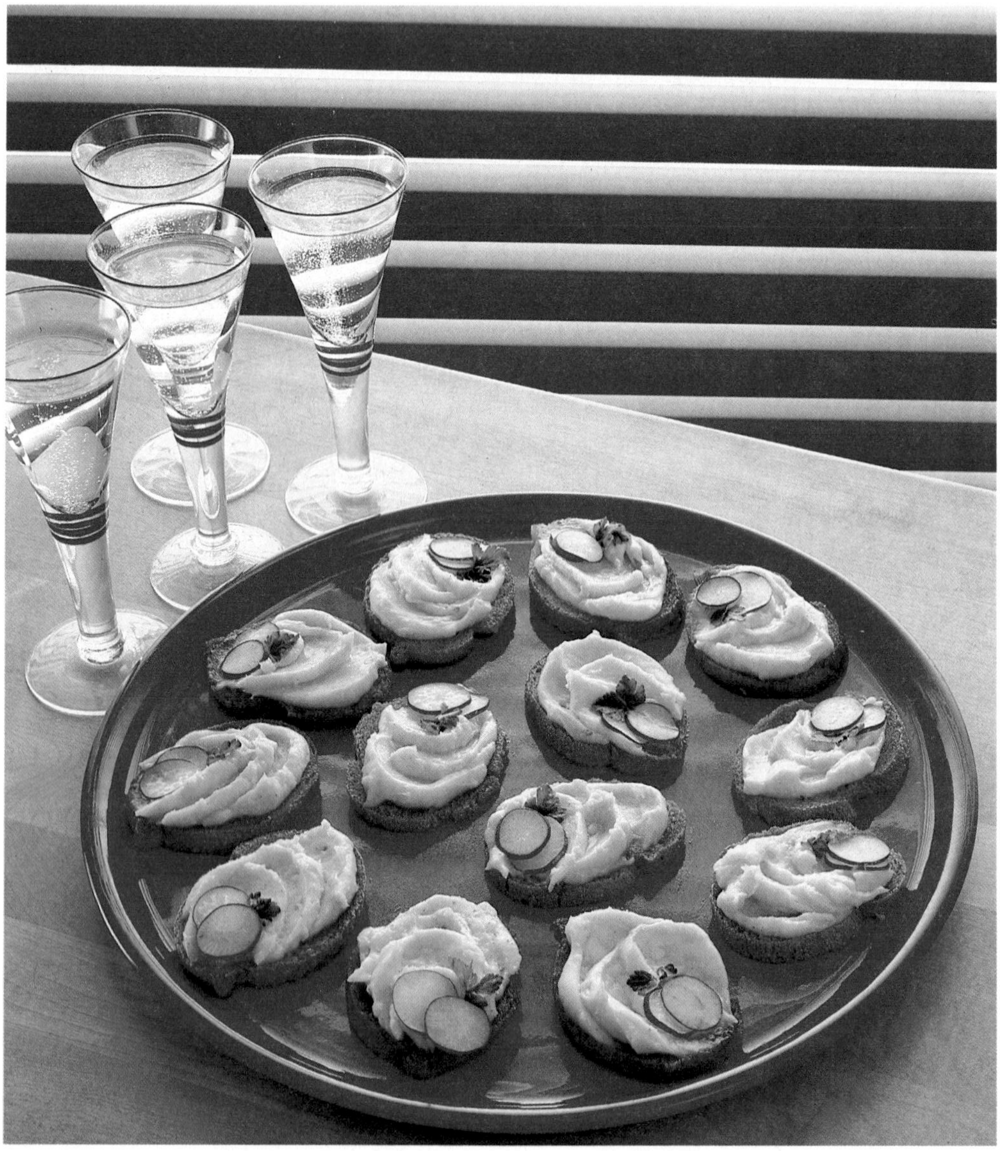

Greek cheese pastries

This recipe has been adapted to puff pastry because it is more readily available than the paper-thin, Greek filo pastry.

20 minutes, plus cooling, then 30 minutes

Makes 18–20 pastries

10 ml /2 tsp flour, plus extra for dusting
225 g /8 oz frozen puff pastry, thawed
1 medium-sized egg yolk
100 g /4 oz Feta cheese, drained
10 ml /2 tsp chopped fresh parsley
a pinch of grated nutmeg
25 g /1 oz unsalted butter
50 ml /2 fl oz milk

1 On a floured surface, roll out the puff pastry into a large square, about 38 × 30 cm / 15 × 12 in. Cut it into 7.5 cm /3 in squares. Chill the squares of pastry until needed.

2 Beat the egg yolk in a small bowl, and reserve. In a larger bowl, mash the cheese and then mix in the parsley and nutmeg.

3 Put the butter in a heatproof container, then stand it in hot water, and stir until the butter melts. Remove it from the heat.

4 Put 10 ml /2 tsp of the melted butter in a small saucepan. Mix in 10 ml /2 tsp flour and stir over a gentle heat for 2 minutes. Gradually stir in the milk and continue stirring until the sauce is boiling and very thick.

5 Mix the hot sauce with the cheese, little by little, until it is smoothly blended. Blend in the egg yolk and allow the mixture to cool.

6 Heat the oven to 200C /400F /gas 6. Lay the pastry squares flat on the work surface. Divide the filling among them, putting it in the centre of each square.

7 Damp the edges of each square with water. Forming triangles, fold them in half, firmly pressing the edges with a fork to seal them.

8 Place the pastries on a lightly greased and floured baking sheet. Brush them with the remaining melted butter. Bake for 15–20 minutes, or until the pastries are crisp, puffed and golden brown.

Canapés with Brie

Petits chèvres frais

🔪 15 minutes,
plus chilling

Serves 6
75 g /3 oz cottage cheese
150 g /5 oz goat's cheese
5 ml /1 tsp lemon juice
a pinch of cayenne pepper
freshly ground black pepper
10 ml /2 tsp melted butter

1   Twist the cottage cheese in muslin to drain it well, then sieve it. In a bowl, thoroughly combine both the cheeses.
2   Add the lemon juice, cayenne pepper and black pepper to taste, and then the melted butter. Mix until smooth.
3   Form the mixture into a roll with your hands and wrap it in greaseproof paper. Chill it in the refrigerator or freezer until firm.
4   Remove the greaseproof paper and cut the chilled cheese roll into 12 portions. Shape each portion into a small, neat round cake. Chill until just before serving.

Fresh pineapple and melon boats garnished with strawberries, Boccancini di Dolcelatte (see page 52) and Petits chèvres frais

● Try serving Fresh pineapple and melon boats with the Petits chèvres frais: vertically cut a 1 kg /2¼ lb pineapple into 6 pieces. Remove and discard the core, cut the flesh carefully from the skin, slice it into bite-sized chunks and return it, attractively arranged, to the shells. Do the same with a 1.5 kg /3 lb melon. Serve both garnished with fresh strawberries.

Cream cheese and red caviar

🔪 5 minutes

Makes 20–24
60 ml /4 tbls red caviar or red lumpfish roe
225 g /8 oz cream cheese
½ small onion, grated
30 ml /2 tbls finely chopped fresh parsley
salt and freshly ground black pepper
baked bread tartlets, to serve (see note below)

1   Reserve a little caviar or roe for decoration, then cream together the cream cheese, onion, parsley and caviar or roe. Season to taste with salt and black pepper.
2   Fill the tartlet cases with the cream cheese and red caviar or roe mixture. Garnish with the reserved caviar or roe.

● Baked bread tartlet cases are made with 8 cm /3 in bread rounds, buttered on both sides and pressed into tartlet tins. Bake them at 180C /350F /gas 4 for about 20 minutes, until they are crisp and golden.

Greek cheese pastries

Liptauer cheese

🕐 15 minutes,
then overnight chilling

Serves 6–8
225 g /8 oz curd cheese
175 g /6 oz unsalted or lactic butter, softened
3 anchovy fillets, drained and chopped
10 ml /2 tsp Dijon mustard
salt and freshly ground black pepper
7.5 ml /1½ tsp paprika
5 ml /1 tsp caraway seeds, crushed
15 ml /1 tbls capers, drained and chopped
whole capers, to garnish
crudités, to serve

1   In a large bowl, beat together the cheese and butter until they are soft.
2   Beat in the anchovies, mustard, black and paprika peppers, caraway seeds and chopped capers. Taste and add salt if necessary. Cover and chill overnight.
3   Turn the cheese into a serving bowl, garnish with capers and serve with crudités.

Camembert soup

🍴 45 minutes

Serves 4–6
40 g /1½ oz unsalted butter
½ medium-sized onion, chopped
1 celery stick, chopped
15 ml /1 tbls flour
60 ml /4 tbls milk
425 ml /15 fl oz hot chicken stock, home-made or from a cube
600 ml /1 pt dry white wine
125 g /4½ oz half-round Camembert cheese
150 ml /5 fl oz thick cream
salt and ground white pepper
5 ml /1 tsp chopped fresh chives

1   Melt 25 g /1 oz butter in a large, heavy saucepan, over very low heat. Add the onion and celery, cover and simmer for 5 minutes.

2   Carefully stir in the flour, and cook for 3 minutes, stirring continuously. Do not let the flour colour. Remove it from the heat.
3   Bring the milk to the boil. Off the heat, stir in the stock. Gradually mix the liquid into the butter and flour. Add the wine.
4   Return the mixture to a low heat and simmer it for 15 minutes. Meanwhile, cut the rind from the cheese. Chop the cheese into small pieces. Stir it into the soup and cook for 10 minutes more.
5   Strain most of the liquid into a clean saucepan. Purée all the solids with the rest of the liquid and then add this purée to the strained liquid.
6   Just before serving, bring the soup to the boil. Remove it from the heat and stir in the remaining butter and thick cream. Stir it until the butter melts. Season it to taste. Garnish with chopped chives and serve.

Brie pâté

🍴 4–6 hours soaking, 2 hours
chilling, then 10 minutes

Serves 4
225 g /8 oz Brie cheese
150 ml /5 fl oz dry white wine
75 g /3 oz unsalted butter, softened
salt
ground white pepper
a few drops of Worcestershire sauce or cognac
2 plain oatcakes
4–6 slices hot toast, to serve

1   Cut or scrape the rind from the cheese and discard the rind. Soak the cheese in the dry white wine for 4–6 hours. Drain it and discard the wine.
2   Mash or beat together the cheese and butter until blended. Season the mixture with the salt and white pepper and add Worcestershire sauce or cognac to taste.
3   Line a 225 g /8 oz cottage cheese carton with a thin cloth. Press in the cheese mixture, and level the top. Chill until it is

Greek pepper salad

Liptauer cheese with crudités

firm, about 2 hours. Meanwhile, put the biscuits in a plastic bag and crush them to fine crumbs with a rolling pin.
4   Remove the pâté from the carton by pulling up the corners of the cloth. Turn it out onto a board. Coat the pâté all over with crumbs and press them on firmly.
5   Serve the pâté at once, accompanied by the slices of hot toast.

Rigatoni with ricotta and sage

🍴 20 minutes

Serves 6 as a starter
500 g /1 lb rigatoni
salt and ground white pepper
1 small onion, finely chopped
50 ml /2 fl oz olive oil or 125 g /4 oz butter
250 g /8 oz ricotta cheese
125 ml /4 fl oz milk
4–5 fresh sage leaves, finely chopped

1   Simmer the rigatoni in a large pan of boiling, salted water for 16–20 minutes until it is cooked but still firm when tested.
2   Meanwhile, in a small saucepan, cook the onion in olive oil or butter over a low heat for five minutes. Mix the ricotta with the milk and sage, add this to the onion and cook the mixture for 8 minutes over a low heat, stirring it continuously. Season with salt and pepper.
3   Drain the rigatoni and place it in a large, warmed serving dish. Pour the ricotta sauce over the rigatoni and serve immediately.

Greek pepper salad

🍴 45 minutes,
including salting

Serves 4
1 cucumber, sliced
salt
3 large peppers, seeded and cut into rounds
500 g /1 lb firm tomatoes, cut into quarters
a bunch of spring onions, trimmed
50 g /2 oz black olives
75 g /3 oz Feta cheese, cubed
For the dressing
2 sprigs of fresh mint, chopped
2 garlic cloves, crushed
105 ml /7 tbls olive oil
juice of 1 large lemon
salt and freshly ground black pepper

1   In a colander, layer the sliced cucumber with salt between the layers. Leave to drain, then rinse and dry the slices.
2   Arrange the prepared peppers, cucumber and tomatoes in layers in a bowl.
3   Chop the spring onions in half lengthways and add them to the salad. Top the salad with olives and Feta cheese.
4   Mix together the mint, garlic, olive oil and lemon juice. Add salt and pepper to taste, pour over the salad and serve.

Chicken stuffed with herbs

 1¾ hours

Serves 8

4 double poussins, weighing 800–900 g /
  1 lb 12 oz–2 lb each
100 g /4 oz button mushrooms
25 g /1 oz freshly chopped parsley
45 ml /3 tbls freshly chopped tarragon
45 ml /3 tbls freshly snipped chives
4 spring onions, finely chopped
100 g /4 oz Petit Suisse cheese
salt
freshly ground black pepper
15 ml /1 tbls olive oil
mange tout, to serve (see note
  below)

For the sauce

425 ml /15 fl oz chicken stock, home-made or
  from a cube
150 ml /5 fl oz white wine
15 ml /1 tbls cornflour
1 clove of garlic, peeled
15 ml /1 tbls freshly chopped parsley or
  tarragon
25 ml /1 fl oz thick cream

1 Heat the oven to 190C /375F /gas 5.
2 Rinse the chickens inside and out and pat
them dry. Wipe the mushrooms, trim the
stalks and slice the caps finely.
3 Combine the mushrooms, parsley,
tarragon, chives, spring onions, cheese and
salt and pepper to taste. Mash the ingredients
together to make a stiff paste.
4 Working from the neck end, lift the skin
away from the chicken flesh without tearing
it. Work your hand around the breast and
along the thighs so that the skin is loose all
over the body.
5 Divide the herb paste into four. Push a
portion under the skin over the breast and
spread it with your hand all round the body
of the chicken and down into the thighs.
Repeat with the other chickens. Put the
chickens on a roasting rack in a roasting tin.
Brush with oil and roast them for 50–60
minutes until the juices run clear. Transfer
the cooked chickens to a warm serving dish
and keep them hot.
6 To make the sauce, add the stock and
wine to the roasting tin. Bring it to the boil
on top of the hob and scrape the sediment
from the bottom of the tin.
7 Dissolve the cornflour in a little water
and add a spoonful of the stock and wine
liquid to it. Stir and then turn the mixture
into the roasting tin. Add the garlic and

simmer the sauce for a few minutes. Remove
the garlic, then stir in the parsley or tarragon
and cream and transfer it to a sauce-boat.
8 Cut each bird in half and pour a little
sauce over each portion. Serve with mange
tout and the sauce handed separately.

● To serve the mange tout, top and tail
the vegetables, then drop them into a pan
of slightly salted boiling water. Cover and
simmer for 3–4 minutes, drain and serve.
● Substitute the grated zest of a lemon for
the tarragon and chives in the stuffing. Use
15 ml /1 tbls lemon juice in the sauce.

Aubergine-layer bake

 3¼ hours

Serves 4

1 kg /2 lb aubergines, sliced 5 mm /¼ in thick
salt
olive oil
225 g /8 oz cottage cheese, sieved, or ricotta
  cheese
60 ml /4 tbls finely chopped fresh parsley
50 g /2 oz Parmesan cheese, freshly grated
175–225 g /6–8 oz Mozzarella cheese, thinly
  sliced

For the tomato sauce
1 Spanish onion, finely chopped
2 garlic cloves, finely chopped
30 ml /2 tbls olive oil
45 ml /3 tbls tomato purée
400 g /14 oz canned peeled tomatoes
1 bay leaf
30 ml /2 tbls finely chopped fresh parsley
4 ml /¾ tsp dried oregano
1.5 ml /¼ tsp dried basil
a small strip lemon zest
45 ml /3 tbls dry white wine
salt and freshly ground pepper

For the bechamel sauce
40 g /1½ oz butter
30 ml /2 tbls finely chopped onion
30 ml /2 tbls finely chopped ham or veal
30 ml /2 tbls flour
425 ml /15 fl oz milk
¼ chicken stock cube
½ bay leaf
6 white peppercorns
a good pinch of freshly grated nutmeg

1 To make the tomato sauce, sauté the onion and garlic in olive oil in a large, thick-bottomed frying-pan, until they are transparent and soft but not coloured. Stir in the tomato purée and continue to cook the sauce for 1–2 minutes, stirring constantly.
2 Pour in the canned tomatoes and juice.

Stir in the bay leaf, parsley, oregano, basil and lemon zest. Add the white wine and 45 ml /3 tbls water and season to taste with salt and black pepper. Simmer gently, stirring from time to time, for 1–2 hours, until the sauce has reduced. Remove the bay leaf and lemon zest.
3 Meanwhile, make the bechamel sauce. Put the butter in a small pan over a low heat. Melt the butter and then add the finely chopped onion. Sauté it very gently until it is soft, without letting it colour. Stir in the finely chopped ham or veal and the flour and cook for 2–3 minutes, stirring constantly with a wooden spoon.
4 In another pan, bring the milk almost to boiling point. Away from the heat, stir one-quarter of the heated milk into the roux of flour and butter. Return it to a low heat and bring it to the boil, stirring vigorously.
5 As the sauce begins to thicken, add the remainder of the milk, a little at a time, stirring briskly until the sauce bubbles and is cooked.
6 Crumble the stock cube and add it to the sauce. Next, add the bay leaf, the peppercorns and the pinch of nutmeg. The sauce must now infuse and reduce in quantity to 275 ml /10 fl oz. If you are using a double boiler, leave the pan at the back of the stove over gently simmering water for about 30 minutes, stirring occasionally. If not, stir the sauce more frequently, over a low heat, for 10–15 minutes.
7 Strain the sauce through a fine sieve and reserve it until it is needed.
8 Meanwhile, salt the aubergine slices and leave them for 30 minutes in a colander. Next, rinse the aubergines and pat them dry. Heat the grill to high. Brush the aubergine slices with olive oil on both sides. Place them on a grill pan and grill them for about 3 minutes on each side until lightly browned.
9 In a bowl, combine the sieved cottage or ricotta cheese with the parsley and half the Parmesan cheese. Heat the oven to 180C / 350F /gas 4.
10 Pour one-third of the tomato sauce into a large, shallow heatproof casserole or gratin dish. Place a layer of lightly browned aubergine slices on top of this, followed by one-third of the cheese mixture, and half of the bechamel sauce. Repeat these layers, then top the dish with the remaining tomato sauce,

aubergines and cheese mixture, and end with a layer of the sliced Mozzarella cheese.
11 Sprinkle the top of the layer bake with the rest of the grated Parmesan cheese and bake it for 50 minutes, until the cheese has melted and the top is brown.

Spinach and cheese pie

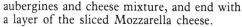 1½ hours

Serves 6
1 kg /2 lb fresh spinach
1 large onion, finely chopped
6 spring onions, finely chopped
60 ml /4 tbls olive or a light vegetable oil,
    plus extra for greasing and brushing
30 ml /2 tbls dill or fennel leaves, finely
    chopped, or 10 ml /2 tsp dillweed (dried dill)
225 g /8 oz Feta or cottage cheese
4 medium-sized eggs, lightly beaten
salt and freshly ground black pepper
a pinch of grated nutmeg
500 g /1 lb frozen puff pastry, defrosted

1 Wash the spinach in plenty of water, remove the large stems, drain and squeeze out the excess water.
2 Fry the onion and spring onions gently in the oil until they are soft and transparent but not coloured. Add the spinach to the pan with the dill or fennel leaves and let it all cook in the water from the spinach and the natural juices. Stir regularly. Cook over a medium heat for about 15 minutes or until the spinach has collapsed into a tender mass. Drain off the excess liquid.
3 When the spinach has cooled a little, mash the cheese with a fork and add it to the spinach with the lightly beaten eggs. Season the mixture with some black pepper, a pinch of nutmeg and salt — Greek Feta cheese needs hardly any salt but cottage cheese will need some added.
4 Heat the oven to 180C /350F /gas 4. Cut the pastry in two, one piece slightly larger than the other. Roll out the larger one and use it to line a lightly oiled, large ovenproof dish, about 35 × 25 cm /14 × 10 in. Make sure that the edges come well over the sides of the dish to make a good edge for sealing later.
5 Spread the cooled spinach mixture over the pastry, thinly roll out the rest of the pastry and cover the spinach mixture. Trim the top and bottom edges and seal them together by moistening them with a little water and pressing them together, pinching and twisting the dough at close intervals. Brush the top with oil and prick the crust all over with a fork so that the steam can escape.
6 Place the pie in the centre of the oven for 45 minutes or until the crust is crisp and golden. Serve it hot or warm.

● This recipe, called Spanakopita in Greek, is usually made with filo pastry.
● Filo pastry can be hard to find but is sometimes stocked by large freezer centres, supermarkets and Greek delicatessens.

Chicken stuffed with herbs

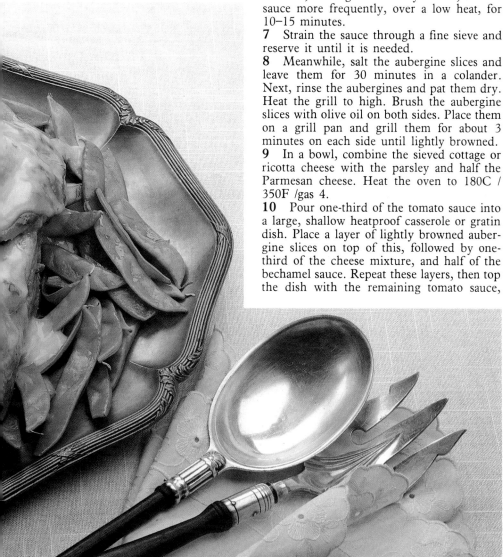

Cucumber ring

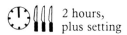 2 hours,
plus setting

Serves 4

½ large cucumber, peeled, seeded and finely chopped
30 ml /2 tbls tarragon or white wine vinegar
salt
500 g /1 lb cottage cheese
150 ml /5 fl oz soured cream
10 ml /2 tsp powdered gelatine
3 spring onions, finely chopped (including green parts)
30 ml /2 tbls snipped fresh chives
45 ml /3 tbls finely chopped fresh parsley
45 ml /3 tbls finely chopped watercress
freshly ground black pepper
oil, for greasing

For the filling
wedges of tomato and stoned black olives
½ × Vinaigrette (see page 38)

1   Place the cucumber in a bowl, sprinkle it with the vinegar and 15 ml /1 tbls salt and toss the mixture well. Place the cucumber in a sieve, weight it down with a plate and leave it to drain, over a bowl, for at least 1 hour. Remove the plate and press the cucumber gently to extract any remaining liquid. Discard the juices and reserve the salted cucumber pieces.
2   Mix together the cottage cheese and the soured cream and process them in an electric blender until smooth. Put the mixture in a large bowl.
3   Sprinkle the gelatine over 45 ml /3 tbls water in a small, heavy-based saucepan and leave it to soak for 5 minutes. Next, set the pan over a very low heat for 2–3 minutes

Cucumber ring

until the gelatine has completely dissolved. Remove the saucepan from the heat.
4   Stir a few spoonfuls of the cheese mixture into the dissolved gelatine, then pour this onto the mixture in the bowl, stirring continuously. When the gelatine has been incorporated, fold in the chopped cucumber, the spring onions, chives, parsley and watercress. Season generously with the black pepper.
5   Pour the mixture into a lightly oiled 700 ml /1¼ pt ring mould; smooth the surface, cover it with cling film and leave it in the refrigerator overnight to set or for at least 8 hours.
6   Turn the cucumber ring out of the mould onto a serving plate. Toss the tomato wedges and black olives in the vinaigrette dressing and then fill the centre of the mould with them.

Brie and herb quiche

30–35 minutes

Serves 6
100 g /4 oz full-fat Brie cheese with herbs
125 g /4½ oz low-fat curd cheese
25 g /1 oz softened butter
45 ml /3 tbls thick cream
2 medium-sized eggs
15 ml /1 tbls finely snipped fresh chives
5 ml /1 tsp finely chopped fresh parsley
salt
freshly ground black pepper
a small pinch of cayenne pepper
22 cm /8½ in half-baked pastry case (see page 16)

1   Heat the oven to 190C /375F /gas 5. Mash the Brie cheese thoroughly, including the rind. Beat in the curd cheese, butter and cream. Continue to beat the mixture until it is well blended and smooth.
2   Beat in the eggs, then the chives and parsley. Taste the mixture, then season it with salt, black pepper and cayenne pepper.
3   Turn the cheese mixture into the pastry flan case. Bake it for 20–25 minutes, or until the filling is set and lightly browned. Serve the quiche at once while it is hot, or allow it to cool and then serve it cold.

● If you have plain Brie, mix in 2.5 ml / ½ tsp Fines herbes to 100 g /4 oz Brie.

Half-moon pizza

30 minutes, plus rising, then 20 minutes

Serves 4
15 g /½ oz fresh yeast, or 7.5 ml /1½ tsp dried yeast and 2.5 ml /½ tsp sugar
200 g /7 oz flour
15 ml /1 tbls olive oil
5 ml /1 tsp salt
For the stuffing
50 g /2 oz ricotta cheese
75 g /3 oz Italian salami or prosciutto, cut into 10 mm /½ in cubes
100 g /4 oz Mozzarella cheese, coarsely grated
45 ml /3 tbls olive oil
salt and freshly ground black pepper

1   If you are using fresh yeast, dissolve it in 100 ml /4 fl oz warm water (37C /98F). If you are using dried yeast, dissolve the sugar in 100 ml /4 fl oz warm water, add the yeast and leave in a warm place for 10–15 minutes, until the liquid becomes very frothy.
2   Pour the flour onto a work surface, make a hollow in the centre and put in the oil, salt and dissolved yeast. Work it with your hands to form a smooth ball. Knead the dough for 10 minutes, until it is smooth and elastic. Transfer the dough to a lightly floured bowl. Cover the bowl with a damp cloth folded in half. Leave the bowl in a warm, draught-free place for about 3 hours, until the dough has risen and doubled in bulk.
3   When the dough is ready, heat the oven to 240C /475F /gas 9. With a fork, break up the ricotta cheese and mix in the salami or prosciutto, the Mozzarella cheese and 15 ml / 1 tbls of the oil. Season the mixture to taste with salt and freshly ground black pepper.
4   Carefully roll out the dough to a 25–28 cm /10–11 in round, 6 mm /¼ in thick. Brush the round with 15 ml /1 tbls of oil. Spoon the stuffing onto one half of the disc, leaving a clear border about 25 mm /1 in all round. Fold over the disc to form a half moon. Seal the edge, first with your fingers then with a fork. Brush the dough all over with the remaining oil.
5   Place the crescent on a baking tray. Bake it for 15–20 minutes or until the edge of the pizza is golden. Serve the pizza hot.

● Try serving the pizza with a tomato sauce. To make a quick tomato sauce, in a pan combine 500 g /1 lb canned tomatoes, 1 crushed garlic clove, 15 ml /1 tbls oregano, 125 ml /4 fl oz olive oil, 5 ml /1 tsp sugar, salt and pepper to taste. Boil for 15 minutes and serve immediately.

Fluffy cottage-cheese dessert

1¼ hours, plus 24 hours draining

Serves 4–6
250 g /9 oz cottage cheese
100 ml /3½ fl oz thick cream
75 g /3 oz caster sugar
3 medium-sized egg whites
a pinch of salt
To serve
grated lemon zest
sugar
cream or crème fraîche (see note below)

1   Drain the cottage cheese in a sieve for 10–15 minutes.
2   Next, rub the cottage cheese through the sieve into a large bowl and beat the cream into it until the mixture is smooth and thick. Gradually add the sugar and reserve.
3   Beat the egg whites with the salt until they are stiff, and then fold them into the cream and cheese mixture. Turn onto a muslin square and suspend it in a sieve over a bowl in the refrigerator for 24 hours to allow it to drain.
4   Scoop the dessert into rounded portions and serve topped with a sprinkling of lemon zest, sugar and cream or crème fraîche.

● To make crème fraîche, mix 275 ml /10 fl oz thick cream with 150 ml /5 fl oz soured cream. Cover and stand in a warm room until set (6 hours). Chill well.

Half-moon pizza

Sicilian chocolate cream pie

🍴 1 week to preserve the peel, making the pastry case, 15 minutes, plus chilling

Serves 6–8

325 g /12 oz ricotta or low-fat curd cheese
125 g /4 oz cottage cheese
a pinch of salt
45 ml /3 tbls cognac or rum
75 g /3 oz caster sugar
50 g /2 oz bitter chocolate, grated
50 g /2 oz preserved orange peel, bought or
*   home-made (see note below)*
45 ml /3 tbls apricot jam, for brushing
22 cm /8½ in fully-baked pastry case (see
*   page 16)*
grated chocolate, to decorate

1 In a bowl, sieve the ricotta or low-fat curd cheese, if using, and the cottage cheese and salt. Stir in the cognac or rum and the sugar and chocolate.
2 Drain the orange peel if using home-made preserved peel. Chop it finely and stir it into the cheese mixture. Chill for 1 hour.
3 Heat the apricot jam in a small pan until it is liquid, then brush it over the inside of the pastry case. Fill the case with the cheese mixture and chill until it is needed.
4 Scatter grated chocolate and extra chopped peel over the dessert just before serving.

● To make the preserved peel, start 7 days in advance. Remove the whole peel (rind and pith) from 2 oranges. Cut it into small, neat strips. Put a layer of strips in a jar with a screw-top lid. Cover the strips with a 3 mm / ⅛ in layer of sugar. Repeat the layers until all the strips are used. Close the jar securely, and shake well. Leave aside for 24 hours. Turn the jar upside down on a saucer. Leave for 24 hours. Repeat the turning process at 24 hour intervals for 6 days. Leave the jar in a cool, dark place until needed. Remove as much peel as you need, and top up the jar with new peel and sugar if wished. Repeat the turning process for 6 days for the new batch and store until required.

Coeurs à la crème

🍴 25 minutes, plus chilling

Serves 4–5

135 g /4½ Gervais Demi-Sel cheese
15 ml /1 tbls lemon juice
125 ml /4 fl oz thick cream
a pinch of salt
50 g /2 oz caster sugar
2 medium-sized egg whites
5 ml /1 tsp sifted icing sugar
150 ml /5 fl oz thin cream, to serve

1 Line a 500 ml /1 pt perforated heart-shaped mould or sieve with long strips of muslin which go across the base, up the sides and overhang at the edges.
2 Whisk the cheese with a fork to break it up, then whisk in the lemon juice.

3 In a separate bowl, whip the cream with the salt until it holds light but firm peaks. Fold it into the cheese with the caster sugar.
4 Whisk the egg whites until stiff. Fold them into the mixture. Gently turn the mixture into the mould. Fold the strips of muslin across the top of the dessert and then chill for at least 1 hour.
5 Half an hour before serving, fold the icing sugar into the thin cream.
6 Immediately before serving, unwrap the muslin strips from the top of the mould, folding them back to leave the surface of the cheese completely free. Now loosen the cheese by pulling up the strips at the edges. Place a serving plate upside down on the mould and invert the mould and plate together so that the dessert lies on the centre of the plate. Carefully peel away all the muslin and discard it — or boil it thoroughly so that it can be used again. Serve the dessert immediately, accompanied by the sweetened, thin cream.

● Serve this delicious French dessert at a St Valentine's Day celebration.

Sicilian chocolate cream pie

22 cm /8½ in cake tin. Do not fit on the sides of the cake tin at this point.

2 Put the biscuit crumbs in a bowl and work in the butter and sugar with a wooden spoon. Pat or spread the mixture in an even layer over the cake tin base.

3 Bake the biscuit mixture for 8 minutes in the oven. Allow it to cool completely (about ½ hour), then fit on the sides of the tin.

4 Meanwhile, strain the orange juice into a heatproof measuring jug and then make up the liquid to 275 ml /10 fl oz with warm water. Sprinkle on the gelatine and leave it to soften for a few minutes.

5 Stand the jug in a pan of very hot water and stir until the gelatine dissolves. Remove the jug from the heat. Add the Cointreau and leave to cool.

6 Turn the cheese into a mixing bowl. Add the grated orange zest and 60 ml /4 tbls of the jam. Beat the mixture until it is thoroughly blended.

7 Gently stir in the orange juice-gelatine mixture. Whip the cream until it just holds soft peaks. Fold it into the cheese mixture. Chill, if necessary, until just beginning to thicken (about 5–10 minutes).

8 Spread the remaining 30 ml /2 tbls jam over the biscuit base in the cake tin. Turn the cheesecake mixture onto the jam-covered base. Chill until the cheesecake is set (about 2 hours). While setting, drain the fruit well.

9 Run a sharp knife around the inside of the cake tin to loosen the cheesecake. Remove the sides of the tin and slide the cheesecake onto a serving plate. Arrange the apricots on the top of the cheesecake and serve.

Ricotta cheesecake

50 minutes,
plus cooling

Serves 6
oil, for greasing
500 g /1 lb ricotta cheese
a pinch of salt
15 ml /1 tbls flour
125 g /4 oz soft brown sugar
2 medium-sized eggs, separated
2.5 ml /½ tsp saffron
5 ml /1 tsp grated orange zest
25 g /1 oz raisins
25 g /1 oz candied orange peel
2.5 ml /½ tsp powdered cinnamon, to garnish
30 ml /2 tbls icing sugar, to garnish

1 Heat the oven to 190C /375F /gas 5 and grease a 20 cm /8 in round, loose-bottomed cake tin. Mix together the ricotta cheese, salt, flour, brown sugar, egg yolks, saffron and the orange zest. Mix in the raisins and candied orange peel.

2 Whisk the egg whites until they are stiff but not dry and fold them into the mixture with a metal spoon. Turn the mixture into the greased tin and bake it in the centre of the oven for 40 minutes or until firm.

3 Remove the cake from the oven, allow it to cool (3–4 hours) and then turn it out onto a dish. Sprinkle with cinnamon and icing sugar before serving.

Orange-apricot party cheesecake

1 hour 10 minutes,
plus cooling

Serves 8–10
oil, for greasing
175 g /6 oz rich tea biscuits, crumbled
60 g /2½ oz softened butter
35 g /1½ oz caster sugar

For the filling
juice and grated zest of 1 large orange
20 g /¾ oz powdered gelatine
45 ml /3 tbls Cointreau
2 × 200 g /7.5 oz Philadelphia full-fat soft cheese
90 ml /6 tbls smooth apricot jam
75 ml /3 fl oz thick cream

For the topping
400 g /14 oz canned apricot halves, drained

1 Heat the oven to 180C /350F /gas 4. Grease and line the base of a loose-bottomed

Truffled tuna pâté

Serves 6
200 g /7 oz canned tuna, drained
100 g /4 oz cream cheese
30 ml /2 tbls soured cream
1 small onion, grated
juice of ½ lemon
5 ml /1 tsp mustard powder
30 ml /2 tbls melted butter
salt and freshly ground black pepper
2 small truffles, coarsely chopped (see below)
3 black olives, halved and stoned, to garnish
hot toast fingers, to serve

1   In a bowl, pound together the drained tuna, cream cheese, soured cream and grated onion until it is smooth and well blended. Alternatively, use a pestle and mortar.
2   Beat in the lemon juice, mustard powder and melted butter. Season to taste with salt and black pepper.
3   Fill 6 individual ramekins with the mixture, smoothing the tops with a palette knife. Chill the pâté until needed.
4   Just before serving, decorate each ramekin with a halved black olive. Arrange the coarsely chopped truffles around the olive. Serve the pâté with hot toast fingers.

● Truffles are extremely expensive and are usually sold in tiny cans. It is often possible to buy slightly cheaper cans of truffle parings which are very good for flavouring pâtés. Keep any unused truffle in the refrigerator, covered with its own juice or a little sherry, and tightly covered with cling film. Use within 1 month.

Deep-fried cheese wheels

Serves 4–6
1 cos lettuce
1 head of chicory
12 sprigs of watercress
olive oil, for deep frying
125 g /4 oz goat's cheese (choose a cylindrical shape), without rind
1–2 eggs, beaten
50–75 g /2–3 oz fresh breadcrumbs
For the vinaigrette dressing
30 ml /2 tbls lemon juice
120 ml /8 tbls olive oil
salt and freshly ground black pepper

1   Thoroughly wash and dry the lettuce, chicory and watercress. Wrap them in tea-towels and store them in the refrigerator to crisp for at least 1 hour.
2   Meanwhile, make the vinaigrette dressing. Combine the lemon juice, olive oil and salt and black pepper to taste. Mix well.
3   Toss the lettuce, chicory and watercress individually in the vinaigrette. Arrange the lettuce around the edge of a serving dish. Arrange the chicory leaves in the centre and scatter with sprigs of watercress. Now refrigerate the salad while the cheese wheels are being cooked.
4   Heat sufficient olive oil for deep frying to 180C /350F on a deep-fat thermometer, or until a cube of stale bread dropped into the oil turns brown in 60 seconds.
5   Use the goat's cheese straight from the refrigerator as it is easier to handle. Cut it into 8 wheels 5 mm /¼ in thick. Coat the cheese wheels first in beaten egg and then in breadcrumbs. Deep fry the wheels for 2 minutes, or until they are golden brown. Be careful not to overcook them, otherwise the breadcrumb casing will split.
6   Drain the cheese wheels on absorbent paper. Place them on top of the salad and serve it all immediately.

 15 minutes,
plus chilling

 1¾ hours,
including chilling

Italian pork chops with Mozzarella

Serves 4
50 g /2 oz ham
4 × 175 g /6 oz pork loin chops
salt
freshly ground black pepper
30 ml /2 tbls olive oil
75 ml /3 fl oz thick cream
100 g /4 oz Mozzarella or Fontina cheese, diced
a pinch of nutmeg
1 egg, beaten
watercress sprigs, to garnish

1   Heat the grill to high. Cut the ham into julienne strips.
2   Sprinkle the pork chops with salt and black pepper, then brush them with the olive oil. Place the chops on the grill pan 7.5 cm /3 in from the heat and cook them for 5–6 minutes on each side.
3   Meanwhile, in a double boiler, heat the thick cream with the diced Mozzarella or Fontina cheese. When the cheese is melted, add about half the strips of ham, black pepper and nutmeg to taste. Stir in the beaten egg and set aside.
4   When cooked, place the chops on a heatproof serving dish, spoon the sauce down the centre of the chops and put them under the grill until the sauce is lightly browned. Garnish with the remaining ham strips and sprigs of watercress.

30 minutes

Sweet cheese fritters

Serves 6
200 g /7 oz curd cheese
3 eggs, separated
60 ml /4 tbls caster sugar
a pinch of salt
75 ml /5 tbls flour
30 ml /2 tbls rum or lemon juice
finely grated zest of 1 lemon
1.5 ml /¼ tsp ground cinnamon
oil, for deep frying
sifted icing sugar, to serve
For the batter
150 g /5 oz flour
a pinch of salt
30 ml /2 tbls olive oil
1 egg white

1   Wrap the cheese in a double thickness of fine muslin and squeeze out as much liquid as possible — the cheese should be dry and crumbly in texture.
2   Prepare the batter. Sift the flour with a pinch of salt into a bowl. Make a well in the centre, add the oil and 175 ml /6 fl oz water. Beat the liquid with a wire whisk, incorporating the flour. Carry on beating until the batter is smooth.
3   In a bowl, whisk the egg white until it is stiff but not dry. Gently but thoroughly fold it into the batter, using a large metal spoon. Leave the batter to rest.
4   In a bowl, beat the crumbly curd cheese with the egg yolks, the caster sugar, salt, flour, rum or lemon juice, until smooth and well blended.
5   Beat in the prepared batter, the finely grated lemon zest and the ground cinnamon.
6   Heat the oil in a deep-fat frier to 190C /375F — a 15 mm /½ in cube of day old bread takes 50 seconds to become crisp and golden brown at this temperature.
7   In a clean, large bowl, whisk the egg whites until they are stiff but not dry. With a large metal spoon, fold them carefully but thoroughly into the batter mixture.
8   To put the mixture into the hot oil, hold a tablespoon of mixture still and ease it off with a knife. This ensures the fritters keep their round shape and do not ribbon out. Next, flip them over immediately and deep fry for 4–5 minutes, or until crisp and golden brown. Do about 5 fritters at a time, then drain them on absorbent paper and repeat the process with the remaining mixture, keeping the cooked fritters warm.
9   Pile the fritters either onto a serving dish or individual dishes. Dust them with icing sugar and serve immediately.

45 minutes

SEMI-HARD & SEMI-SOFT CHEESES

Cheese from the families of semi-hard and semi-soft cheeses fall between the soft, quick-ripening cream cheeses and the hard cheeses, but they are equally good for eating raw and for cooking.

A semi-hard cheese is one that has an inside 'paste' which is semi-hard, close and firm, but pliant, which gives this group of cheeses the name of 'yielding' cheeses. Most are just lightly pressed and not cooked, so they contain a good deal of liquid. As they grow older this evaporates, they become denser and stronger and more like a hard cheese.

Semi-soft cheeses, of which one of the best known is Bel Paese, are softer and creamier but even at their peak, they will still slice. Some of them are close to the yielding cheeses in texture. Others are closer to the soft, rinded and brine-washed cheeses of the Camembert type (see pages 26–39). However, semi-soft cheeses do not spoil so quickly. Many of them have a natural rind, but they do vary considerably.

Most of the cheeses in these two groups are easily available in the shops as they are becoming increasingly popular. Easy to store, they are good to eat and can make moist and tasty sandwich fillings, so they are made and exported by every cheese-making country.

Dutch semi-hard cheeses
Dutch Edam and Gouda are world-renowned for being mild and mellow in taste and semi-hard in texture.

Edam has been made in Holland since the 13th century. With Gouda and their cumin-flavoured cousin, Leiden, it was developed to use up surplus milk. Ball-shaped and weighing about 1.5 kg /3½ lb, the red jacket (once dye, now wax) is added for export as it protects the cheese in transit.

Edam is one of the lowest-calorie cheeses, as it is made with pasteurized, skimmed evening milk, to which full fat morning milk is added. The butterfat content is only 40 per cent, although it has a close buttery texture. It is usually sold while young and bland, but

is sometimes matured. When well-aged it can eventually darken and become very hard indeed. History says it has even been used for cannon balls!

Gouda, like Edam, is named after a small port that shipped cheeses abroad. It now accounts for two-thirds of Dutch cheese. Made with pasteurized full milk, it has a butterfat content of 48 per cent. It is shaped like a wheel, with a smooth yellow rind. It is also sold while still young and bland, although a certain quantity of 'mature Gouda' of high quality is now exported. Like Edam, Gouda is used for cooking in almost any kind of dish.

Copies: it's not surprising that cheeses which have proved so popular should be copied in many of the countries to which they have been sent. Dozens of Edam-type cheeses are made: in France a large Edam-type is manufactured and called Mimolette. It is coloured orange. There is also a Gouda Français, very similar to the original. In parts of Central and South America, Edam has been adopted so fully that it is often the only cheese sold except soft, fresh local cheese, and it is even called Puerto Rican cheese.

Italian semi-hard cheeses
The ancient Romans, who were sophisticated cheesemakers, imported and exported a great many varieties. Most of these cheeses were hard, but the army supplied soldiers with semi-hard cheeses, which were smoked for greater flavour. The forerunner of today's Provolone was one of these smoked cheeses, as was Caciocavallo, already popular and a great favourite of the Emperor Augustus.

Provolone: usually made with raw cow's milk, this type of cheese is called *formaggio de pasta filata* in Italian, because the curd, which is heated in whey, sliced and then heated again, is kneaded by the cheesemaker, rather like bread, until it becomes elastic and 'stringy'. It is then moulded into various shapes — ovals, pear shapes, cones, cylinders, even baby piglets — which are sold under a variety of names. Once moulded, the cheeses are tied with string and hung up to dry. Most modern Provolone is preferred young and yielding, so the cheeses are then dipped in paraffin wax to preserve the moisture content, although in the past they were matured until they were hard and then they were smoked.

Caciocavallo is a cheese much copied in the Eastern Mediterranean and Balkans. The

1 Gjetost, 2 Mimolette, 3 Jarlsberg,
4 Provolone, 5 Havarti, 6 Limburger, 7 Edam,
8 Tilsit, 9 Munster, 10 Tomme de Savoie,
11 Gouda, 12 St-Albray, 13 Port Salut,
14 St-Nectaire, 15 Morbier, 16 Tourte
Paysanne, 17 Bel Paese, 18 Taleggio,
19 Danbo, 20 Tomme au Marc de Raisin,
21 Swedish Fontina

name means 'cheese on horseback' as it was traditionally hand-moulded in the shape of two saddlebags. It is saltier than Provolone, but the pummelling given by the cheese-maker makes both cheeses have an unusual close, smooth, buttery texture.

Fontina, from the Aosta Valley, near the St Bernard pass leading to Switzerland, is one of the half a dozen most beautiful cheeses in the world. It is copied in Sweden, as a paler, blander and moister Fontina, which has a bright-red jacket. In various parts of Italy there are reasonably similar copies called Fontal or Fontinella.

Fontina was originally made from sheep's milk, but is now made only from cow's milk. In summer it is produced in mountain chalets, when the cows are grazing on high ground, and in winter it is made in the village creameries. It is flat and round cheese with a smooth rind, the colour of creamy coffee. The interior is ivory, with tiny holes. The flavour has been described as having 'the sweetness of Gruyère with a hint of Port Salut'.

Fontina does not run or ooze at room temperature, but it is also never really solid. It is a marvellous, subtle table cheese and also a wonderful melter in cooking. It is an essential ingredient of the Italian version of Swiss fondue called *fonduta*, which is made with fresh white truffles, Fontina, eggs and milk. It can also be used as a substitute for Mozzarella.

French semi-hard cheeses
Mild yielding cheeses are in the minority in France. Two newcomers are Bonbel and Baby Bel from *La Vache qui Rit* — 'the laughing cow' label. The first is a blander popular version of Port Salut, the second is not unlike mild Gouda.

Port Salut dates back to the early 1800s, when the monks at the Abbey of Port du Salut started making a mild, fruity cheese with an orange-ochre rind and a pale paste. It became so popular that pirate versions appeared, so in 1878 the name was reserved for the monks who then helped to found a creamery using the cheese's original name.

Like many of the yielding cheeses, Port Salut changes as it matures. When young it is very mild indeed, and the baby versions remain so. The large cheeses get stronger. It is widely exported and much copied, not only by the Danes, but also in the U.S.

Tommes are soft and creamy and are made in many different parts of France; some are made from goat's or sheep's milk. Tomme de Savoie is particularly worth looking out for. Firmer than some, and easily sliced, it is a raw cow's milk cheese, ripened in damp cellars, and it has an aroma of mould. The version most often exported is Tomme au Marc de Raisin from Burgundy. It is easily recognized by the grape pips pressed into the crust of the young cheese which give it a distinctive smell of brandy as it matures.

Morbier is an unusual cheese, imported for its appearance. It has a natural, linen-patterned grey rind and a thin dark line of sooty ash through the middle. This originated when the mountain herdsmen used to cover the curds of the morning milk with ash to protect them, but it was found to improve the cheese's flavour, and the habit has been continued since then.

Other semi-hard cheeses

Other countries produce their versions of semi-hard cheeses which may be more difficult to buy, but it will be rewarding if you can manage to track them down in specialist cheese shops.

Tilsit is the most famous German semi-hard cheese to be exported and is rather like Port Salut. In Central Europe it is called Ragnit.

Weisslacker Bierkase has long been the Germans' preferred national cheese, although it was originally Belgian. The cheese is a fairly firm cube or loaf with a shiny, dryish rind and can be stored for up to a year.

Grevé, from Sweden, is a similar cheese to Tilsit, but with larger holes than Emmental.

Jarlsberg, from Norway, is the most familiar Scandinavian cheese. Mild and semi-hard, it has large eyes like Emmental, but a distinctively different flavour.

Gjetost, 'goat's milk', is also from Norway. It is a sweet, toffee-coloured unpressed cheese made mostly from whey. Its flavour is an acquired taste.

Havarti: derivative of the German Tilsit, it is a supple and creamy cheese with irregular holes, and it is usually eaten after three months, as it becomes harder and more pungent with age.

Esrom, often described as a version of Port Salut, is based on an old Danish formula. Slightly stronger than Port Salut, it is sometimes sold under the name Ambassadeur.

Samsø, made in a big wheel, is the 'grandfather' of the mild cheeses — the family includes Danbo (which can be plain or with caraway seeds), Fynbo, Elbo (mild and packed with small holes, it has a red coat), Tybo and Molbo. Samsø is a softer, milder, moister version of Swiss Emmental with smaller holes. As it ages it develops a full flavour of its own. Mini-sized versions are sold in red coats. Maribo is a mild Danish cheese which is good to use when cooking.

Other cheeses: Greek Kasseri is not unlike Provolone, while Portugal's Oeija de Serra or 'mountain cheese' is also one of the filata type. Neither of these, nor the Spanish Aragon, is generally exported.

French semi-soft cheeses

Aromatic cheeses, developed long ago by monks for their own use, are the best of French semi-soft cheeses. Many of them are soft. Others have a natural or brushed rind and are lightly pressed or heavily drained to give a cheese that is sliceable at room temperature when at its best. You can cook with most of them, but they tend to impose their own character on the dish, so they need care in handling.

Munster is one of the oldest cheeses, dating back to the earlier Middle Ages. It is the national cheese of French Alsace (not to be confused with German Münster or Muenster or American Munster — which are all very different). It was first made by Irish Benedictine monks in the Vosges mountains in Alsace and its name comes from the Latin word for monastery. By law the name is reserved for cheeses from this small area.

Flat discs made of cow's milk from mountain pastures, Munster and Petit Munster are rich cheeses with 45 per cent butterfat. The farm-made cheese (Munster Fermier) has an ochre, bloomy rind, while the creamery version, made with pasteurized milk, has a reddish rind. It is sometimes made with cumin seeds, but is at its best when plain and young.

Géromé is a near-relation of Munster, almost as handsomely flavoured; there is a variant called Chaumont.

St-Nectaire, another fine mountain cheese, seems positively fragile when compared to Munster. Made in the Auvergne, it comes from the milk of cows reputed to be the richest milk-producers in France. Matured on rye straw in cool, damp cellars, after three months it develops a natural, colourful mouldy crust, which is red, yellow and white. It is best eaten about six months old, when its flavour has developed and its aroma is quite strong. Lightly pressed, with a 45 per cent butterfat content, it has various cheese 'cousins' of which the nearest are Savoron and Vachard. Another relation is Murol, which looks like a raised doughnut with a hole in the middle.

Other cheeses which are exported are Fromage de Curé, from Brittany, square with a spicy flavour, St-Albray which comes from the Pyrenees and is made in the same way as Camembert and Tourte Paysanne, a cow's milk cheese from eastern France.

Italian semi-soft cheeses

The semi-soft group of cheeses described in Italy as *Italico* are creamy but still firm enough to slice.

Bel Paese is one of the few modern factory cheeses to achieve and deserve international status. Mild, reliable and unchanging, it is easily recognized by the label showing the map of Italy — the *bel paese* or 'beautiful country'. Created in 1921 by a cheese-maker called Galbani who was a keen mountaineer, it is based on the peasant and monastery cheeses of the mountains near Lake Como. Good for eating, it has a smooth rind and its fat content of 48 per cent makes it a quick melting cheese, ideal for cooking. Bel Paese can also be bought in a harder form and as a cheese spread. It is often used as a substitute for Mozzarella in fondues.

It is exported and copied throughout the Americas and the Far East, and there are at least three other Italian versions, a German version and a French one.

Stracchino cheeses were first made from the milk of cows being driven south as winter approached; the name comes from the word *stracco* which means 'tired'. The milk was thin and cheeses from it were fresh and delicate. Cheeses made from raw milk mature and deteriorate quickly, so these days most stracchino cheeses are made all the year round, from pasteurized milk.

Taleggio is the finest of the white stracchino cheeses. Made from a mixture of ripened evening and fresh morning milk, Taleggio is not pressed, but is turned in its vat to drain it. It has a flaky, soft, rosy rind and a compact, pale paste. The best Taleggio is made in north Italy — the name is protected by law, although its alternative name, Talfino, is not. It has a rich aroma and flavour, and a melting, delicate and easily spoiled consistency.

Stracchino crescenza is a square-shaped, rindless and quick-maturing cheese; one version is a cream cheese, the other, firmer.

Robiola, delicious and quick-maturing, is not strictly a stracchino cheese, but is very similar. The original Robiola gave birth to the various Italico cheeses and was made from partly skimmed ewe's, goat's and cow's milk. Now only the latter is used.

Made in cool conditions because it spoils easily, the curd is hardly cut. The cheese is rubbed with a brine cloth, while curing in a

linen-lined box. It can be eaten, while delicate and mild, after ten days. However, it is worth waiting a month for its full, truffle-like flavour to develop. The delicious, milder Robiola is exported in a 'baby' version called Robbiolina.

Other semi-soft cheeses

Three other general kinds of semi-soft cheese are worth mentioning here.

Vacherin Mont d'Or is produced in Switzerland in the mountain foothills. This fine, creamy winter cheese is one of the softest of the group. Do not confuse it with the French cheese of the same name, or the other nine cheeses also called Vacherin!

The Swiss cheese is made of milk from cows on winter feed and the hay gives the cheese a sweet quality. It is drained on pinewood shelves and it develops a pinkish rind after ten days. The thin, washed rind does not stop the cheese collapsing, so it is packed in pinebark cylinders which add to its faint balsam flavour. It deteriorates easily, so it is only made and exported in the cold months — Vacherins bought at the other times of the year are not likely to be Swiss ones.

Limburger is a group of cheeses rather than a single one. Chiefly renowned for their smell, there are at least seven types of German Limburger, as well as versions from six other countries — but not all of them are smelly. In fact they vary enormously, from an almost fresh cheese to Romadur, generally agreed to be pretty odorous. Limburgers also vary enormously in butterfat content — from 20–85 per cent. Limburger itself is delicate and spoils quickly.

Münster is the only other German cheese seriously exported (the umlaut distinguishes it from its French counterpart). Baby German Münsters are sold as fat, round little cheeses with a smooth, mild paste, a reddish skin and a butterfat content of between 30–50 per cent.

Storing the cheeses

Semi-soft cheeses may generally be stored in the refrigerator, but should always be removed at least two hours before eating to allow the flavour to develop. Dense, semi-hard cheeses can be stored uncut for 3–4 weeks — Edam and Gouda will usually keep much longer. After cutting, cover the surface with foil (not cling film or they will sweat) and keep them for 3–4 days. Keeping semi-hard cheeses for a maximum of 3–4 days in the refrigerator is a good rule to follow.

Curried chicken salad

making the mayonnaise, then 15 minutes

Serves 4
100 g /4 oz Leiden or Edam cheese
100 g /4 oz cooked chicken
1 large courgette
2 large celery sticks
50 g /2 oz button mushrooms
a handful of young spinach leaves
For the dressing
about 125 ml /4 fl oz mayonnaise (see note below)
20 ml /4 tsp lemon juice
2.5 ml /½ tsp curry powder
7.5 ml /½ tbls grated onion

1 Grate 25 g /1 oz of the cheese and keep it aside for garnishing. Cut the remaining cheese and the chicken into 10 mm /½ in dice and mix them together in a bowl.
2 Dice the courgette and add it to the bowl. Thinly slice the celery and mushrooms and add these to the bowl.
3 Measure out 125 ml /4 fl oz mayonnaise in a bowl. Whisk in the lemon juice, curry powder and grated onion, taste and add more mayonnaise if it tastes too sharp. Pour the dressing over the salad and toss to coat.
4 Remove any stems from the spinach leaves, then make a bed of leaves on a salad platter. Pile the chicken mixture on top. Sprinkle with the reserved grated cheese and serve the salad immediately.

● To make 150 ml /5 fl oz mayonnaise, put one egg yolk in a blender with 7.5 ml /1½ tsp wine vinegar or lemon juice, a pinch each of mustard powder, salt and freshly ground black pepper and 15 ml /1 tbls cold water. Blend until well mixed. Remove the centre of the lid and, with the motor at maximum, trickle in 150 ml /5 fl oz olive oil.

Curried chicken salad

Cheese in vine leaves

🍴 40 minutes preparation,
plus 20 minutes cooking

Makes 24
200 g /8 oz sealed pack of preserved vine leaves
350 g /12 oz Fontina cheese, rind removed
75 ml /5 tbls olive oil
6 slices medium white bread

1 Remove 24 leaves from the pack of vine leaves, and reserve the rest for future use. To remove the brine preserve, rinse the vine leaves thoroughly in cold water. Shake off the excess water, then pat each one dry.
2 Cut the cheese into twenty-four 25 mm / 1 in thick cubes.
3 Place a cube of cheese in the middle of each dry vine leaf. Fold the two sides of the leaf over the cheese. Bring up the stem end, then roll the parcel towards the tip of the leaf to form a neat little package.
4 Lightly oil a shallow, ovenproof serving dish large enough to take the leaves in a single layer. Place the packages, seam-side down, in the dish. Brush them all over with olive oil. Cover with cling film and chill.
5 Heat the oven to 200C /400F /gas 6.
6 Bake the cheese and vine leaf packages for 20 minutes, or until they feel soft to the touch.
7 Using a plain 4 cm /1½ in biscuit cutter, cut 24 rounds from the bread. Put the rounds of bread to crisp in the oven 5 minutes before the end of the cooking time. Now, place the cheese packages on top of the croûtes. Leave them to cool slightly, then serve.

● If wished, use Gruyère cheese or Bel Paese instead of Fontina. Goat's cheese coated in finely ground walnuts is another delicious variation.

Four seasons pizza

🍴 35 minutes making the dough,
then 45 minutes

Makes a 32.5 × 22.5 cm /13 × 9 in pizza
For the dough
15 g /½ oz fresh yeast
25 mg tablet ascorbic acid
225 g /8 oz strong, plain flour, plus extra
for dusting
5 ml /1 tsp salt
5 ml /1 tsp sugar
15 g /½ oz butter
oil, for greasing
For the topping
225 g /½ lb fresh tomatoes, skinned
100 g /¼ lb mushrooms
15 g /½ oz butter
225 g /½ lb canned tuna
100 g /¼ lb sliced salami
50 g /2 oz Edam cheese, grated
5 ml /1 tsp freshly chopped basil or oregano

1 Warm a scant 150 ml /5 fl oz water to blood heat (37C /98F). Crumble the yeast into the water.
2 Crush the ascorbic tablet between 2 spoons, then stir the powder into the yeast

liquid and whisk it with a fork until it is completely dissolved.
3 Into a large mixing bowl, sift the flour, salt and sugar and stir them together with a round-bladed knife. Cut the butter into the flour until the pieces are pea-sized and coated with flour, then rub in the fat until the mixture resembles breadcrumbs.
4 Make a well in the centre of the flour mixture and add the yeast liquid. Mix together until the dough binds and cleanly leaves the sides of the bowl.
5 Turn the dough onto a floured surface and knead it by stretching the dough, pushing it away from you with the heel of your hand. Give the dough a quarter turn, folding it back and kneading it. Repeat the kneading and turning for 10 minutes, using a rocking action. (Alternatively, use the dough hook of an electric mixer to knead the dough. Mix it at speed 1 for 1 minute and speed 3 for 3 minutes.)
6 Put the dough in a greased polythene bag and tie it loosely. Put the bag in a warm place for 5–10 minutes to allow it to rise.

7 Brush a 32.5 × 22.5 cm /13 × 9 in baking sheet with oil. Knock back the risen dough with your knuckles and then roll it into a ball.
8 Heat the oven to 200C /400F /gas 6. Roll out the dough to fit the baking sheet. Transfer the dough to the greased baking sheet. Pinch the outer edge of the dough to form a slight rim.
9 Cut the tomatoes into thin slices and reserve. Cut the mushrooms into slices. Melt the butter in a small frying-pan and add the mushrooms. Sauté them until they are golden brown, then drain and reserve them.
10 Drain the oil from the tuna and reserve it. Flake the fish. Remove the skin from the salami and cut each slice into quarters.
11 Brush the top of the pizza dough very lightly with a little of the reserved tuna oil and, with the back of a large round-bladed knife, mark the dough into 4 equal strips.
12 Place the tuna on one strip, the tomatoes on the next, followed by the salami, with the mushrooms on the last one.
13 Sprinkle the cheese all over the pizza

and finish by sprinkling the basil or the oregano over the top of the cheese.

14 Drizzle about 2.5 ml /½ tsp reserved oil from the tuna over each quarter. Bake the pizza in the centre of the oven for 20–25 minutes until it is well risen and the topping is bubbling.

● Try a 4-cheese pizza. Cover the surface of the pizza with a fresh tomato sauce (see page 12). For the topping, use 50 g /2 oz of a different cheese on each section of the pizza. Accompany each cheese with a different herb: Lancashire with chives, Emmental with marjoram, Gouda with parsley, and Mozzarella with oregano. Drizzle the pizza with olive oil and garnish with black olives.

Hot cheese and tomato loaf

 40 minutes

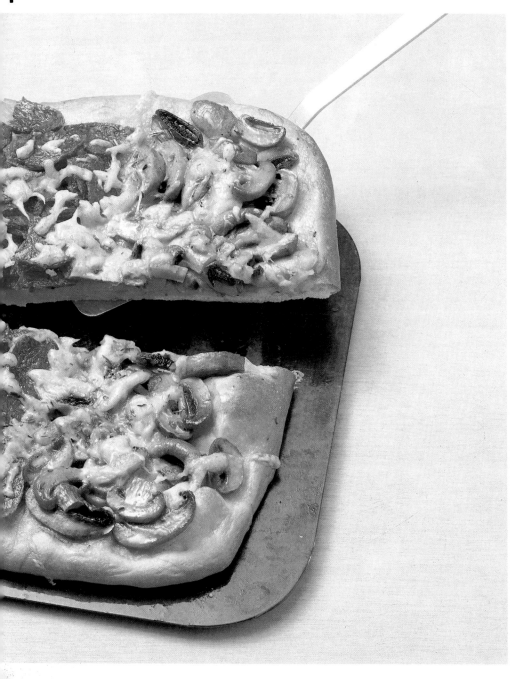

Serves 6
15 ml /1 tbls oil
450 g /1 lb small bloomer loaf
225 g /8 oz Edam cheese
225 g /8 oz thinly sliced ham
225 g /8 oz firm tomatoes, blanched, skinned and sliced
15 ml /1 tbls freshly chopped basil
50 g /2 oz softened butter

1 Heat the oven to 200C /400F /gas 6. Using the oil, grease a large baking tray.
2 Cutting at 12 mm /½ in intervals, slice the bread almost but not quite through, leaving the slices attached at the bottom.
3 Cut the cheese into as many thin slices as there are cuts in the bread. Place a slice of cheese in each slit in the bread. Add a slice of ham and 4 slices of tomato.
4 Sprinkle a little basil into each slit. Spread the outside of the loaf with butter.
5 Wrap the loaf in foil. Place it on the baking tray. Cook for 20 minutes. Serve hot.

Four seasons pizza

Italian toasted sandwiches

 15 minutes

Serves 2
50 g /2 oz butter, plus extra for greasing
4 slices white bread
4 thin slices salami
8 green or black olives
4 thin slices Bel Paese or Edam cheese
salt and freshly ground black pepper

1 Set the grill at low.
2 Butter each slice of bread, then put 2 slices of salami on each of 2 slices of bread.
3 Stone the olives and chop them finely. Sprinkle them on top of the salami.
4 Cover the olives with the cheese slices. Sprinkle the cheese with salt and pepper. Cover the filling with the second bread slice, buttered side down. Press lightly, to make firm sandwiches.
5 Lay the sandwiches on a well-buttered flameproof plate.
6 Toast the sandwiches under the grill, using a gentle heat, until the upper slices brown. Turn them over and toast the bottom slices. Serve at once.

Cheesy sausages with noodles

40 minutes

Serves 4
8 large turkey sausages
50 g /2 oz Bel Paese or Tilsit, rinded
2 large tomatoes, blanched, skinned and seeded
15 ml /1 tbls olive oil
3 leaves fresh sage, finely chopped
25 g /1 oz butter, plus extra for greasing
salt
225 g /8 oz egg noodles

1 Split each sausage down one side, making a deep socket along its length. Cut the cheese into matchsticks and stuff them into the slits. Press the sausages to reshape them.
2 Heat the oven to 220C /425F /gas 7.
3 Mash the tomato flesh, together with any seedless juice, in a bowl.
4 Sprinkle the oil in a baking tin. Put the sausages, cut side up, in the tin and bake in the oven for 10 minutes.
5 Sprinkle the sausages with the sage and pour the tomatoes over the top. Cover the tin with greased foil. Reduce the oven to 160C /325F /gas 3 and bake for 20 minutes.
6 Meanwhile, bring a large pan of salted water to the boil and cook the noodles for 8–12 minutes until just tender.
7 Drain the noodles. Spread them on a warmed platter, dot them with butter and then cover them loosely with buttered paper.
8 When the sausages are done, place them, cut side up, on top of the noodles. Spoon any remaining tomato sauce over them and then serve them immediately.

Dutch fondue

🍴 40 minutes

Serves 4

250 g /9 oz flat mushrooms with their stalks,
    plus extra for garnishing
600 ml /1 pint chicken stock, home-made or
    from a cube
60 ml /4 tbls cornflour
150 ml /5 fl oz milk
250 g /9 oz Gouda cheese, finely grated
15 ml /1 tbls finely chopped fresh parsley
5 ml /1 tsp Worcestershire sauce
salt
freshly ground black pepper
a sprig of parsley, to garnish

To serve

1 small French loaf, cut into 2.5 cm /1 in cubes
500 g /1 lb pork sausages, fried and thickly
    sliced
broccoli spears and cauliflower florets

1 Finely chop 250 g /9 oz of the mushrooms and slice the rest for the garnish.
2 In a saucepan, put the chopped mushrooms and the stock and bring them to the boil. Lower the heat, cover the pan and simmer gently for 10 minutes.
3 In a small bowl, blend the cornflour to a smooth paste with a little of the milk. Stir this into the mushroom and chicken stock, then add the remaining milk. Bring to the boil, lower the heat and simmer for 2 minutes, stirring all the time.
4 Turn the heat down to low. Add the grated cheese to the pan a little at a time, stirring well until all the cheese has melted. Do not allow the mixture to simmer or the mixture will become stringy and separate.
5 Remove the pan from the heat and stir in the parsley, Worcestershire sauce and salt and pepper to taste. Pour the fondue into a warmed serving bowl or 4 warmed individual bowls, garnish with the mushroom slices and parsley and serve with the bread cubes, sausages, broccoli and cauliflower.

● For additional information on fondues, see page 15.
● As a variation, mix 50 g /2 oz grated Cheddar cheese with 200 g /7 oz Gouda, stir in 15 ml /1 tbls sherry before serving.

Dutch fondue

46

Brandy onions

 45 minutes

Serves 4

4 large onions
salt
100 g /4 oz chilled French Munster or 1 Petit
  Munster, rinded
100 g /4 oz fresh white breadcrumbs
50 g /2 oz watercress leaves, finely chopped
60–75 ml /4–5 tbls melted butter, plus 20 ml /
  4 tsp softened butter
15 ml /1 tbls brandy

1 Boil the onions in their skins in salted water for 25 minutes or until they are tender when pierced with a skewer. Drain and allow them to cool.
2 Meanwhile, cut the cheese into tiny pieces. Mix it with the breadcrumbs and the chopped watercress.
3 Grease four 7.5 cm /3 in ovenproof pots or ramekins with about 10 ml /2 tsp of the melted butter. Stir the remaining melted butter into the breadcrumb mixture. It should hold together when squeezed but not be soggy. Add the brandy and mix it in very thoroughly.
4 Heat the oven to 180C /350F /gas 4.
5 Remove the roots from the onions so that

Brandy onions

they stand upright. Skin the onions and cut off the tops. Put them, root end down, in the pots or ramekins. With a pointed spoon or grapefruit knife, dig out all but the 3 outside sheaths of the onions, leaving cups of onion flesh. (Reserve the insides of the onions for use in another recipe.)
6 Press the buttered breadcrumb mixture firmly into the onion cups, and pile any mixture that is left over on top of them. Dot the stuffing with the softened butter. Put the onions in the oven and bake them for 15–20 minutes until the stuffing is bubbling and browned. Serve the onions immediately.

Savoury Dutch cheese truffles

Makes 12
100 g /4 oz butter, slightly softened
75 g /3 oz Edam cheese, grated
salt and freshly ground black pepper
a pinch of paprika
a pinch of cayenne pepper
a few drops of Tabasco
2–3 slices of stale, dark pumpernickel bread, crumbled
To serve
curly endive
red and green apple slices, brushed with lemon juice to prevent
  discoloration
celery sticks

1　Cream the softened butter with a wooden spoon until it is smooth, add the cheese and mix well.
2　Add the salt, freshly ground black pepper and paprika to taste. Now add just a hint of cayenne pepper and a few drops of Tabasco. Mix well.
3　Roll the cheese mixture into 12 balls. Next, roll them several times in the dark pumpernickel breadcrumbs, so they look like truffles. Make sure that the balls are completely covered. Chill the truffles in the refrigerator to allow them to become firm.
4　Serve the cheese truffles on a plate decorated with curly endive, apple slices and celery sticks.

● These Savoury Dutch cheese truffles can be served at the end of a meal instead of the usual cheeseboard.

 30 minutes,
then chilling

Cheese fondue

Serves 4
1 garlic clove
300 ml /½ pt dry white wine
15 ml /1 tbls flour
225 g /8 oz Gouda or Gruyère cheese, finely grated
225 g /8 oz mature Cheddar cheese, finely grated
5 ml /1 tsp kirsch
a pinch of freshly grated nutmeg
salt and freshly ground black pepper
To serve
a selection of raw, crisp vegetables (celery sticks, cauliflower
  florets, carrot sticks)
French bread, cut into cubes

1　Halve the garlic clove and rub the cut surfaces of the clove around the inside of the heavy-based fondue pan or saucepan. Discard the garlic.
2　Pour the wine into the pan and heat it until it starts to boil.
3　Put the flour in a polythene bag, add the Gouda or Gruyère and the Cheddar cheese, and shake well.
4　Turn the heat to low and slowly add the cheese to the wine, stirring constantly.
5　Add the kirsch, the nutmeg and salt and pepper to taste, then cook for 10–15 minutes on the lowest possible heat to allow the fondue flavours to develop. Do not let the mixture become too hot or the cheese will separate and turn stringy.
6　To serve, place the fondue pan over a spirit burner, or pour the fondue into warmed individual bowls. Serve at once with crisp vegetables and cubes of bread to dip into the fondue.

● For additional information about fondues, see page 15.
● This recipe is an inexpensive version of the traditional Swiss fondue which uses Gruyère and Emmental cheeses.

 30–40 minutes

Calzone

Makes 4
oil, for greasing
175 g /6 oz prosciutto or Parma ham
175 g /6 oz Bel Paese
2 × ingredients for Pizza dough and follow steps 1–6 (see page 44)
1 small egg, beaten
15 ml /1 tbls freshly chopped mixed herbs
salt and freshly ground black pepper
20 ml /4 tsp olive oil

1 Heat the oven to 220C /425F /gas 7. Generously grease a large baking sheet and set it aside.
2 Thinly slice the ham and the cheese and reserve them.
3 Knock back the dough, then divide it into 4 equal pieces. Roll or press out each piece to a circle about 15 cm /6 in in diameter.
4 Brush around the edge of each circle of dough with beaten egg.
5 Place a quarter of the ham on one half of each circle to 12 mm / ½ in of the edge of the dough. Top the ham with the sliced cheese.
6 Sprinkle the herbs over the filling and season to taste with salt and black pepper.
7 Drizzle 5 ml /1 tsp olive oil over each filling.
8 Lift up the unfilled half of each circle of dough and fold it over so the filling is completely enclosed. Now press firmly round the edge to seal the calzone to prevent the filling spilling out during cooking.
9 Brush each calzone with the remaining beaten egg. Use a skewer or the prongs of a fork to make a steam vent on the top of each one.
10 Carefully transfer the calzone to the prepared baking sheet with a fish slice, spacing them well apart to allow for expansion during cooking. Cover the calzone with foil and allow them to relax for about 15 minutes in a refrigerator.
11 Bake the calzone for about 20 minutes or until they are risen and browned. Serve immediately.

 making the dough,
plus 50 minutes

Stuffed meat loaf

Serves 6–8
1 slice white bread without crusts
1 kg /2 lb minced beef
1 garlic clove
1 medium-sized onion, finely chopped
30 ml /2 tbls finely chopped fresh parsley
salt and black pepper
4 eggs, beaten
olive oil, for greasing
broccoli spears, to serve

For the stuffing
2 hard-boiled eggs, chopped
50 g /2 oz salami, skinned and cut into small strips
50 g /2 oz Provolone or Caciocavallo cheese, cut into small dice

For the sauce
15 ml /1 tbls olive oil
1 onion, chopped
15 ml /1 tbls tomato purée
225 ml /8 fl oz red wine

1 Moisten the slice of bread with a little water, then squeeze it dry and crumble it over the meat. Crush the garlic clove in a garlic press and scatter it over the bread and meat. Add the onion and the parsley. Season the mixture to taste and stir. Mix in the beaten egg.
2 Grease a large, double sheet of thick foil with a little olive oil and pat out the meat mixture into a flat, square layer on the foil — it should be about 15 mm /½ in thick.
3 Pile the hard-boiled eggs, salami and cheese dice in the centre of the meat layer. Lift 2 opposite edges of the foil and fold the sides of the meat layer over the stuffing. Pat it into a neat roll, completely covering the stuffing. Fold the foil over the roll, enclosing it completely. Fold up the ends to make a neat parcel.
4 To make the sauce, heat the oil in a flameproof casserole. Fry the onion in the oil until soft. Add the foil-wrapped meat.
5 Mix the tomato purée with the wine, then pour into the casserole. Add 50 ml /2 fl oz water. As soon as the liquid bubbles, reduce the heat to low and cover the casserole tightly. Simmer for 1½ hours.
7 Top up the sauce with boiling water if it appears to be drying out.
8 Remove the parcel from the casserole. Undo the foil, and tip the meat roll onto a warmed platter. Pour the sauce over the roll and serve it with broccoli spears.

● To eat the meat loaf cold, loosely cover the roll with the foil and leave it to cool. Cool the sauce and strain off any excess fat, then serve the roll cold, with the cold sauce handed round separately.
● This meat loaf, *polpettono all Siciliana*, can be rolled in a whole thin slice of beef or veal but it is easier to wrap it in foil.

2 hours

BLUE CHEESES

Blue cheeses are the aristocrats of the cheeseboard. Though usually served in peak condition with biscuits, blue cheese can also lend its distinguished flavour to a number of interesting dishes, both sweet and savoury.

If you have never acquired a taste for blue cheese or are unenthusiastic about the idea of eating a specially cultivated 'mould', pause to discover why these are called the connoisseur's cheeses. The blues — three in particular — are the cheeses which experts appreciate most for their flavour, and which go best with fine wines. Indeed, they are so good that wine-tasters are not supposed to eat them when tasting, because these cheeses will enhance the taste of any wine, whatever its actual quality.

The three greatest blue cheeses with the longest traditions are French Roquefort, Italian Gorgonzola and English Stilton. There are about 50 other varieties, all subtly different, but these three are the classic blues. French Bleu de Bresse comes close behind them in popularity, followed by Danish Blue. There are many other, newer cheeses, all worth trying. The blue veins in all these cheeses may be thin, delicate threads or broad bands or nuggets of colour. The flavour may vary from mildly piquant to forceful, the texture from blandly creamy to dry and crumbly.

How blue cheese is made

Different types of blue cheese vary considerably. They may be made from cow's whole milk, semi-skimmed milk, from ewe's milk (like true Roquefort) or from cow's and goat's milk mixed (like some Gorgonzola).

All cheeses are living food, made by harmless bacteria which feed on the sugar in the milk and turn it into lactic acid. This process separates the milk into liquid (whey) and clots of curds which make the cheese. Blue cheeses are created by special bacteria added to the curds, which make distinctive blue or greenish-blue veins of mould threaded through the cheese inside the rind. Although the same bacteria are almost always used, the blue veins, and consequently the flavour, will vary. What makes blue cheese special is the care and time given to its development. (Otherwise, the blue veins may not grow sufficiently before the cheese becomes overripe and bitter.)

Penicillin-type bacteria are added to the milk curds, which are then cut and drained and packed into moulds called hoops. These are turned over and drained regularly until the recognizable cheeses are formed. At this stage, they are white and almost tasteless. The cheeses are then pricked deeply all over by metal spikes to make air channels for the mould to travel through. They are then kept at a controlled temperature in moist air for weeks or months, depending on the cheese. They are regularly turned and checked, until the mould is fully developed.

All modern blue cheeses are made this way, which is based on old methods, but their forerunners were quite ordinary, dull white cheeses which developed blue mould by luck from the bacteria which occurred naturally in the caves or other cool places where the cheeses were stored.

Types of blue cheese

Different methods and different milks give a great variety within the category of blue cheeses.

Roquefort is unique as the only world-renowned cheese made with sheep's milk. The white cheeses come from as far away as Corsica to be matured in the limestone caves of Columbou near Roquefort, where the mould first occurred naturally. The cheese curds are layered with breadcrumbs covered with *Penicillium roqueforti*, salted, lightly pressed and deeply spiked. They mature for three months in moist mountain caves.

This process gives the genuine, piquant flavour of true Roquefort. This cheese is widely copied, and even some true Roquefort is oversalted for export, so to taste the real flavour you have to buy cheese made for the French.

Gorgonzola was traditionally made from the 'tired milk' of cows on the move to summer pasture. The milk curds from an evening milking were covered with the warm new curd from the fresh morning milk. The bacteria introduced, called *Penicillium gorgonzola*, were first found in the cheese when it was matured in the caves of Valassina, near the town of Gorgonzola.

Modern methods have not spoiled the delicate, creamy, yet piquant, flavour of Gorgonzola. Its most delicate form is Dolcelatte (meaning sweet or mild milk). Try it as a simple but sophisticated party nibble (see Boccancini di Dolcelatte) or in a creamy, brandy-flavoured sauce to complement veal (see Veal scaloppine with Gorgonzola).

Stilton, from cow's milk and cream, is the richest of the great blue cheeses. No one knows how or where Stiltons were first blued. The salted curds are first set in their final shape in hoops, but are then given a short period tightly wrapped in calico bandages and are scraped down to prevent too thick a rind from forming. They are stacked on slatted shelves in cool, damp rooms to let the mould develop for 4–6 months at an undisclosed temperature.

Bleu de Bresse is an outstanding, mild French blue cheese, with a character all its own. Made from full-cream cow's milk, it has dark veins with droplets of blue suspended in its creamy, honey-coloured paste. In France, it is used to make an excellent little biscuit (see recipe). Bleu de Bresse quickly becomes over-ripe and you cannot tell this until you unwrap it. If the rind smells strong or the paste just inside is pinkish, return the cheese to your supplier.

Danish Blue, which is less expensive than French and Italian cheeses, is used for everyday and especially for cooking. Sometimes

called Danablu, it is buttery-textured, rich in cream and has dense but clearly traced blue veins all through. It is sold pre-packaged and so it is always consistent in flavour. Danablu is saltier than most blue cheeses and has a sharp flavour so it is often best blended with some cream, cottage or curd cheese. More of a rarity is the milder Danish Mycella, with a yellowish paste and more banded veining.

Other blue cheeses: mild French Pipo Crème, sold from a big cylinder, is perhaps the gentlest of all blues. It is called Grièges

yellow paste and the blue veins run in broad bands or streaks. Blue Wensleydale, once highly valued, is less well known now, because farmhouse production stopped during the Second World War and has never picked up. Its veins are lacy, like a fine web in the white paste, and its flavour is lighter and slightly more acid than other blues. Blue Shropshire is a fairly new cheese, with an even yellower paste than Blue Cheshire; it has branching blue veins.

Cambozola, from West Germany, also known as German Blue Brie, is a full-fat soft cheese with an edible mould crust, manufactured in a similar way to French Brie. Bavarian Blue is a creamy, rich, full-fat, spreadable cheese with blue veining and a white mould surface.

Buying and storing blue cheeses

A good store or a speciality shop usually sells some blue cheeses cut to order from a large drum or cylinder. This way you can see from the surface whether the cheese is just ripe or over ripe. It may be creamy or crumbly, white or yellowish, but it should never have greyish patches in the paste or (except for Stilton) be darker nearer the rind. Both conditions are signs of age. The veining should be an even colour and well-distributed right through to the centre. The rind must not be cracked and the paste should never be sweating or have a dull bloom. This would show that the cheese has not been cut for some time (indicating poor turnover in the store); or it may mean that the cheese is being kept too warm and may be over-ripe. Continental cheeses bought from a drum are at their best between November and April.

Packaged portions should always fill their wrappings but without seeping through the packaging. The wrappings should never be torn. If you buy cheese which smells of ammonia or is stained under the rind, return it to the supplier.

If you are purchasing blue cheese with a specific recipe in mind, remember that the rind cannot be used. For example, with a small Bresse Bleu weighing 125 g /4½ oz, about 25 g /1 oz will be lost as rind.

Keep mature cheeses in a cool, dark place. Blue cheeses cut from a large piece in good condition should keep well for several days under a well-aerated cover, and a drum will keep several weeks. Try to avoid keeping blue cheese in the refrigerator. If you really have no choice, wrap the cheese in foil, not cling film, and allow it to come to room temperature before you serve it.

Never freeze blue cheese. Not only will its texture spoil, but it will cross-flavour other foods. It will also go bad very quickly once it has been thawed.

A selection of blue cheeses: top row, left to right: a slice of Stilton, Danish Blue, Dolcelatte; middle row: Stilton and Blue Cheshire; bottom row: Blue Wensleydale and Gorgonzola

in France and is creamy with delicate blue veins. Bleu d'Auvergne is also well known. It is a cheaper little brother to Roquefort, with something of the same character, but it is made from cow's milk. Fourme d' Ambert, sometimes called Fourme de Cantal, is ripened in caves and is salty and quite sharp. You may find Bleu des Causses in speciality shops and restaurants. There are at least a dozen more good French blues, including a group of similar cheeses, of which the best known is Gex, made from cow's milk or mixed milk from mountain regions.

All the British blue cheeses are strongly flavoured except Lymswold, which is always soft and mild with a white surface. Blue Cheshire, once rare, is now widely sold. Rich and vigorous in flavour, it has a darkish-

Using blue cheese

If you are serving a cheeseboard with a selection of cheeses, one should be a blue cheese; for a meal with white wine, choose a mild blue cheese. Always supply a separate knife for cutting blue cheese; this prevents its strong flavour affecting the other cheeses. If you serve a fine blue cheese on its own, offer your guests plain crackers rather than cheese-flavoured ones. Fruit goes particularly well with blue cheeses, whether to start a meal (see Pears with Stilton, Stuffed cocktail grapes, Pears with Roquefort and watercress dressing) or to finish it (see Peaches Gorgonzola).

If you have a drum (or part of one) of blue Stilton, always serve it on its own. Cut off the top rind in one level slice, and cut the cheese at table in horizontal slices. Scooping it out with a spoon may be popular, but this method does not allow the cheese to be eaten at its best after the first few servings. After the meal, replace the rind as a cover. Some people favour pouring port into the shell of a Stilton as it nears its end, but this sours the cheese. A better alternative is to pot the remnants with port (see Potted Stilton).

All blue cheeses, in fact, can be turned into a preserve with alcohol and can then be served as a dessert or used for cooking. It is also possible to mix different types of cheese when preserving. Take care to increase the quantity of butter you add to suit the fat content and saltiness of the cheese. Use a spicy Madeira or a sherry, rather than port, if you pot a cheese that is of a lesser quality than Stilton, especially if it is salty. Do not try to compensate for the saltiness of the cheese by using a very rich, sweet alcohol when you are preserving cheese.

Many people think you cannot cook with blue cheese or that it is a shame to do so. It is true that the three great aristocratic blue cheeses, when in peak condition, are best enjoyed as they are. But they are soon past their prime, especially if they are imported. It is a pity to waste them, so try one of my recipes, from this chapter, using raw or cooked blue cheese.

Dried-out texture, darkening or over-strong flavour near the rind can be corrected by mixing the crumbled blue cheese with a soft, bland curd or cottage cheese in a cooked dish (see Cheese-stuffed mushrooms). This will also balance a cheese that has been over salted to preserve it for export and the rigours of long travelling.

Most blue cheeses have a marked flavour, even when cooked. A dish containing blue cheese, especially if it is rich and creamy, needs placing carefully in the menu, where it will not overwhelm the dishes served with or after it. Because its flavour is so strong, a little goes a long way, as in Roquefort salad dressing or a savoury butter for grilled steaks (see recipes).

Pears with Stilton

A good starter is light yet tangy, to stimulate appetites at the beginning of the meal. In this recipe, the sharp flavour of the cheese contrasts well with the delicate flavour and succulence of the fruit.

10 minutes

Serves 4
4 thin slices dark rye bread
25 g /1 oz butter, softened
2 firm dessert pears
30 ml /2 tbls lemon juice
50 g /2 oz Stilton cheese, slivered
8–12 sprigs of watercress, to garnish

1 Trim the bread to oval shapes a little larger than the pears. Thinly spread the softened butter on 1 side of each slice.
2 Peel the pears and halve them lengthways. Using a teaspoon, scoop out the cores with a circular movement of your wrist. Cut a thin slice off the rounded side of each pear half to make it stand level.
3 Heat the grill to high. Put the pear halves in a saucepan of water sharpened with the lemon juice and bring the water to the boil. Remove the pears with a slotted spoon, or tip them into a sieve to drain. Pat them dry with absorbent paper.
4 Place each pear half, cut side up, on a bread slice. Cover the pears with cheese, making sure none hangs over the edge.
5 Place the pears, still on the bread, in the grill pan. Grill them until the cheese bubbles.
6 Place each pear on a small, warmed plate, garnish the narrow ends with watercress and serve at once.

Stuffed cocktail grapes

20 minutes, plus 8–12 hours chilling

Serves 4–6
50 g /2 oz Gorgonzola or Dolcelatte cheese, without rind
45 ml /3 tbls cream cheese
2.5 ml /1/2 tsp finely grated onion
2.5 ml /1/2 tsp medium-dry sherry
450 g /1 lb large, firm dessert grapes
fresh geranium leaves, to garnish

1 Work together the Gorgonzola cheese, cream cheese, onion and sherry with the back of a spoon. Sieve the mixture to make a smooth paste. Cover and chill for 8–12 hours.
2 Remove any pips from the grapes and slit them deeply lengthways. Stuff them with paste and re-shape. Chill until needed.
3 Serve on a bed of fresh geranium leaves and garnish with a single leaf.

Boccancini di Dolcelatte

15 minutes, plus chilling

Serves 6
175 g /6 oz Dolcelatte cheese
25 g /1 oz butter, softened
40 ml /2½ tbls finely chopped fresh parsley

Stuffed cocktail grapes

1   Press the Dolcelatte cheese through a wire sieve into a bowl, using the back of a wooden spoon. Beat in the softened butter until the mixture is well blended.
2   Divide the mixture into 12 portions and shape each into a ball with your hands.
3   Roll the cheese balls in the finely chopped parsley to coat. Place them on a serving dish, cover them with cling film and refrigerate until they are firm.
4   Serve the boccancini as soon as possible after removing them from the refrigerator, providing wooden cocktail sticks for your guests to eat with.

Roquefort turnovers

 1½ hours

Makes 30
550 g /1¼ lb made-weight flaky pastry
flour, for dusting
1 egg yolk, beaten with 15 ml /1 tbls water,
*   for egg glaze*
cayenne pepper
For the filling
75 g /3 oz Roquefort cheese
¼ Spanish onion, finely chopped
30 ml /2 tbls finely chopped red pepper
10 ml /2 tsp finely chopped fresh parsley
1 egg yolk
10 ml /2 tsp thick cream
freshly ground black pepper

1   Place the Roquefort cheese in a mixing bowl and mash it with a fork until it is quite smooth. Add the finely chopped onion, red pepper and parsley, the egg yolk and thick cream and season with freshly ground black pepper to taste. Mix them well.
2   On a lightly-floured board, roll out the pastry until it is 3 mm /⅛ in thick. With a 4 cm /1½ in cutter, cut 30 rounds. From the remaining pastry, cut 30 rounds with a 5 cm / 2 in cutter. Brush off any excess flour.
3   Place a teaspoon of the filling on each of the smaller rounds. Brush the edges of the larger rounds with egg glaze, being careful that it does not drip over the sides. Place the larger rounds on top of the cheese filling, glaze side down. Use the turned end of the smaller cutter pressed down over the top to seal the edges lightly. Decorate around the edge with the back of a knife.
4   Place the turnovers on a baking sheet and leave them in the refrigerator for 30 minutes to relax.
5   Meanwhile, heat the oven to 220C /425F / gas 7.
6   Sprinkle the baking sheet with water, brush the turnovers with the egg glaze and bake them for 10 minutes or until the pastry is puffed and golden brown.
7   Sprinkle the turnovers lightly with cayenne pepper and serve immediately.

Danablu dip

bringing to room temperature, then 5 minutes, plus 30 minutes chilling

Makes about 175 g /7 oz
100 g /4 oz Danish Blue cheese
75 g /3 oz full-fat cream cheese
15 ml /1 tbls lemon juice
a pinch of salt
To serve
carrots, celery and cucumber, cut into 7.5 cm /
*   3 in sticks*
whole celery sticks, with leaves on
bread sticks

1   Bring the Danish Blue and cream cheeses to room temperature. Beat the cheeses with a wooden spoon to soften them, blend in the lemon juice and salt to make a smooth cream.
2   Transfer the dip to a serving bowl, cover with cling film and chill for 30 minutes.
3   When you are ready to serve, place the bowl of dip in the centre of a large platter and surround it with the sticks of carrot, celery and cucumber. Accompany it with whole celery sticks and bread sticks.

●   To vary the theme, mix in 50 g /2 oz stoned black olives or stuffed green olives, coarsely chopped, or 15 ml /1 tbls finely chopped fresh chives before chilling.
●   Other raw vegetables suitable for dipping include courgette sticks, cauliflower florets, button mushrooms, strips of green and red pepper, and very thin slices of turnip.

Roquefort salad dressing

Creamy salad dressings made with blue cheese can be a pleasant change from mayonnaise and are an excellent way to use up left-over cheese.

7–8 minutes, plus 2 hours chilling

Makes 150 ml /5 fl oz dressing
40 g /1½ oz Roquefort cheese
125 ml /4 fl oz soured cream
15 ml /1 tbls lemon juice
1 large spring onion, white part only,
*   finely chopped*

1   Sieve the Roquefort cheese into a bowl. Smoothly work in the soured cream and lemon juice, little by little. Lastly, add the finely chopped spring onion.
2   Pour the dressing into a scalded jar with a screw-top lid. Close the lid tightly and shake the jar well. Chill for 2 hours. Shake the jar again before use and transfer the dressing to a small jug to serve, if required.

Danablu dip

Potted Stilton

This recipe is at least 200 years old and a superb way to make the most of left-over fragments of England's greatest cheese.

🔪 20 minutes

Makes 700 g /1½ lb potted cheese
125 g /4 oz softened butter
450 g /1 lb Blue Stilton cheese without rind
a pinch of salt
a large pinch of ground mace
30–60 ml /2–4 tbls ruby or vintage port
cooled, melted clarified butter (see page 24)
crackers, to serve

1 In a mortar, pound together the butter, cheese, salt and mace until they are evenly blended. Moisten the mixture with just enough port to give a good flavour and smooth texture — the cheese must not 'weep'.
2 Press the mixture into scalded small pots; tap the pots on the table while filling them to knock out any air holes. Leave 12 mm /½ in headspace.
3 Cover the potted cheese with about 3 mm / ⅛ in clarified butter. Chill it in the refrigerator until needed. The preserve can safely be kept for 2 weeks. When ready to use, serve with crackers and break and remove the butter coating.

● For a pretty alternative for a party, make a firm mixture and shape it into a mound, smoothing the outside. Stud the entire surface with half walnuts. Eat within 24 hours.

Bresse Bleu biscuits

These rich little cheese biscuits are called *galettes de Bresse* in France. They are quick and easy to make. Serve them plain or spread with full-fat soft cheese.

🔪 1 hour,
including resting

Makes 30–40 biscuits
125 g /4½ oz Bleu de Bresse cheese
100 g /4 oz softened butter or margarine
1 medium-sized egg, separated
175 g /6 oz flour, plus extra for dusting

1 Scrape all the rind off the cheese and discard it. Put the cheese in a mixing bowl with the butter or margarine. Mash them together until they are well blended.
2 Work the egg yolk evenly into the cheese mixture. Work in the flour, little by little. Use a beater or fork at first, then your hand. You will have a very soft dough.
3 Wrap the dough in greaseproof paper, and chill it in the refrigerator for 30 minutes or until firm.
4 Heat the oven to 220C /425F /gas 7. On a lightly-floured surface, roll out the dough 6 mm /¼ in thick. Cut it into 4 cm /1½ in rounds with a cutter.
5 Place the biscuit rounds on a lightly-

Potted Stilton

greased baking sheet. Beat the reserved egg white lightly, and brush it over the rounds. Bake them for 8 minutes or until lightly browned. Serve warm or cold.

Veal scaloppine with Gorgonzola

🔪 25 minutes

Serves 4–6
12 small, thin veal slices (40 g /1½ oz each)
7.5 ml /1½ tsp flour, plus extra for dredging
45 ml /3 tbls olive oil
125 ml /4 fl oz brandy
75 g /3 oz unsalted butter, chilled
100 g /4 oz Gorgonzola cheese without rind, chopped
125 ml /4 fl oz thick cream

1 If the veal slices are English cut, beat them out with a meat bat until very thin.

This can be done between two sheets of greaseproof paper if wished. Dredge them well with flour.

2 Heat 15 ml /1 tbls olive oil in a large frying-pan which will hold 4 slices side by side. Over a fairly high heat, fry the scaloppine for 30 seconds on each side, until just cooked through. Remove the meat with tongs to a heated serving platter, and keep it warm. Cook the remaining scaloppine in 2 batches, using olive oil as before, and remove them to the heated platter.

3 Reduce the heat under the frying-pan to low, add the brandy and sprinkle it with 7.5 ml /1½ tsp flour. Stir the mixture with a wooden spoon to scrape up any crusty bits, and boil it rapidly until the sauce is reduced by half.

4 Cut the butter into small pieces and add to the pan. Cook, stirring, until it melts, then immediately stir in the cheese and cream. Cook, stirring, until the cheese is fully melted but do not allow the mixture to boil. Coat the scaloppine with the sauce and serve.

Danish Blue and pepper quiche

1¾ hours, including resting

Serves 4–6
butter, for greasing
shortcrust pastry (see recipe page 12) or
  275 g /10 oz made-weight pastry
flour, for dusting
100 g /4 oz Danish Blue cheese, crumbled
25 g /1 oz full-fat cream cheese
½ green pepper, cut into rings
1 medium-sized tomato, seeded and chopped
  (optional)
2 eggs, beaten
150 ml /5 fl oz thin cream
salt and freshly ground black pepper
a pinch of grated nutmeg

1 Grease a straight-sided, loose-bottomed 18 cm /7 in flan tin. Roll out the pastry and line the tin. Chill it for 30 minutes.

2 Heat the oven to 200C /400F /gas 6. Line the pastry case with greaseproof paper and dried beans to bake blind for 10 minutes. Remove the greaseproof paper and dried beans, lower the oven heat to 180C /350F / gas 4 and bake the case for a further 8 minutes, to crisp the base.

3 Meanwhile, mash the cheeses together with a fork, breaking up any lumps. Keep 2 green pepper rings for garnishing and chop the remaining rings. Mix the chopped pepper and the tomato (if used) with the cheeses. Mix the beaten eggs and the cream into the cheeses until well blended and season to taste with salt, pepper and nutmeg.

4 Pour the cheese mixture into the case. Bake the quiche for 20–30 minutes or until the filling is set.

5 Let the quiche cool for 6–7 minutes before removing it from the tin. Serve it hot or cold, garnished with the reserved green pepper rings.

Peaches Gorgonzola

15 minutes, plus chilling

Serves 4
5 fresh peaches
45 ml /3 tbls brandy
25 g /1 oz Gorgonzola or Dolcelatte cheese
  without rind
30 ml /2 tbls thick or whipping cream
15 ml /1 tbls icing sugar

1 Dip the fresh peaches in boiling water to loosen the skin, then peel, halve and stone them. Put 8 peach halves in a bowl and sprinkle them with 15 ml /1 tbls brandy. Leave them for 1–2 hours.

2 Blend the remaining 2 peach halves, the Gorgonzola, the remaining brandy, the cream and the icing sugar to a smooth purée. Chill the mixture for at least 1 hour.

3 Put 2 peach halves into each of 4 individual glasses and top each serving with the brandied cheese cream.

Pears with Roquefort and watercress dressing

Serves 4
75 g /3 oz watercress
100 g /4 oz Roquefort cheese
2 egg yolks
150 ml /5 fl oz olive oil
30 ml /2 tbls lemon juice
freshly ground black pepper
2 large, ripe pears
30 ml /2 tbls chopped walnuts
For the garnish
1 bunch of watercress, washed and dried

1 Trim the watercress, discarding any discoloured leaves. Wash it thoroughly and dry it carefully in a tea-towel.
2 In a blender, combine 50 g /2 oz Roquefort cheese, the watercress and the egg yolks and blend slowly, adding the olive oil gradually as for mayonnaise. Blend the mixture until it is smooth, then pass it through a sieve. Add 10 ml /2 tsp lemon juice and freshly ground black pepper to taste. Set it aside until needed.
3 Peel the whole pears and place them in a bowl containing 275 ml / 10 fl oz water sharpened with the remaining lemon juice, to prevent discoloration.
4 When ready to serve, cover the base of 4 individual serving plates with the Roquefort and watercress dressing. Quarter the pears, remove the cores and slice the fruit thinly. Arrange overlapping slices of pear across each plate.
5 Crumble the remaining Roquefort cheese and sprinkle it over the pear slices with the chopped walnuts. Decorate each plate with a small bouquet of watercress.

Blue cheese roulade

Serves 6
100 g /4 oz Danish Blue cheese
100 g /4 oz full-fat cream cheese
50 g /2 oz butter, softened
5 ml /1 tsp brandy
a pinch of cayenne pepper
50 g /2 oz walnuts, finely chopped
1 radish rose and 1 slice of cucumber, to garnish
crackers or toast, to serve

1 Blend the blue cheese and cream cheese thoroughly in a blender, food processor or by beating with a wooden spoon. Add the softened butter and blend again to a smooth consistency.
2 Flavour the cheese mixture with the brandy and add cayenne pepper to taste.
3 Place the cheese mixture on a sheet of greaseproof paper. Use the paper to shape it into a firmly-packed roll, 15 cm /6 in long. Secure the ends by twisting the paper. Chill the roll until it is firm — allow about 2 hours.
4 Remove the paper and gently press the chilled roll in the chopped walnuts to coat it evenly. Place the roulade on a serving dish and garnish it with a radish rose set on a slice of cucumber.
5 To serve, cut the roulade into 12 slices with a sharp knife, wiping the knife between each cut. Serve with crackers or slices of toast.

● Making this roulade is rather like making your own cheese! Serve it instead of a cheeseboard, before or after dessert, or as a starter.

 40 minutes

15 minutes, plus 2 hours chilling, then 5 minutes

Cheshire-filled celery boats

Serves 8
2 heads of celery
225 g /8 oz Blue Cheshire cheese, heavily veined
225 g /8 oz butter, softened
10 ml /2 tsp paprika
30–45 ml /2–3 tbls cognac
12–16 black olives, stoned and halved, to garnish

1 Discard the outer stalks of the celery heads. Separate the tender inside stalks, wash them thoroughly and dry them. Trim off the leaves and reserve the best-looking ones for garnishing. Cut the stalks into equal lengths, about 6 cm /2½ in long.
2 In a bowl, beat together the Blue Cheshire cheese and the softened butter until smooth and creamy. Add the paprika, followed by the cognac a little at a time, mixing well. Chill the mixture for at least 30 minutes.
3 Fill the celery pieces with the cheese mixture, using a knife to give a rounded effect. Garnish them with the halved black olives. Arrange the celery boats on a serving platter, garnish with the reserved celery leaves and serve.

Stuffed potatoes Stilton

Serves 6
6 large, floury potatoes
125 g /4 oz butter, softened
175 g /6 oz Stilton cheese, crumbled
90 ml /6 tbls thick cream
freshly ground black pepper
15 ml /1 tbls finely chopped fresh parsley, to garnish
bouquet of parsley, to garnish

1 Heat the oven to 190C /375F /gas 5.
2 Scrub the potatoes until absolutely clean. Pat them dry with absorbent paper or a clean tea-towel and prick them all over with a sharp fork.
3 Bake the potatoes for 1–1¼ hours, or until they are tender.
4 Meanwhile, towards the end of the cooking time, combine the softened butter and the crumbled Stilton cheese in a bowl. Beat them with a wooden spoon until the mixture is well blended.
5 Remove the fully-cooked potatoes from the oven and leave it on. Cut a thin slice from the top of each potato and discard. Scoop out the potato flesh with a sharp spoon, taking care not to break the skin and leaving a shell about 6 mm /¼ in thick.
6 Mash the potato flesh to a purée or push it through a sieve. Blend the puréed potato thoroughly with the butter and Stilton mixture. Beat in the thick cream and add freshly ground black pepper to taste.
7 Spoon the potato and cheese mixture into a piping bag fitted with a 12 mm /½ in star nozzle and pipe it into the potato shells. Return the stuffed potatoes to the oven for 10–15 minutes until they are heated through.
8 Arrange the potatoes on a heated serving dish and sprinkle them with finely chopped parsley. Garnish the dish with a bouquet of parsley and serve immediately.

● Do not use salt in the stuffing, as Stilton is already quite strong and salty.
● For a change from Stilton, try using another creamy blue cheese like Fourme d'Ambert, Bleu d'Auvergne or the more expensive Roquefort.

35 minutes,
plus 30 minutes chilling

1½–1¾ hours

Grilled steaks with savoury butter

Serves 4
4 thick rump steaks (175 g /6 oz each)
freshly ground black pepper
olive oil, for brushing
salt
fresh salad vegetables, to serve
For the savoury butter
50 g /2 oz butter, softened
5 ml /1 tsp flour
25 g /1 oz Danish Blue cheese, crumbled
30 ml /2 tbls finely chopped fresh parsley
lemon juice

1 Take the steaks out of the refrigerator well in advance of cooking to bring them to room temperature (allow about 2 hours). Wipe them with a clean, damp cloth. Trim off the excess fat, then nick the remaining fat around the edge of each steak to prevent the meat curling during cooking. Lay the steaks on a wooden board and beat them on both sides with a wooden rolling pin or meat bat to tenderize the meat. Season the steaks with freshly ground black pepper.
2 While the steaks are coming to room temperature, make the savoury butter. Blend the softened butter and the flour in a small bowl, using a wooden spoon. When smooth, add the crumbled Danish Blue cheese and the finely chopped fresh parsley and blend again to a smooth consistency, adding lemon juice to taste.
3 Place the mixture on a piece of greaseproof paper and pat it into a small roll shape. Wrap the savoury butter in the paper and chill it in the refrigerator until it is needed.
4 When you are ready to cook the meat, heat the grill to high and brush the grid of the grill pan with olive oil. Season the steaks with salt and more pepper. Place the steaks on the grid and grill the meat 7.5 cm /3 in from the heat for 2 minutes on each side for rare, 3 minutes for medium-rare and 4 minutes each side for well done.
5 Meanwhile, slice the chilled savoury butter into neat pats. Transfer the steaks to heated dinner plates, garnish the meat with the pats of butter and serve immediately with fresh salad vegetables arranged attractively on the plates.

15–20 minutes,
plus bringing to room temperature

Cheese-stuffed mushrooms

Serves 8–10
75 g /3 oz Roquefort cheese
250 g /9 oz cream cheese
30 ml /2 tbls thick cream
7.5 ml /1½ tsp brandy
freshly ground black pepper
20 button mushrooms
20 small pineapple triangles, to garnish
a sprig of flat-leaved parsley, to garnish

1 Bring the Roquefort and cream cheeses to room temperature. In separate bowls, beat the cheeses with a wooden spoon. Mix them together well and blend in the thick cream and the brandy until smooth. Season to taste with freshly ground black pepper.
2 Wipe the mushrooms. Remove the stalks, reserving them for another recipe.
3 Fill each mushroom cap with the cheese mixture, piling it up neatly with a teaspoon.
4 Top each mushroom with a small triangle of pineapple and place them on a plate garnished with a sprig of flat-leaved parsley. Cover them with cling film and keep in the refrigerator until ready to serve.

● This creamy cheese mixture also makes a tasty filling for hollowed-out cherry tomatoes or chunks of celery.

bringing to room temperature,
then 20 minutes

Wine

UNDERSTANDING WINE

Which wine best complements certain food; how should you store and serve different types; which glasses bring out the best in the wine? These are just some of the basic essentials I cover in this invaluable chapter.

Although it is perfectly possible to drink any wine with any food, it is well worth considering my guidelines to help increase your combined enjoyment of food and wine.

The extensive chart below provides invaluable suggestions about the kind of wine to serve with various hors d'oeuvres, main courses, cheeses and desserts. Bear in mind that a dish from a particular region will often go well with a type of wine from the same region. Also, if you use a certain wine in the making of a dish, it is likely to be the best choice to accompany it.

I give tips on which glasses to use, to show

to full advantage the colour, bouquet and taste of the wine of your choice. My advice on how to serve wine should ensure that it is at its best when it arrives in the glass.

Wine bottles are as varied as their contents; I show you some traditional shapes associated with specific wines, as well as information about a new dry-to-sweet white wine guide.

Better quality wines, even quite modest ones, do benefit from 'laying down'; follow my suggestions on how, where and what wines to store.

Serving wine to complement the food

FOOD AND WINE CHART

HORS D'OEUVRES Pâté, quiche, etc.	Fairly strong dry white, such as Traminer; a Rhine wine, such as Rüdesheimer; a rosé, such as Rosé d'Anjou, or a light red, such as Beaujolais
Salad or cold hors d'oeuvres	Dry white, such as Alsace Sylvaner or Yugoslavian Zilavka or Riesling
SOUP	Dry sherry or a light Madeira is served with consommés, otherwise wine is not usually served with soup
FISH Grilled or lightly poached fish	Light white, such as Chablis, Pouilly Fuissé or Moselle
Fish in a rich cream sauce	Heavy white, such as white Burgundy (Meursault, Montrachet), or Rhine wine, such as Niersteiner
Shellfish	Light white, such as Muscadet; Italian Soave or a slightly flinty Loire, such as Sancerre or Vouvray. Chablis is traditional with oysters
Shellfish served as a risotto or with a rich sauce	Rosé, such as Tavel; a white Loire wine, such as Pouilly Fumé, or a white Burgundy, such as Puligny Montrachet
Smoked Fish	Heavy white, such as white Burgundy; Alsace Traminer or a spicy Rhine spätlese wine
DARK MEAT Beef, roasted or grilled	Bordeaux, such as Haut Médoc or St Emilion. (Any good Bordeaux is perfect with a roast.)

Beef casseroles and stews

Steaks

Lamb, roasted or grilled

Lamb casseroles, stews and risottos

Game (grouse, partridge, pheasant)

Hare, venison

WHITE MEAT
Pork

Veal

Ham

POULTRY
Chicken, cooked simply

Sturdy red Burgundy, such as Nuits St Georges; a Rhône wine, such as Châteauneuf-du-Pape; a heavier Italian red, such as Barolo, or a Hungarian Egri Bikaver	Chicken cooked with red wine or in a very rich stew with vegetables	Light red, such as Fleurie or another Beaujolais
Bordeaux, such as St Estèphe; a red Burgundy, such as Nuits St Georges, or a Cabernet Sauvignon	Duck	Heavy white Burgundy, such as Meursault, or a rosé, such as Tavel
Bordeaux, such as a Margaux; a light red, such as Beaujolais or Mâcon, or a light Italian wine, such as Bardolino	Goose	White, such as a Rhine wine, or a red Burgundy, such as Beaune
	Turkey	Heavy white, such as Traminer; a Rhine wine, or a rosé, such as Côtes de Provence
Bordeaux, such as a Médoc; a Bulgarian Cabernet Sauvignon; an Italian wine such as Chianti or Valpolicella	CHEESE Soft (Brie, Camembert, etc.)	Medium red Burgundy, such as Beaune, or a Bordeaux, such as St Julien
Red Rhône; Bordeaux, such as St Emilion, or a red Graves	Medium (Port-Salut, Cheddar, etc.)	Light, fruity red, such as Fleurie, or a spicy white, such as Alsace Gewürztraminer or a Tavel
Strong red, such as Côtes du Rhone, or a heavy Burgundy, such as Chambertin	Cream or Goat's	Medium white, such as Graves; an Alsace Traminer or a Rhine wine
Medium-sweet white, such as Graves, or Orvieto, or a rosé, such as Côtes de Provence or Mateus	Blue cheese (Stilton, etc.)	Light red such as Bardolino; a medium red such as Brouilly, or a Cabernet Sauvignon
Strong white, such as Montrachet; Pinot Chardonnay; Rully, or a light red, such as Valpolicella, Zinfandel or Beaujolais	DESSERT	Sauternes or Barsac are traditional dessert wines, but any sweet Loire wine or a German wine marked spätlese or auslese would be suitable. For an extra rich dessert, try a Hungarian Tokay Generally, wine is not served with desserts containing chocolate
Rosé, such as Tavel or Rosé d'Anjou, or a light red, such as Mâcon		
Heavier white, such as Hungarian Riesling, or a white Burgundy	AFTER-DINNER	Port; the heavier Madeiras or, for a change, a mature Hungarian Tokay, or the 'queen of Sauternes', Château d'Yquem

GLASSES

A whole array of gleaming glasses in the drinks cupboard may look inviting, but unless you know how to select and use glasses to best advantage they will add little to the pleasures of drinking. Just as you use a different sort of knife for meat or for cheese, so there are different glasses available to suit the particular drink you intend to serve. The picture below shows some of the glasses I mention in this chapter.

General points

The three notable qualities of any drink are its colour, bouquet and taste. Consequently, the best glasses are always clear, to show the true colour without any distortion. This is especially valuable in the case of wines and fortified wines, which reveal a lot about their age, style and freshness through their colour.

With the exception of tumblers, the best glasses are bowl-shaped, tapering towards the rim to contain and concentrate the bouquet for you to inhale. Bowl-shaped glasses should also be large enough to hold a good measure without being more than a third to half full. This is because, before you take the first sip, you should swirl the wine around in the glass to fill the glass with the bouquet.

All wine and fortified wine glasses have stems, so that you can hold the glass by the stem not the bowl. This is so that your hand does not affect the temperature of the wine and it will also prevent you from smearing the bowl with your fingertips.

The one point that all glasses should have in common is that they are sparkling clean and stored away from cupboard smells and any trace of dust. Glasses should be dried hot with an immaculate, fluff-free cloth.

The basic sizes and shapes of glasses for wine drinking are: a small-stemmed glass which narrows towards the rim for sherry, port or Madeira; and a bowl- or tulip-shaped stemmed glass for white or red wine.

Fine, thin wine glasses are an enjoyable luxury but uncut, plain glasses with a stem are cheap, easily obtainable and quite adequate for all table wines including champagne. However, over the years it can be rewarding to collect a much wider range.

Glasses for table wine

There are many designs of glasses associated with wines from different regions; here I describe some of the more common types.

Champagne: the best glass to use for champagne or sparkling wine is the tall, slim flute which preserves the 'mousse' or bubbles for as long as possible. The once-fashionable wide-brimmed, bowl shape is not suitable for serving champagne since it encourages the bubbles to die quickly in the glass besides being easy to spill, however it is suitable for champagne cocktails.

Paris goblet: this round, bowl-shaped glass is the commonest wine glass available. It is best suited to red wines, although it will suffice for white wine too.

Alsace: the glass traditionally used for the delicate, young white wines made near the eastern border of France has an extra-long stem of green glass, supporting a wide bowl. The wines of the area are very fresh and are complemented by the greenish reflection.

Anjou: a long stem is also a feature of the typical straight-sided glass used for the white wines of Anjou and the Loire. The stem is not merely for elegance, it keeps the wine clear of any warmth from your hand.

Moselle: cut glass is frowned upon by some as distorting the appearance of wine. However, in the Moselle area cut glass is entirely typical and gives an added glint to the colour of these, or any other, white wines.

Hock or Rhine: hock was a Victorian name for the German wines of the Rhine. In their homeland, these aristocratic white wines are served in an unwieldy glass with a thick, bobbly stem. However, it is unlikely that you will come across these unusual, old-fashioned glasses outside Germany. This wine looks attractive served in a very long stemmed glass with a round bowl.

Glasses for fortified wines

Do justice to your fortified wines by serving them in the correct glasses.

Sherry: in public-houses and bars, sherry is often served to the brim of a waisted schooner — a glass which fulfils few of the essentials of good glasses. Instead, the traditional sherry glass or *copita* is funnel-like in its design, tall, elegant and tapering towards the top to channel the bouquet.

Port: being primarily an English drink, port is often served in small crystal glasses which, although very decorative, do not display the wine quite as well as a plain flute.

NEW WINE GUIDE

The Wine Development Board, a non-commercial independent body, has developed a dry-to-sweet guide, mainly for white wines, which has the endorsement of the wine trade. The major white wines of the world, as well as rosés, sherry and vermouth, have been numbered from 1–9 in terms of dry to sweet. Number 1 signifies very dry wines and Number 9 indicates maximum sweetness. The guide is used by many wine merchants and supermarkets, though in some outlets you may find wines numbered slightly differently to the numbers suggested, because their wine is drier or sweeter. The numbers and symbols will usually appear on a description card underneath the wine. It is hoped in the future that the symbol will appear on all labels, to help you choose the wine you prefer and to allow you to taste unfamiliar wines without the likelihood of disappointment and consequently financial loss.

1	2	3	4	5	6	7	8	9
Muscadet	Soave	Brut Sparkling wine	Vinho Verde	Vouvray Demi-Sec	Demi-sec Champagne	Asti Spumante	Austrian Beerenauslesen	Malmsey Madeira
Champagne	White Burgundy	Gewürztraminer d'Alsace	Moselle Kabinett	Liebfraumilch	Spanish Medium	Rhine Auslesen	Spanish Sweet White	Muscat de Beaumes de Venise
Chablis	Fino Sherry	Dry Amontillado Sherry	Rhine Kabinett	Medium British Sherry	All Golden Sherry types	Premières Côtes de Bordeaux	Sauternes	Marsala
Dry White Bordeaux	Sercial Madeira	Medium Dry Montilla	Yugoslav Laski and Hungarian Olasz Riesling Medium Dry	Verdelho Madeira		Tokay Aszu	Barsac	
Manzanilla Sherry	Rioja	Dry White Vermouth	Portuguese Rosé			Pale Cream Sherry	Cream and Rich Cream Sherry types	
Tavel Rosé	Penedes	Anjou Rosé				Montilla Cream		
		Medium Dry English				Bual Madeira		
						Rosso, Rosé and Bianco Vermouths		

BOTTLES

Nowadays there is a wonderful variety of wine bottle shapes available, as well as the more traditional shapes which are associated with specific wines or with wines from certain areas.

The picture opposite shows some of these traditional shapes. From left to right are: the typical, fairly squat bottle used for both red and white wine from Burgundy, wine from the Rhône and certain Loire wines. Inexpensive table wines are in litre-sized bottles of this shape too;

the classic champagne bottle which also comes in a variety of sizes, from a ¼ bottle to one containing 20 single bottles — the latter is called a Nebuchadnezzar;

the rather exotic bottle used for all wines from the Provence region of France, whether red, white or rosé;

the tall, slender green bottle for German Moselle wines;

the similarly elegant brown bottle for white Rhine wine;

the straw-covered flask which is used for several wines from Italy, such as Orvieto (as in the picture) and Chianti;

the distinctive, round-shaped bottle for rosé wine from Portugal;

and the tall, square-shouldered bottle that is the classic shape for wines from the Bordeaux region of France. French wines are usually sold in quantities of 75 centilitres. Each bottle yields about 8 glasses.

The 'standard' capacity of a wine bottle varies from country to country — German wines can be sold in bottles holding from 68 cl to 75 cl. Most bottles, however, hold either 70 cl or 75 cl. Half bottles are available, but they tend to be comparatively more expensive than a full bottle.

SERVING

Whatever wine you are serving, it is worth making sure that it is at its best when you come to drink it. This need not be a complicated ritual, just a matter of ensuring that the bottle is opened at the right time and the contents poured at the right temperature into an appropriate glass.

Temperature
The rules about the temperature for serving wine are basic and easy to remember: white wines and rosés should be served chilled and the red wines at room temperature.

As a general rule, the cheaper or sweeter the white wine, the cooler it should be, but about 7C /45F should be cold enough for any wine. Better-quality white wines, champagne and other sparkling wines, as well as rosés, need only be as cool as the ideal cellar — 10C /50F — or, more realistically for most of us, the temperature of the bottle after an hour or so in the refrigerator. Never leave a bottle of wine to become extremely cold as this will hide the wine's flavour and bouquet.

A quicker way to chill white wine is to plunge it into a bucket filled with water and a handful of ice-cubes. A few minutes in the freezer or a couple of ice-cubes in the glass are acceptable only as emergency measures.

The chemicals that give red wine its bouquet and flavour come alive at higher temperatures than those in white wine, so it makes sense to serve red wine rather warmer. Think of 'room temperature' as a term coined in the days before central heating — 15C /60F is quite warm enough for red wine, if not for living-rooms. Allow the bottle to warm up gradually, perhaps in the kitchen as you cook, but not next to the cooker or on a radiator. If you are buying a bottle of red wine and do not have time to bring it to the right temperature, look for a beaujolais or a red Loire wine, or an Italian Valpolicella, all of which can be served cool.

Most red wines improve with being allowed to 'breathe' for an hour or two before they are drunk, whether you simply draw the cork to let the air in or decant the wine into another glass container. Before wine-making techniques improved, decanting was essential to get rid of all the sediment; nowadays most wines are crystal clear in their bottles and only fine claret, old burgundies and vintage port are likely to need decanting. For most purposes, therefore, decanting is just a useful way of getting air to the wine and an equally useful way of disguising its possibly humble supermarket origins. All in all, it is a matter of personal choice. Similarly, the wicker baskets that are designed to stop the sediment being shaken up as the wine is poured, are, in the vast majority of cases, unnecessary.

Opening a wine bottle
Opening the bottle is often the most difficult part of serving wine, particularly if you are confronted with a plastic covering which has to be sliced with a knife. A conventional lead covering (the capsule) should be scored with the point of a knife and then peeled off. Any mould should be wiped away from the rim of the bottle with a clean cloth.

The best corkscrew is a simple, sturdy spiral with a good, sharp point. If a cork refuses to move, run hot water over the neck of the bottle until the glass expands and allows the cork to be gently eased out with a corkscrew.

The best way to open sparkling wine is to take off the wires, hold the cork wrapped in a clean cloth in one hand and twist the bottle in the other until the cork eases out. There is no need for dramatic explosions.

STORING

Inexpensive, everyday wine is nowadays ready to drink as soon as it is bottled, so don't fill up a wine cellar with it, buy it and drink it as and when you need it. However, better-quality wines, even quite modest ones, do benefit from 'laying down'.

How and where

The first question for most wine drinkers is how and where to store even a limited number of bottles. The ideal, of course, is a cool, dark cellar with a steady temperature of about 10C /50F. Since very few modern houses have cellars, the alternative is to look around for a dark place where the bottles can lie undisturbed.

The storage place must be dark — because light can affect the colour of the wine — and free from strong smells (paint or detergent) that could penetrate the cork. There should also be no local vibrations that may shake up the bottles and stir up the sediment.

The temperature of the 'cellar' is crucial too, although it is more important that it should be constant rather than particularly cool. Anywhere free from draughts that is not near a radiator, central heating boiler or hot water tank should be adequate — in practice this means the back of a broom cupboard or a recess under the stairs. A shed or garage may be suitable, but it is vital that it be well enough insulated for there to be no risk of the bottles freezing in winter.

Wine bottles really should be stored lying horizontally. This is to ensure that the corks are kept in contact with the wine, so that they do not dry out and let in too much air. Wine merchants' cardboard boxes lying on their sides will just about do for a limited number of bottles, but for a more serious cellar, wine racks are essential.

Organize your cellar by storing white wines below red wines because they like to be cooler and heat rises. Keep all necks pointing outwards, labels uppermost so that you can see what is where. You may even find it useful to keep a 'cellar book', with the dates of purchases and comments on the wines as you drink them.

What to store

Fine clarets and red burgundies, excellent white burgundies, Sauternes and vintage port used to be the staples of the traditional cellar, laid down to mature for a decade or so, or much longer in the case of very great wines. During these years, tiny amounts of air seep in through the cork and combine with the wine. Gradually the raw elements knit together and the marvellous bouquet builds up, to be savoured when the bottle is eventually opened and the wine poured.

The most important reason for storing wine is that certain wines improve dramatically with keeping. Some cheap young reds will taste much better after six months or a year — which is much longer than they will have been 'in bottle' before appearing on the wine merchants' shelves. Red wines like those from the northern Rhône, Italian Barolos, Chiantis and Barbarescos, and

Spanish red Riojas will benefit from keeping considerably longer. Look out for any wines from these areas that you particularly like, with a view to laying down. Of course, if you are going to invest money in a large volume of wine, make sure you taste it carefully before you buy it.

Lighter reds, anything that says 'fresh and fruity' to you when you taste it, may well benefit from just a few months 'rest' in their bottles, but need not be kept any longer. Southern Rhône wines (except Châteauneuf-du-Pape), *vins de pays*, Valpolicella and beaujolais fall into this category. As a general guide, the 'bigger' and 'heavier' a wine tastes, the longer it needs to mature.

Generally speaking, most of the more ordinary white wines will not benefit from more than a very few months rest. Drink light, dry whites such as Muscadet, Mâcon, any Sauvignon and the Italian whites as soon as you like. Sweet dessert white wines and good white Burgundy, however, do improve with keeping. Non-vintage champagne does not need laying down — unless you drink it in large quantities, just buy it when you need it. Vintage champagne does benefit from laying down, however.

Apart from the definite improvement in taste, there are several good reasons for buying wine in bulk and keeping it in your cellar: wine prices tend to rise all the time; wine merchants will often give a discount on bulk purchases — generally a case or more, sometimes a mixed case of several different wines; and finally, if you have a comfortably stocked cellar, there is no chance of running out of wine in the middle of a party!

Since exposure to air causes a wine to deteriorate, do try to finish up any bottle on the day that it is opened. If you wish to keep a half-finished bottle for another couple of days, then transfer the wine to a smaller bottle and re-cork it (see diagram below) as soon as possible — or use it for cooking.

Re-corking a bottle

To re-cork a half-drunk bottle of wine, cut a V from the base of the cork to make it easier to re-insert. Most wines will keep for 24 hours. Red wines keep better than whites.

BURGUNDY

Most wine experts are agreed that the best of Burgundy's wines are among the greatest in the world. Almost all burgundy is very expensive nowadays but there are still bargains to be had from fringe areas.

Burgundy is the English word for the district in France which produces a great, soft, fruity but full-bodied wine. Big and rich, the wine is sold in green bottles with sloping shoulders. Unlike claret, most burgundies do not improve with long keeping. Five to six years old is a good bet for most fine red burgundies, but some white burgundies should be drunk younger.

You need to plan a little for a full-bodied wine, rather than buying and drinking it on the spur of the moment — this is because it is best enjoyed with food. It goes perfectly with game, good, rare beef steaks and roasts and rich meat pâtés. It also rounds off a meal with blue cheese and fruit very well. A white burgundy goes well with fish, seafood and chicken (see the section on Chablis).

To get the best from a full-bodied red wine, allow it to come to room temperature, a pleasant 20C /68F is ideal. Open the bottle about two hours before the meal. A white burgundy is best served at cellar temperature, 7–10C /45–50F.

The regions of Burgundy

Burgundy is one of France's two great wine-producing regions. Both red and white burgundies are world famous.

Burgundy is almost in central France, but it is closer to the Swiss border than to the Atlantic. The most famous burgundies come from the Côte d'Or (golden slopes) which is the name given to the areas Côte de Nuits and Côte de Beaune together. The areas of Chablis, the tiny Côte Challonnaise and Mâconnais make up the rest of Burgundy (although Chablis only produces white wine). South of Burgundy is the area of Beaujolais. This chapter contains articles on each of these regions and also some recipes to go with the different wines.

Describing burgundy

What are the characteristics of a good burgundy — red or white? The incomparable whites make up less than a quarter of Burgundy's total output. As a rough description, the wines are firm and balanced and are powerfully suggestive of the noble Chardonnay grape.

Most can be laid down for several years, as they have exceptional staying power. Well-made reds are fruity and emphatic, but not heavy or 'soupy'. The adjective most often used to describe red burgundy is 'velvety'.

Producing burgundy

Burgundy costs so much because the total area producing wine entitled to bear one of the 114 burgundy appellations is small. The best burgundies come from the vineyards of the Côte d'Or. They lie along a south-east-facing strip of hillside — Côte de Nuits is 20 kilometres long and Côte de Beaune is much the same again and both are often

as little as 1 kilometre wide. The very best vineyards, which produce the red *grand crus* (best growths), lie in the centre of this strip.

Some of these vineyards, with world-famous names, are no bigger than large gardens. Romanée-Conti, for example, generally thought of as the peak of burgundy, covers a mere 1.8 hectares. Bad weather often dramatically reduces the potential yield, and then a large percentage of what is eventually produced is sold direct to individual buyers. In some years it is remarkable that any burgundy reaches the market at all and what little they manage to produce has to satisfy a burgundy-thirsty world.

Burgundy is said to be very variable in quality. In the past 'burgundy' was often doctored with heavy reds from Midi, or even Algeria, to give it the weight that the customers expected. Now, with the law tightened up, any wine with a burgundy *Appellation Contrôlée* label must be made entirely from grapes grown in the area.

Variability still remains, however, but this is partly because, unlike Bordeaux where large properties often belong to a single owner, burgundy vineyards may have dozens of owners, each responsible for a tiny parcel of land. Even wine made from grapes in adjoining rows may taste quite different because the grapes may have been tended and harvested differently. The grapes are then sold to different middlemen, *négociants*, each of whom will blend wines according to his own house-style and bottling standards. The wines will then be marketed with his name on the label.

When buying burgundy, a careful scrutiny of the label is the only guide. If you are buying a *grand cru* or one of the better *premier crus*, a wine that is made and bottled by the grower at the property is the best choice (see box).

General classifications

The appellation system which governs the way Burgundy's wines are labelled and sold is complex. The most basic appellation is Bourgogne Grand Ordinaire. Next in price and quality comes the red Passe-tout-Grains; this means 'all grapes included' and in practice the wine will be a mixture of two-thirds from the Gamay grape — the more prolific grape of the area — and one-third of the superior grape, Pinot Noir.

The second grade for white wine is Bourgogne Aligoté; this is made from the Aligoté grape, the lesser of the two grapes used in the region for the white wine. AC Bourgogne comes next, made entirely from the noble Pinot Noir grape for red and Chardonnay for white. AC Bourgogne from a well-known and reliable shipper is often a good buy.

From the hilly countryside beyond the main slopes come two more basic appellations — Hautes Côtes de Beaune and Hautes Côtes de Nuits. These wines can also be very worthwhile; in good years, when the grapes have had plenty of sun to ripen them, they will compare favourably with their aristocratic relatives.

From the Côte d'Or, the heartland of Burgundy, come the three topmost appellations of the region. At the very top are the 30 grands crus, the best vineyards with famous names like Chambertin, Le Musigny and Le Montrachet. *Premier cru* is the grade immediately below. The third rank is *appellation communale*, in other words, having the right to use the name of the commune. These are still fine wines, although not in quite the same exalted class as those wines that are produced from either grand cru or premier cru vineyards.

UNDERSTANDING FRENCH WINES

While every region has its own methods and words for classifying their wines, there are many pieces of information that remain the same. These are found on the label of the bottle and are your guide to the wine inside.

Vin de table: a basic-quality, good wine.
Vins de Pays: a better-quality local wine.
VDQS (*Vin Délimité de Qualité Supérieure*): the production of these wines is strictly governed and conforms to high standards.
AC (*Appellation Contrôlée*): the finest wines of guaranteed origin, standard and degree of alcohol.

Bottling

The best wines are '*mise en bouteille à la propriété*', '*mise en bouteille au château*' or '*mise en bouteille à la domaine*', which mean that the grower bottled them himself. '*Mise en bouteilles dans nos caves*' or '*mise en bouteille dans nos chais*' means *not* bottled at the property. '*Nos caves*' (our cellars) could

be anywhere. '*Mise par le négociant*' or '*mise par Monsieur X*' means that a shipper bought the wines and blended and bottled them.

Vintage

Few people can remember all the information about every vintage of wine, and there are plenty of books that set it all down. But it is worth having a rough idea of what should be ready when and the best years.

Degree of sweetness and sparkle

Brut: bone dry
Sec: dry
Demi sec: medium sweet
Doux: sweet
Champagne: made in the Champagne area of France by the *méthode champenoise*
Mousseux: sparkling
Crémant: less sparkling than Mousseux
Pétillant: with a tingly fizz
Perlant: with just a touch of fizz

COTE DE NUITS

The Côte d'Or ('golden slope'), stretching between Dijon in the north and Santenay in the south, has been producing legendary wine for hundreds of years. The northern part is known as Côte de Nuits.

There are eight important wine communes in this Côte. For the commune appellation titles some hyphenate the names of their most famous vineyard to their village name, giving resounding combinations like Chambolle-Musigny and Nuits-St Georges.

The two northernmost communes are Fixin and Gevrey-Chambertin. Gevery-Chamertin is often described as the typical red burgundy and its commune has nine *grand cru* vineyards. The *appellation communale* wine of Gevrey has a high reputation and the wines from Fixin, north of Gevrey, are dark red, strongly perfumed and age well.

Beyond Gevrey-Chambertin lies Morey-St Denis, where the wines are like the Gevrey-Chambertin wines, with a trace of softness.

Chambolle-Musigny, just to the south, is elegant and perfumed, but full-bodied. The great vineyard in this commune is Les Musigny which also produces a small quantity of white wine. Among the *premiers crus* are the prettily named Les Amoureuses and Les Charmes. Next door the small commune of Vougeot is almost taken up by the vineyard Clos de Vougeot.

Between Vougeot and Vosne-Romanée lies Flagey-Echézaux. Most of the wines from this commune are sold as Vosne-Romanée. The commune has five grands crus and Romanée-Conti is thought by some to be the very greatest red wine of all. The other equally famous names here are la Romanée and Romanée-St Vivant.

The last important commune of the Côte is Nuits-St Georges, centred on the town of Nuits. The wines of Premeaux, the neighbouring commune, are also sold as Nuits-St Georges. These are big wines, typically Côte de Nuits, firm and tannic and with a deep colour. They take time to mature, but are worth waiting for.

Certain inferior vineyards along the length of the Côte are only allowed to sell their wines as Côte de Nuits-Villages. (Remember that 'inferior' is a relative term when talking of the Côte d'Or.) These are still of a higher standard than AC Bourgogne.

Boeuf bourguignon

Serve this Boeuf bourguignon, adapted from an old Burgundy recipe book, with a full-flavoured Nuits-St Georges.

 3½ hours

Serves 4
30 ml /2 tbls oil
225 g /8 oz onions, chopped
4 feather steaks, cut from the blade, each weighing 175 g /6 oz
250 g /8 oz carrots, sliced
1 leek, rinsed and sliced
1 garlic clove, chopped
a sprig of thyme
a sprig of parsley
bay leaf
100 g /4 oz streaky bacon, chopped
200 ml /7 fl oz beef stock, home-made or from a cube
300 ml /10 fl oz Madeira
salt and freshly ground black pepper
creamed potato, to serve

1 Heat the oven to 150C /300F /gas 2. Heat the oil in a frying-pan and cook the onion until transparent and soft. Remove it from the pan and reserve. Increase the heat, add the steaks and brown well.
2 Put the meat into a shallow ovenproof dish, large enough for it to fit in a flat layer. Add the onions, carrots, the leek, the garlic, thyme, parsley, bay leaf, streaky bacon, beef stock, Madeira and salt and pepper.
3 Cover the dish tightly with foil, and then cover with a lid. Cook for 3 hours.
4 Remove the steaks from the dish and place them on a warmed serving dish. Pipe the creamed potato around the edge of the dish. Arrange the sliced carrots over the pieces of meat, then spoon some of the sauce over the meat and serve the rest separately.

Chicken sauté chasseur

 1½ hours

Serves 4
1.4 kg /3 lb oven-ready chicken
salt and freshly ground black pepper
45 ml /3 tbls olive oil
40 g /1½ oz butter
1 medium-sized onion, finely chopped
1 shallot, finely chopped
1 garlic clove, finely chopped
15 ml /1 tbls flour
225 ml /8 fl oz red wine
60 ml /4 tbls finely chopped fresh parsley
4 tomatoes, blanched, skinned, quartered and seeded
275 g /10 oz mushrooms

1 Cut the chicken into 4 serving portions and season them with salt and black pepper.
2 Heat the olive oil and butter in a flameproof casserole large enough to take the chicken portions in one layer. When the foaming subsides, sauté the chicken over a high heat for 2–3 minutes each side until browned. Remove the chicken from the casserole and keep warm.
3 Add the onion, shallot and garlic to the casserole and cook over a medium heat for 10 minutes or until golden, stirring occasionally.
4 Stir in the flour and cook for 2–3 minutes over a low heat, stirring constantly. Pour in the wine, whisking vigorously, and boil for 1–2 minutes. Stir in the parsley and tomatoes. Season with salt and black pepper to taste.
5 Replace the chicken in the casserole, cover and simmer for 20 minutes, stirring occasionally.
6 Meanwhile, trim the stalks from the mushrooms, slice them, then wipe the caps with a clean damp cloth and slice them thinly. Add to the casserole, cover and cook for a further 15 minutes.
7 Transfer the chicken portions to a heated serving platter. Adjust the seasoning of the sauce and pour it over the chicken.

Boeuf bourguignon

COTE DE BEAUNE

Burgundy's southern half, the Côte de Beaune, is world famous for its white wine. To many people the white wine from this region is the greatest in the world, and the many classic wines from the area, with their distinctive dry but lusciously rich flavours, command high prices.

The neighbouring communes of Puligny-Montrachet and Chassagne-Montrachet at the southern end of the Côte de Beaune are the best known. These communes take their names from the villages, with the name of the most illustrious vineyards tacked on. Le Montrachet is the greatest of the white *grands crus* vineyards. It is split between the two communes of Puligny and Chassagne, with its only marginally less illustrious grand cru neighbours clustered around it. Even Appellation contrôlée commune wines from this area are very expensive so it is wise to take a look at wines from the neighbouring commune at St-Aubin. Its wines, white and red, are dependable, cheaper and still provide an echo of the Montrachet distinction.

Next to Puligny-Montrachet lies the commune of Meursault, producing soft white wines with a distinctive flavour described as either 'mealy' or 'buttery'. The single-vineyard wines — les Genevrières, les Charmes, les Perrières — are excellent but the commune AC wines can be disappointing if they come from the low vineyards bordering the main road. Meursault is popular and sometimes overpriced; neighbouring Auxey-Duresses is a cheaper alternative. Red wines from Meursault are generally sold as Volnay, and Volnay's whites as Meursault.

North of Meursault lie the famous red wine communes of the Côte — Volnay, Pommard and Beaune. Pommard is the most expensive and most imitated. Volnay's reds are attractive, short-lived but with a delicate roundness and a fragrant bouquet. A cheaper alternative to these red wines can be found in Auxey-Duresses or Monthélie.

Beaune is a large commune centred on the town of Beaune, the administrative centre of the Burgundy wine trade. It is a famous name and almost all the wines from the commune get *premier cru* rating. AC Beaune is the lowest appellation and tends to be overpriced for its variable quality — better buys are to be found amongst the reds of Savigny-lès-Beaune, or Santenay. The commune of Santenay is at the southern end of the Côte and produces lower priced wines. These may be light and fruity, or powerful and long-lived according to the variability of the soil.

At the northern end of the Côte is the village of Aloxe-Corton, with the hill of Corton rising above it. On the slopes of this hillside lie a wonderful concentration of both red and white vineyards. The red wines of Le Corton rival the very best of the Côte de Nuits. Corton-Charlemagne — legend has it that this land was once the property of the Emperor Charlemagne — produces superb white wine.

The Côte de Beaune is a larger area than the Côte de Nuits so its basic wines are more

Salmon with mousseline sauce

plentiful and therefore cheaper. Immediately below commune level is AC Côte de Beaune-Villages, from several of the villages around the town of Beaune. Some of these villages are also entitled to their own individual appellations. Plain AC Côte de Beaune is the product of 16 villages on the edges of the Côte proper. If the blending is done by one of the big *négociants*, these wines can also be good value. Finally, there is Bourgogne Hautes Côtes de Beaune, from the country over the hill beyond the Côte d'Or itself. If they are carefully made in a good year, generic wines like these are excellent and can provide the only really accessible burgundies for the average drinker.

Salmon with mousseline sauce

Serve this impressive dish at a buffet and accompany it with a white Burgundy — perhaps a Puligny Montrachet.

 1 hour, plus chilling

Serves 12

1 salmon, weighing about 2.8 kg /6 lb
30 ml /2 tbls dried dill
salt and freshly ground black pepper
oil, for greasing
1 large cucumber, peeled
watercress, to garnish
10 ml /2 tsp fresh dill, finely chopped

For the mousseline sauce
1 cucumber
550 ml /1 pt Mayonnaise (see page 43)
300 ml /10 fl oz thick cream, whipped
5 ml /1 tsp lemon juice
30 ml /2 tbls dried dill
salt and white pepper

1 Keep the fish whole and clean it well. Season it inside and out with dill, salt and pepper. Place the fish on a piece of lightly oiled foil and wrap it up, sealing the edges.
2 Place the foil-wrapped fish in a fish kettle, or ease it gently into a very large pan. Pour boiling water into the kettle or pan to come three-quarters of the way up the sides of the foil packet. Cover the kettle or pan and simmer for 30 minutes.
3 Remove the fish kettle or pan from the heat and leave the fish to cool just a little in the kettle or pan for up to 15 minutes.
4 Carefully lift the fish out, holding it by the foil. Place it on a large serving platter and unwrap it. There will be some liquid in the foil which you should drain away carefully, keeping a firm hold on the fish. Ease the foil away from under the fish and discard it.
5 Remove the skin of the fish, leaving the head intact. Clean the serving dish with absorbent paper and leave until cold.
6 Make the mousseline sauce. Peel and finely grate the cucumber, then mix it with the mayonnaise and whipped cream. Stir in the lemon juice and dill and season to taste. Chill the sauce until required.
7 Thinly slice the peeled cucumber and use it to decorate the fish. Garnish with watercress and a fine sprinkling of fresh dill. Serve with the mousseline sauce.

CHABLIS

Chablis

Chablis comes from an isolated little pocket of northern vineyards, a mere 160 kilometres south-east of Paris. It is one of the smallest fine-wine-producing areas. The local conditions demand that the land has to be 'rested' from time to time, so that even this small area is not always under cultivation.

Although Chablis is made from the same grape as the great white burgundies, the Chardonnay, its taste is very different. The crucial factor is the mixture of chalk and limestone in the soil.

Chablis is an elegant wine with a bouquet which is fresh and clean but comparatively light, and the colour is particularly attractive, pale straw-gold with greenish highlights.

Chablis has its own system of classification. The best (and very expensive) wine comes from the seven grand cru vineyards. The level immediately below grand cru is premier cru and there are about a dozen of these. The Chablis appellation laws state that grand cru wines must reach a level of 11 per cent of alcohol and premier cru must reach 10.5 per cent. In bad years the wine may not reach the required minimum strength, in which case it has to be sold off as Petit Chablis, the lowest of the local appellations, because it only needs to reach a strength of 9.5 per cent.

The apellation laws also set out the maximum yield per hectare for grand cru and premier cru vineyards and it is a strictly limited output.

Fortunately, plain AC Chablis is rather more accessible. This wine comes from the less well-placed slopes of any of the 20 communes in the region, and the bulk of it is handled by négociants. This wine needs only reach a level of 10 per cent.

The lighter wines of the Chablis region should not be left too long before they are drunk. A year or so in bottle is plenty for Petit Chablis and the ordinary AC wines. Premier cru wines are ready to drink after two years and most grands crus can be drunk after three years in the bottle. The best Chablis does have remarkable staying power, however, and can go on giving of its best for ten years, or longer.

Cold seafood platter

Serve this platter as a main course for two at a special supper and accompany it with a white Burgundy.

45 minutes, plus cooling

Serves 4 as a starter
500 g /1 lb or 1 pt mussels, scrubbed
150 ml /5 fl oz Chablis or another dry white wine
8 raw scampi, with heads and shells on
8 large scallops
For the sauce
25 g /1 oz butter
15 ml /1 tbls oil
1 onion, finely chopped
1 garlic clove, crushed
1 green pepper, finely diced
500 g /1 lb tomatoes, blanched, skinned and chopped
10 ml /2 tsp lemon juice
1.5 ml /¼ tsp ground coriander
2.5 ml /½ tsp paprika
2.5 ml /½ tsp cumin
salt and freshly ground black pepper

1 To make the sauce, in a saucepan, heat the butter and oil and sauté the onion until soft (about 5 minutes). Add the garlic and the green pepper and continue cooking, stirring occasionally, for 5 minutes. Add the tomatoes, lemon juice, coriander, paprika and cumin. Stir well and season with salt and black pepper. Simmer the sauce for 20 minutes, stirring occasionally.
2 Meanwhile, put the mussels in a large saucepan with 150 ml /5 fl oz water and the dry white wine. Cover the pan tightly and steam over a high heat, shaking the pan occasionally, for about 5 minutes or until the mussels have opened. Strain the mussels, reserving the liquor. Discard any mussels that have not opened and set the remainder aside to cool.
3 Bring the reserved liquor to the boil, add the scampi and turn the heat down. Simmer for 1½–2 minutes. Remove with a slotted spoon and set aside to cool.
4 Separate the orange corals from the scallops, then remove and discard the black membrane. Poach the scallops for 3–5 minutes in the liquor, adding the corals for

the last minute of the cooking time. Drain and leave to cool.
5 Remove the sauce from the heat and allow it to cool. Remove the mussels from their shells and discard the shells.
6 To arrange, pour the sauce into individual ramekins and place each on a plate. Arrange the scampi and mussels on the plates. Slice the scallops in half horizontally and arrange them with the corals decoratively on top. Serve the platter and provide finger-bowls and large napkins.

Sole in white wine sauce

35 minutes

Serves 6
oil, for greasing
25 g /1 oz shallots, finely chopped
12 fillets of lemon sole
salt and freshly ground black pepper
50 g /2 oz butter
275 ml /10 fl oz Chablis or another dry white wine, mixed with 150 ml /5 fl oz water
175 g /6 oz boiled, shelled prawns
5 ml /1 tsp lemon juice
12 asparagus tips, cooked or canned
25 g /1 oz flour, blended to a paste with 40 g /1½ oz butter
200 ml /7 fl oz thick cream
25 g /1 oz Gruyère cheese, grated

1 Heat the oven to 180C /350F /gas 4. Grease a large ovenproof dish and sprinkle half the shallots over the base. Rub the sole fillets with salt and pepper and arrange it in the dish. Sprinkle it with the remaining shallots and dot with 25 g /1 oz butter.
2 Pour in enough of the wine and water mixture to just cover the fish. Poach in the oven for 8–10 minutes.
3 Meanwhile, heat the prawns in 25 g /1 oz butter and the lemon juice. At the same time, warm the asparagus tips.
4 Transfer the poached fish to a serving dish and keep it warm in the oven. Strain the cooking liquid into a pan and boil it until it has reduced to 275 ml /10 fl oz.
5 Remove the pan from the heat and beat in the flour and butter paste a little at a time. Return to the heat and boil until thickened. Stir in the cream and bring to just below boiling point. Reserve 24 prawns for garnishing, and stir the remaining prawns into the sauce. Season the sauce to taste, then pour it over the fillets.
6 Sprinkle the Gruyère over the top and heat it under a hot grill until it is bubbling and golden. Garnish with the asparagus tips and the reserved prawns. Serve immediately.

Hot and cold chicken loaves

 cooking and cooling, then several hours' preparation

Serves 12

3 × 1.4 kg /3 lb chickens
1.1 L /2 pt chicken stock, home-made or from
  cubes
6 celery sticks, with leaves, sliced
2 large carrots, sliced
2 large Spanish onions, sliced
2 bay leaves
12 black peppercorns

For cold jellied chicken loaf

5 ml /1 tsp powdered gelatine
300 ml /10 fl oz Chablis or dry white wine
salt and freshly ground black pepper
stuffed green olives, sliced, to garnish
lettuce, finely shredded, to garnish

For hot curried chicken loaf

20–25 ml /4–5 tsp garam masala
a pinch of cayenne pepper
150 ml /5 fl oz milk
25 g /1 oz butter
175 g /6 oz fresh white breadcrumbs
30 ml /2 tbls coarsely chopped fresh parsley
45 ml /3 tbls diced celery
45 ml /3 tbls diced green pepper
2 canned pimento, diced
4 eggs, beaten
salt and freshly ground black pepper
oil, for greasing
6 black olives, stoned, to garnish
hot carrots and asparagus tips, to garnish

For the curry sauce

20 ml /4 tsp garam masala
1 chicken stock cube, crumbled
425 ml /15 fl oz Bechamel sauce (see page 33)
1.5 ml /¼ tsp tumeric

1 In a large, heavy-based flameproof casserole or another pan which is large enough to take the chickens side by side, place the chickens, stock, celery, carrots and onions, bay leaves and peppercorns. Bring to the boil and simmer for 50–60 minutes, or until cooked through, the juices run clear, and the flesh is just tender. Leave to cool in the stock for about 3 hours.

2 Remove the chickens from the casserole. Strain the stock through a sieve lined with muslin. Skim off the surface fat.

3 Prepare the cold jellied chicken loaf. Cut the breast meat from the chickens. Remove and discard the skin and cut the meat into large, even-sized pieces. Arrange them in a 850 ml /1½ pt loaf tin.

4 In a small bowl, sprinkle the gelatine over 30 ml /2 tbls cold water. Leave to soften. Place the bowl in a saucepan of simmering water until the gelatine is dissolved. Leave to cool slightly.

5 Add the dry white wine to the strained stock, then season to taste with salt and freshly ground black pepper. Stir in the dissolved gelatine. Pour the mixture over the chiken pieces to fill the tin. Cover with cling film and put in the refrigerator to set.

6 To prepare the hot curried chicken loaf, heat the oven to 180C /350F /gas 4.

7 Separate the remaining meat from the bones and remove and discard the skin. Cut the meat into pieces. Place in a large bowl and sprinkle with garam masala and cayenne pepper. Cover and leave, in a cool place —

not the refrigerator — for at least 2 hours to allow the meat to absorb the flavour.

8 In a saucepan, combine the milk and butter. Heat until the butter has melted.

9 Pour the mixture over the chicken pieces and add the breadcrumbs, and the parsley, celery, green pepper and pimento. Add the beaten egg and mix well. Season to taste with salt and ground black pepper.

10 Lightly grease a 1.8 L /3 pt loaf tin. Spoon the chicken mixture into the tin, smoothing the surface with a spatula. Bake for 50–60 minutes.

11 Meanwhile, make the curry sauce. In a saucepan, combine the garam masala, crumbled stock cube and bechamel sauce and turmeric. Blend well and then heat gently, stirring, until heated through.

12 To serve the jellied loaf, dip the bottom of the tin in a pan of hot water, then turn it out onto a flat serving platter. Garnish with sliced stuffed olive in diagonal lines across the top of the loaf and a couple of slices at each corner and the shredded lettuce along the sides of the loaf.

13 To serve the hot curried loaf, run a knife carefully around the inside of the tin to release the loaf and turn it out onto a heated serving platter. Spoon a little hot curry sauce over it and garnish it with stoned black olives and hot carrots and asparagus tips around the loaf. Serve with the remaining sauce in a heated sauce-boat.

Hot and cold chicken loaves

COTE CHALONNAIS & THE MACONNAIS

The Côte Chalonnais and the Mâconnais produce interesting everyday wines that still have some of the characteristics of ones from the Côte de Beaune.

The Côte Chalonnais is a tiny area lying to the south of the village of Chagny. It is really a continuation of the Côte d'Or, although the countryside in this area is rougher and hillier and the vineyards are broken up between patches of farmland. The Côte produces good-value red and white wine.

The four Chalonnais commune appellations to watch out for are Mercurey, Montagny, Rully and Givry. Montagny's whites are particularly good and clean-tasting, with a tinge of greenish-gold colour that tells of their closeness to Mâcon.

Rully is also beginning to be known for its whites. These are dry and quite full-bodied, with a certain sharpness due to the high level of acidity. Both Rully and Montagny are wines for drinking while they are still young and fresh, although a year or two in the bottle will do no harm.

The best known reds of the Côte are from the vineyards of Mercurey. They are light, but subtle. Givry and Rully also produce reds with slightly more body but less finesse than Mercurey; Givry is the better of the two. Do not leave any of these fresh wines in store for too long, and be wary of any that are more than five years old.

South of the Côte Chalonnais is the much bigger area of the Mâconnais, best known for its white wines — Pouilly-Fuissé in particular. In fact, the villages producing Pouilly-Fuissé — Vergisson, Chaintré, Solutré, Pouilly and Fuissé — are so far to the south of the Mâconnais that they overlap with the Beaujolais area. They lie on soil that gives the wines a distinctive character, known as the *goût du terroir*.

Pouilly wines are praised for being dry and full-bodied, as well as fruity and soft like a good white burgundy. Unfortunately, Pouilly-Fuissé has suffered from being too much in demand. When looking for the characteristic Pouilly taste, it would make economic sense to choose from one of the other three appellations in the area, Pouilly-Loché, Pouilly-Vinzelles or Saint-Véran. (Pouilly-Fuissé is not to be confused with Pouilly-Fumé, made from the Sauvignon grape at Pouilly-sur-Loire on the other side of France.)

Wine from the villages around Chaintré and Saint-Véran may also appear under the label 'Beaujolais blanc'. The appellations here are interchangeable. The rest of the Mâconnais produces less distinctive but perfectly good, rounded white wines made from the noble Chardonnay grape. The reds generally do not reach the same standard because

Veal chops à l'orange

they are made from the prolific Gamay grape, which is also the beaujolais grape.

Apart from Pouilly, where the individual grower predominates, Mâconnais grapes tend to be sold by the grower direct to the local co-operatives, who then turn the grapes into wine. There are about 20 co-operatives in the area, at village centres like Chaintré, Clissé and Viré. Once the wine is made, it is sold to a shipper who arranges the bottling.

A cut above plain white AC Mâcon is Mâcon-Villages, from certain designated villages. About 40 villages producing white wine of this standard are allowed to hyphenate their names onto the basic appellation title — the best known are probably Mâcon-Prissé and Mâcon-Lugny.

Another local appellation, and one that can sometimes be puzzling, is Pinot Chardonnay Mâcon. This is a so-called 'varietal' wine, named after two grape varieties, and it can be particularly good value. It may be made from the Chardonnay grape or from its close relative the Pinot Blanc, and it is so named to set it apart from the other Mâconnais whites made from the Aligoté grape which can taste thin and sharp beside the rich depth of the Chardonnay. The grapes will be identified on the label.

Veal chops à l'orange

 1 hour 20 minutes

Serves 4
15 ml /1 tbls oil
1 large onion, sliced
1 garlic clove, crushed
4 veal chops
1 orange
450 g /1 lb tomatoes, blanched, skinned, seeded and chopped
300 ml /10 fl oz Rully or another dry white wine
10 ml /2 tsp tomato purée
5 ml /1 tsp sugar
15 ml /1 tbls chopped fresh basil
salt and freshly ground black pepper

1 Heat the oven to 180C /350F /gas 4. Heat the oil in a frying-pan, add the onion and garlic and cook over moderate heat until the onions are soft and golden. Transfer the onion and garlic to a roasting tin and set aside. Add the chops, one or two at a time, to the pan and brown them lightly on each side.
2 Finely grate the zest from the orange and add it to the onions in the roasting tin, together with the prepared tomato flesh, the wine, tomato purée, sugar, basil and plenty of salt and pepper. Stir well.
3 Place the browned chops in the tin and cover the tin completely with foil. Put in the oven and cook for 1 hour.
4 Meanwhile, peel the orange, removing all the pith, and cut the fruit into segments, cutting down between the membranes.
5 Remove the tin from the oven, transfer the chops to a serving dish and spoon over the cooking juices. Garnish each chop with orange segments.

BEAUJOLAIS

Light and fruity, beaujolais is a popular and well-known red wine and a very versatile one — suitable for most social occasions and as an accompaniment for many dishes. It comes from an 80-kilometre stretch of country between Mâcon and Lyons. The region is attractive, with rolling hills and small villages which epitomize rural France. Although Beaujolais is next to Burgundy, the French think of it separately, because the wine is lighter. It is made from a different grape, Gamay, and tastes much fresher, though still fruity. Unlike burgundy, beaujolais is drunk slightly chilled and can be opened a few months after it is made.

Generally speaking, the more precisely a bottle of wine is defined by its label, the better it should be. A wine described simply as AC Beaujolais is guaranteed to come from the area, to be made from the Gamay, and to contain at least 9 per cent alcohol. Beaujolais Supérieur is the same, but 1 per cent stronger — over 10 per cent (though it is not necessarily better wine). In the heart of the Beaujolais country there is a group of some 35 communes, or villages, whose product is entitled to be known as Beaujolais Villages. This wine has the same strength as Beaujolais Supérieur but because it comes from a region where the conditions of the soil and climate are especially suited to the Gamay grape, it should have more character.

In terms of quality, there are nine communes in the area, the Grand Crus, which are entitled to their own *appéllation*, that is, a special wine label of their own. Their names are St Amour, Juliénas, Chénas, Moulin-à-Vent, Chiroubles, Fleurie, Morgon, Brouilly and Côte de Brouilly. These wines are undoubtedly the best beaujolais, and a beaujolais expert will tell you that each of them has its own distinctive qualities. As a general guide, Fleurie is perhaps the most immediately appealing — bright, translucent and appetizing. Brouilly and Côte de Brouilly are usually the fruitiest of the group. Morgon is harder and longer lasting and Moulin-à-Vent, the biggest and deepest in flavour, sometimes needs several years to develop its full potential.

As a general rule, even Grand Cru Beaujolais is at its best within two or three years of bottling. Beaujolais also breaks the other rule usually applied to red wine in that it can be served slightly chilled, at 'cellar' temperature (7C /45F), rather than room temperature (20C /68F).

Most beaujolais is bought from individual growers or co-operatives by local *négociants* or merchants. They blend the wines according to the traditions of their firms and the name of the négociant will appear on the label. The Beaujolais of Piat is a well-known wine marketed in a distinctive rounded bottle with a small lip at the top. Other merchants' names worth looking for are Antoine Dépagneux of Villefranche and Georges Duboeuf of Romaneche-Thorins.

Glazed bacon

Beaujolais is cheap so you can drink it cheerfully. It is the great all-purpose wine to drink through the evening at a party, and the perfect wine to order in a restaurant when everyone chooses a different meat for their main course.

Beaujolais nouveau is newly-made wine which is rushed from grape to bottle within the space of about six weeks, and appears on the market around 15 November. It is light, with the purplish colour characteristic of young wine, and with a pleasant scent and fruitiness. Until quite recently you would have been lucky to find it outside the region of origin. Suddenly, through a combination of shrewd marketing and the whims of fashion, it has become a cult. The effect on the beaujolais market has been colossal. It can be easily and cheaply produced, and the grower and négociant see a quick return on their investment. It is therefore hardly surprising that in 1983, 40 per cent of all the AC Beaujolais produced was sold as Beaujolais Nouveau or Primeur, and producers throughout the region feel mounting pressures to jump on the bandwagon. This would be a pity, for Beaujolais nouveau is made to be drunk within weeks rather than months, and when it is all gone there is less of the more worthwhile wine to go round.

Glazed bacon

Serve this delicately flavoured joint with a light red wine such as a beaujolais, to complement the flavours.

🕯 2¼ hours

Serves 8
1.8 kg /4 lb middle gammon or bacon joint, rolled and tied
5 whole black peppercorns
100 g /4 oz brown sugar
20 cloves
15 ml /1 tbls flour
275 ml /10 fl oz cider
salt and freshly ground black pepper
12 apple rings, fried in butter, to garnish
12 parsley sprigs, to garnish

1 Place the joint in a large pan and add enough water to cover it. Add the peppercorns and bring to the boil. Now reduce the heat, cover and simmer for 30 minutes.
2 Heat the oven to 180C /350F /gas 4. Wrap the joint in foil and place it on a rack in a roasting pan. Add enough water to the pan to cover the bottom.
3 Roast for 1 hour, then remove from the oven and open the foil. Discard the water in the pan. Increase the oven heat to 200C / 400F /gas 6. Remove the string and rind from the joint and, using a sharp knife, lightly score the fat in a criss-cross pattern.
4 Cover the fatty surface with brown sugar, pressing it down onto the fat. Stud the sugared surface with the cloves.
5 Exposing the fat only, roast for a further 30 minutes. Remove from the oven and transfer to a serving dish. Keep warm.
6 Pour the juices left in the foil into the roasting pan. Stir in 15 ml /1 tbls flour and cook over a moderate heat for 2 minutes. Remove the pan from the heat and stir in the cider. Bring to the boil, stirring. Season to taste, then pour it into a sauce-boat.
7 Garnish the joint with apple rings, putting parsley sprigs in the centre of each ring.

BORDEAUX

Bordeaux is the largest fine-wine-producing area in the world. The wines range from light, dry reds and whites, to the honeyed white dessert wines of Sauternes and Barsac, with all the subtle variations in between.

Bordeaux wines generally have a more individual bouquet and seem a little more austere than the fuller wines from Burgundy (see page 65). The red wines — often referred to as claret, which is an English term — are made from a blend of three varieties of grape: Cabernet Sauvignon, Cabernet Franc and Merlot.

A bottle of claret is nearly always made from blended wines, with the flavour of the Cabernet Sauvignon grapes used to give a basic style and distinctive taste. The Cabernet Franc grape is added for lightness and fragrance, and the Merlot for its softness. These vines flourish in Bordeaux's poor soil.

St Emilion produces more claret than any other wine district in Bordeaux, simply because it is the largest area. Pomerol, situated to the north-west of St Emilion, is a relative newcomer as a wine area.

The Médoc is the most famous red wine district. One-third of it, lying to the north, is simply known as the Médoc, or Bas-Médoc, and has a proliferation of small chateaux

making sound wine at very reasonable prices. The Haut-Médoc, to the south, produces the greatest red wines in Bordeaux.

For most people, the name Graves used to conjure up a white wine, pale gold in colour and rather sweet. Things have, however, changed in recent years and the Graves district now offers a range of lighter, drier whites, as well as some excellent red wines.

The rich, sweet wines of Bordeaux are one of its greatest glories. The best of them, Sauternes and Barsac, come from the southern areas. To go with a dessert, nothing can compare with a glass of Sauternes.

When they are young, Bordeaux wines have so much tannin in them that they are not very drinkable. After a few years in bottle, however, they become smoother and more complex. Some are good after three or four years, others are better left much longer.

Vintage dates give the wine buyer some useful hints, but are not always infallible.

A bottle of Claret and a Stilton

CLASSIFICATIONS

In 1855, an official classification was drawn up for the best Bordeaux wines. Each of the 60 Médocs and the one red Graves chosen were solemnly graded in order of excellence: First, Second, Third, Fourth or Fifth Growth, or *cru*. The system still gives a roughly accurate guide to the 60 top châteaux in Bordeaux, though many more, especially from St Emilion and Pomerol, would be in-

ST EMILION

The wines of St Emilion have a different character from that of other Bordeaux wines for two reasons: the soil is richer and the grapes used are different from the other Bordeaux wine districts. The Cabernet Sauvignon grapes are little used in St Emilion and they largely give way to Merlot.

The French make a distinction between the wines grown on the hillsides, known as Côtes-St-Emilion, and those grown on the plain, known as Graves-St-Emilion.

The great name in Côtes wines is Château Ausone. The cellars are cut from the hillside with pillars left to support the roof. The vineyards are situated under the brow of the hill, sheltered from the north wind. The wines of Château Ausone, together with those of Cheval Blanc, top the St Emilion classification list and are designated *Premiers Grands Crus Classés A*. (St Emilion was left out of the 1855 classification so it drew up its own league table 100 years later.)

HAUT-MEDOC

The Haut-Médoc is not exciting countryside. To the west, sand dunes and pine forests roll away; to the east the slopes are covered in vines which are beautifully trellised.

St Estèphe, the northern-most commune in the Haut-Médoc, has sturdy, slightly 'harder' wines than the other communes. They contain a great deal of tannin. Bought young, they need to be kept for 10–15 years before they are at their peak. Good *cru bourgeois* wines from the area to the north of the town of St Estèphe itself can be found.

Further south, wine from Château de Pez is well worth looking out for. There is also a good cru bourgeois from Château Meyney.

Adjoining Cos d'Estournel in St Estèphe is the Château Lafite vineyard in the commune of Pauillac. Château Lafite has been classed, by some, as the greatest claret in Bordeaux.

In Pauillac the country is hillier and the vines have to work harder to produce their grapes — leading to heightened quality. Château Latour is strong and full, compared with the perfumed finesse of Château Lafite wines. Château Mouton-Rothschild, on the other hand, is a wonderful wine with great concentration of flavour.

cluded if the league table were ever brought up to date. When a wine is referred to as 'Fifth Growth' in Bordeaux, it does not indicate a fifth-rate wine, but a high-class one.

Classified growths can be very expensive, but below them is a huge range of wines known as *Cru bourgeois*, often wines of real quality that cost much less. Well-made wines from the less highly regarded parts of Bordeaux, such as Blaye, Bourg and Fronsac, can often give more pleasure than the wine of a well-known château in a poor year.

Further down the steep slopes are the vineyards of Château La Gaffelière-Naudes, while across the road and running all the way to the top of the plateau are those of Château Pavie. These are well-known names and the wines expensive, so it is worth looking out for lesser châteaux that are often overlooked but good value.

The 'Graves' wines (not to be confused with the Graves district) are mostly grown from vineyards standing partly on heavy clay, partly on light gravel. The velvety wines of Château Cheval Blanc are one example. However, again, there are many less famous châteaux making good wine for much less.

As if the choice were not already wide enough, the St Emilion name is also shared by seven small communes to the south and east, extending down to the right bank of the Dordogne, and five more to the north-east on slightly higher ground.

The largest wine co-operative, with a total of 400 members, is the Union de Producteurs de St Emilion. Most of its wine is sold as Côtes Rocheuses or Royal Saint Emilion.

Coming a little down the scale, there is Château Pichon Lalande, half in Pauillac and half in the commune of St Julien, and equally well known is the wine of Lynch-Bages. Farther inland are the much smaller Château Batailley and Château Haut-Batailley.

Château Latour makes a second wine, Les Forts de Latour, that makes outstanding drinking. From Mouton, there is Mouton-Cadet, and a co-operative in Pauillac blends and bottles the wine of some 200 farmers.

St Julien is a small commune on the west bank of the River Gironde. It produces less than the other three great red-wine communes of the Haut-Médoc — Pauillac, St Estèphe and Margaux — but they are wonderful wines to lay down.

Château Léoville Las Cases is the most revered name in St Julien, closely followed by Léoville Barton and Léoville Poyferré. Château Beycheville is a wine to buy in a good vintage year.

From farther south comes the magnificent, fruity red wine of Château Margaux — choose a good vintage year to get full benefit of the marvellous bouquet. Château Margaux also produces a dry white wine, Pavillon Blanc, and a second red called Pavillon Rouge; you can even find a distinctive dry rosé from these parts, Rosé de Lascombes.

GRAVES

The Graves district is a flat area stretching from the city of Bordeaux to the pine woods of the Landes and almost to the Pyrenees. The area takes its name from its soil, which is a mixture of gravel and sand.

Many of the white wines are full flavoured, with a hint of vanilla which comes from ageing in oak casks. If you buy a bottle of Graves, don't be misled by the term Graves Supérieur on the bottle — it simply means the alcoholic strength is above 12 per cent!

Generally speaking, white wines are more difficult to make than the reds. There is a risk of oxidation, which darkens the wine and leaves a stale taste in the mouth. Sulphur is the best remedy, but it leaves its traces which are noticeable when you open the bottle and pour the first glass. The art of buying white Graves is to find the wines that avoid both hazards. It may mean choosing one of the new, drier wines like Château Carbonnieux.

The commune of Villenave-d'Ornon also produces several drier, lighter whites, even though this means giving up oak barrels and losing the traditional Graves taste, but if you want an old-fashioned Graves, with its traditional taste, try Graves de Portets.

The best reds come from the north of the Graves area, very near the city of Bordeaux. The greatest is probably Château Haut-Brion.

Other excellent red Graves include Château La Mission Haut-Brion, and Château Pape-Clément, named after the pope who moved the papacy to Avignon in the 14th century.

A few miles south of Pessac, the commune of Léognan produces fine reds, and next to Léognan is Martillac, which is the home of a number of well run estates. A little further south is Château La Garde, which produces a soft red wine, with a pleasant dry finish.

Most of the wines are expensive. A more reasonably priced but still good red Graves is Château Bouscaut.

POMEROL & THE NORTH-EAST

The wines of Pomerol are often grouped with St Emilion, because the best wines of both areas are near their shared border. Yet there is a marked difference in the wines, which is attributed to the soil difference.

The top wines come from Château Pétrus. Château Trotanoy is said to come second in reputation and Vieux-Château-Certan, next door to Château Pétrus, is also held in high regard. Other good names include L'Evangile, Certan-de-May, La Conseillante, La Fleur-Pétrus and Petit-Village.

Pomerol wines need not be hoarded for many years since, made mostly with the soft Merlot grape, they lack tannin. They are drinkable four or five years after the vintage.

Fronsac, Bourg and Blaye are situated on the right bank of the Dordogne and Gironde rivers, where the soil is a little too rich to make wines of distinction. Of the three areas, Fronsac makes the liveliest wines.

Château Canon in the Canon-Fronsac area is a well-known château but is easily confused with a St Emilion wine of the same name. Other wines worth sampling are Châteaux Bodet, Junayme, Rouet, de la Rivière, Mayne-Vieil, Toumalin and La Valade.

The districts of Bourg and Blaye also supply good wines which are at their best when young. Most are made with a blend of Merlot and Cabernet Franc grapes.

Bourg produces more wines than Blaye, the best of them being Château de Barbe and Château Guerry. In Blaye, Haut-Sociondo and Le Menaudat are châteaux of repute, but then it is difficult to go wrong in this area.

SWEET WINES OF BORDEAUX

Sauternes is made by a few hundred growers centred on five tiny communes on the banks of a stream 30 miles south of the city of Bordeaux. The five are: Sauternes, Bommes, Fargues, Preignac and Barsac. Under French law, only they are allowed to put the Sauternes label on their wines; Barsac, the largest commune, has the choice of calling its wines either Sauternes or Barsac.

The lusciousness of the Sauternes white wines is achieved by allowing a mould, called *Botrytis cinerea* or 'noble rot', to form on the grapes. The mould shrivels the grapes so that the sugar content is more concentrated. The picking of the grapes for the great Sauternes is very laborious, as the grapes do not shrivel at the same time and have to be picked individually when ready. This process makes the wines very expensive. The most highly prized wine comes from Château Yquem

where the entire wine-making plant is made of wood. No metal ever comes into contact with the wine in case it affects the taste.

The largest commune, Barsac, makes a slightly different wine from the others. It is a fraction less sweet and not quite so rich.

It is important to check that the label on a bottle of Sauternes bears the name of the commune. The term Haut-Sauternes means nothing at all. Also, any wine calling itself Sauterne, without the concluding 's', is not the genuine article. The best Sauternes should not be highly chilled, otherwise the wine will lose its intensity and flavour.

A district to remember is Cérons, where the wines come halfway in sweetness between Sauternes and Graves and are generally inexpensive. Equally inexpensive are the sweet wines of Ste Croix du Mont and Loupiac, found on the right bank of the Garonne river.

wine into the cornflour mixture, then pour it into the pear liquid. Slowly bring it to the boil, stirring continuously, and simmer for 5 minutes, or until it has thickened. Discard the lemon zest.

5   Allow the soup to cool slightly, then purée it in a blender. Next, press the purée through a fine sieve into a bowl. Leave it to become cold, then chill.

6   To serve, spoon the soup into individual bowls. Swirl 15 ml /1 tbls cream into each bowl, garnish with a fresh sprig of mint and serve at once.

Steak pastry parcels

 defrosting the pastry,
then 1½ hours

Serves 4
4 fillet steaks, each weighing 125 g /4 oz
25 g /1 oz butter, melted
freshly ground black pepper
10 ml /2 tsp freshly chopped mixed herbs
250 g /8 oz made-weight frozen puff pastry,
   defrosted
4 large tomatoes, blanched, peeled, seeded and
   chopped
1 medium-sized egg, beaten
lettuce and tomato wedges, to serve
For the sauce
2 shallots, finely chopped
2.5 ml /½ tsp freshly chopped thyme
2.5 ml /½ tsp freshly chopped tarragon
1 bay leaf
175 ml /6 fl oz red Bordeaux wine
275 ml /10 fl oz beef stock, home-made or
   from a cube
salt and freshly ground black pepper
15 ml /1 tbls tomato purée

1   To make the sauce, put the chopped shallots, thyme, tarragon, bay leaf, red wine, beef stock, salt and black pepper and tomato purée in a saucepan and boil until reduced by a third. Leave the sauce to cool.

2   Brush the steaks with the melted butter. Heat the grill and, when it is very hot, sear the steaks for 1 minute on each side. Season with black pepper, and sprinkle with mixed herbs. Leave until cold.

3   Divide the pastry into 4 and then roll each piece to an oval about 4 cm /1½ in larger than each steak. Divide the chopped tomatoes among the pieces of pastry and place a steak in the centre of each. Dampen the edges of the pastry and fold them over to encase the meat. Trim the edges and press them together. Using a fish slice, transfer the parcels, seam downwards, to a damp baking tray.

4   Re-roll the trimmings and cut them into decorative shapes. Place them on the pastry parcels and brush the surfaces with beaten egg. Refrigerate the parcels for 30 minutes. Reserve the remaining beaten egg. Meanwhile, heat the oven to 200C /400F /gas 6.

5   Brush the parcels again with beaten egg. Cook in the oven for 15–20 minutes until the pastry is golden.

6   Serve the parcels on a bed of lettuce and tomatoes. Reheat the sauce, strain it into a sauce-boat and hand it separately.

Chilled pear soup

 30 minutes,
plus chilling

Serves 8–10
30 ml /2 tbls sugar
10 ml /2 tsp ground ginger
pared zest and juice of 1 lemon
900 g /2 lb pears
60 ml /4 tbls cornflour
850 ml /1½ pt Pavillon Blanc or another dry
   white wine
120–150 ml /8–10 tbls thick cream
fresh mint leaves, to garnish

1   In a medium-sized saucepan, combine the sugar, ground ginger, lemon zest and 1.1 L / 2 pt water.

2   Place the pan over a low heat and bring it slowly to simmering point, stirring occasionally to dissolve the sugar, then cover it and simmer it for 5 minutes.

3   Meanwhile, peel and core the pears and, to prevent them discoloring, put them in a bowl of cold water acidulated with the lemon juice. Drain the pears, discarding the liquid, add them to the simmering syrup and poach them for 3 minutes.

4   Meanwhile, in a medium-sized bowl, mix the cornflour to a smooth paste with a little of the wine. Thoroughly blend the remaining

Pheasant casserole

defrosting the pastry,
then 1¾ hours

Serves 4

50 g /2 oz butter, plus extra for greasing
15 ml /1 tbls oil
100 g /4 oz streaky bacon, chopped
1 large onion, chopped
4 celery sticks, chopped
1 large pheasant, cut into 4
600 ml /1 pt red Graves or another red wine
2 bay leaves
1 bouquet garni
5 ml /1 tsp dried thyme
salt and freshly ground black pepper
250 g /8 oz frozen puff pastry, defrosted
15–30 ml /1–2 tbls cranberry sauce
1 medium-sized egg, beaten
beurre manié, made by blending 25 g /1 oz
   flour with 25 g /1 oz butter
15 ml /1 tbls freshly chopped parsley,
   to garnish

1 Heat the oven to 180C /350F /gas 4. Heat half the butter and the oil in a frying-pan over a moderate heat, add the chopped bacon and cook it until lightly browned. Using a slotted spoon, transfer the bacon to a flame-proof casserole.
2 Add the chopped onion and celery to the frying-pan, and cook over a gentle heat until they are golden brown, then transfer them to the casserole. Add the remaining butter to the frying-pan, add the pheasant joints and cook over a moderate heat for about 5 minutes on each side, until lightly browned. Transfer them to the casserole.
3 Pour the wine over the pheasant. Bring it to the boil on top of the stove, and add the bay leaves, bouquet garni, thyme and salt and pepper to taste. Cover, place in the centre of the oven and cook for 1 hour.
4 Meanwhile, thinly roll out the pastry. Cut it into rounds with a 7.5 cm /3 in fluted cutter. Moisten the edges with water. Place 2.5 ml /½ tsp cranberry sauce in the centre of each round, then fold over the pastry to make a crescent. Lift the crescents onto a greased baking sheet, brush with the beaten egg and refrigerate until needed.
5 When the pheasant is cooked, remove the casserole from the oven and increase the temperature to 220C /425F /gas 7, then place the crescents on the top shelf and cook them for 12 minutes.
6 Meanwhile, transfer the pheasant joints to a serving dish and keep them warm. Remove the bay leaves and bouquet garni from the casserole. Place the casserole over a moderate heat, bring to the boil then reduce to a simmer. Add the beurre manié a little at a time, stirring, until the sauce thickens. Spoon the sauce over the pheasant, sprinkle it with chopped parsley and surround it with the crescents.

Apricot toasts

35 minutes

Serves 4

150 ml /5 fl oz thick cream
30 ml /2 tbls apricot brandy
15 ml /1 tbls orange juice
8 ripe apricots
175 ml /6 fl oz dry white Graves or another
   dry white wine
75 g /3 oz caster sugar
100 g /4 oz butter
8 slices white bread, crusts removed
whipped cream, to serve

1 In a bowl, whip the cream until it is stiff, then add the brandy and orange juice and chill in the refrigerator while you complete the dessert.
2 Peel, halve and stone the apricots. Crack the stones to obtain the kernels. Put the wine, 275 ml /10 fl oz water and the sugar in a saucepan and heat gently, stirring to dissolve the sugar. Bring to simmering point, then add the apricots and kernels and simmer for 3–4 minutes.
3 Melt the butter in a frying-pan and, when it is bubbling, add the bread. Fry, turning once, until it is golden brown (you may have to fry the bread in 2 batches, so keep the first batch warm while you cook the second).
4 Arrange 2 slices of the fried bread on each of 4 warmed plates. Place 2 apricot halves on each piece of bread, one half cut side up with an apricot kernel rounded side up. Spoon a little of the syrup over each apricot toast. Spoon some whipped cream onto each plate and serve at once.

Apricot toasts

CHAMPAGNE

Champagne will turn any event into a special celebration. If you also serve one of my superb dishes prepared with champagne, then you will have a truly sparkling occasion!

The name 'champagne' can only be used for the sparkling wines that come from the Champagne region of north-east France. The finesse and delicacy of the sparkling wines from this region make them stand out from all others. The process by which they are made is long, and therefore expensive, and is known as the *méthode champenoise*. The wine is bottled and, by adding sugar and yeast, is fermented for a second time in the bottle. The expensive part of the production is removing the sediment that collects in the bottle; each bottle has to be gently tilted about 180 times over a couple of months so that the sediment collects at the neck of the bottle. The neck is then frozen and the sediment removed in a block. Next, the bottle is topped up with more wine, which has been sweetened according to the style required.

Champagne is usually made from a mixture of black and white grapes, unless it is a blanc de blancs (white wine from white grapes). When the grapes are particularly good and plentiful, a vintage is declared. This means that a champagne is made from the grapes of that year alone, and the year will be stated on the bottle. It is the vintage champagnes that command the highest prices. (Dom Perignon is always a vintage champagne.) They have more individuality than the non-vintage champagnes, which are blended to maintain a consistent style from year to year. Moët & Chandon and Bollinger are the two most well-known names that produce non-vintage, as well as vintage, champagnes.

On wine lists, champagne is classified into Non-Vintage (NV) and Vintage. Non-vintage champagnes have to be matured in the cellars for a legal minimum period of 18 months, and are blends of wines from several different years. In fact, the NV champagnes exported by the leading champagne houses are usually three years old. If they are left to mature longer in a cool, dark cellar or cupboard, NV champagnes will improve greatly.

Vintage champagnes, selected from a particularly good year, must by law remain in the producer's cellars for at least three years, often more, and may mature well for up to ten years. The leading champagne houses are known as Grande Marques and all are proud of their individual house styles, which have been evolved over many years of production.

Serving

Most important — never try to pull the cork from the bottle. Remove the foil and wire from the cork, then lever the cork upwards with your thumbs, turning the bottle as you gain leverage. When the cork starts to loosen, cover it with a cloth and with the other hand gently turn the bottle away from the cork. The cork should be held back against the escaping gas, to avoid a loud pop, and a wasteful gush of wine.

Depending on the temperature at which the bottle has been stored, it will need only an hour or two in the refrigerator, or less in an ice bucket.

Styles of champagne

Here is a list of different champagnes.

Bollinger: deep, golden colour with an intensity of flavour; dry with great finesse.

Charles Heidsieck: traditional, full-bodied and fruity; not very dry.

Georges Goulet: a racy, youthful wine, very fruity; medium dry.

Krug: subtle bouquet and flavour, silky and well-balanced; dry.

Louis Roederer: great elegance, pale golden with a delicate flavour; notably dry.

Laurent Perrier: light gold, brisk and youthful with a 'leafy' bouquet.

Mercier: slightly flowery bouquet; dry with a good finish.

Moët & Chandon: straw gold in colour, light, well-balanced and not very dry.

Mumm: pale and sprightly with a good finish; medium dry.

Pol Roger: very light gold in colour, with an extremely fine bouquet; dry and elegant.

Veuve Clicquot: pale, well balanced and dry; bright and lively to taste.

Woodcock au fumet

 1½ hours

Serves 2

2 woodcocks, dressed, livers reserved
salt and freshly ground black pepper
2 slices unsmoked bacon
15 ml /1 tbls olive oil
2 shallots, finely chopped
300 ml /10 fl oz champagne
300 ml /10 fl oz port
30 ml /2 tbls tomato purée
2 slices white bread
50 g /2 oz butter
30 ml /2 tbls sieved pâté de foie gras
30 ml /2 tbls cognac

1 Heat the oven to 220C /425F /gas 7.
2 Wipe the birds inside and out with a damp cloth or absorbent paper. Season them inside and out. Bard each bird with a slice of bacon tied with string.
3 Place the birds side by side in a roasting tin and roast in the oven for 15–20 minutes. Cut the threads and discard the bacon.
4 Transfer the birds to a carving board and remove the legs. Now remove the breast and wing portions, leaving the rib cages intact. Reserve the portions and the roasting juices.
5 Chop the carcasses finely and put them in a saucepan with the olive oil and shallots. Simmer until the shallots are soft.
6 Add the champagne, port and tomato

purée, and continue cooking for 5 minutes. Chop the raw livers and add them, together with the juices from the roasting tin, to the chopped carcasses. Simmer for 30 minutes.
7 Cut the bread slices in half; trim the crusts. Heat 25 g /1 oz butter in a frying-pan and sauté the bread slices until golden. Spread with the sieved pâté de foie gras. Place them on a heated serving dish.
8 In a frying-pan, heat the remaining butter. Add the woodcock portions and warm them through for 1 minute. Sprinkle with the cognac and light it with a taper.
9 When the flames have subsided, arrange the woodcock pieces on the croûtes and pour the sauce, through a fine sieve, over the birds. Serve immediately.

Salmon trout in champagne

 50 minutes

Serves 4

60 ml /4 tbls melted butter
1 salmon trout with head, about 1 kg /2 lb, cleaned
375 ml /13 fl oz dry champagne
salt
cayenne pepper
25 g /1 oz flour
600 ml /1 pt thick cream
5 ml /1 tsp lemon juice
8 button mushroom caps
30 ml /2 tbls freshly chopped parsley

1 Heat the oven to 190C /375F /gas 5.
2 Grease a deep, flameproof dish with melted butter. Place the salmon trout in the dish, pour over the champagne and season to taste with salt and cayenne pepper. Cover the dish with a sheet of greaseproof paper buttered with melted butter and with a small hole in the centre. Bring to the boil over a medium heat. Transfer the dish to the oven and cook for 20 minutes, or until the fish flakes easily with a fork.
3 Using a fish slice, transfer the salmon trout to a heated platter. Keep it warm.
4 Pour the champagne cooking juices into a saucepan and boil it rapidly until it has reduced to about 200 ml /7 fl oz; this will take about 6 minutes.
5 Stir 30 ml /2 tbls melted butter into the flour over a medium heat. Pour in the cooking juices and bring to the boil, whisking continuously. Add the cream, mix well and bring to just under boiling point.
6 With a sharp knife, carefully skin the salmon trout, removing all the fins but leaving the head and tail on.
7 In a small saucepan, heat 10 ml /2 tsp melted butter with the lemon juice. Add the mushroom caps and cook until tender. Cut each mushroom cap into 4 slices and dip the top of each slice in chopped parsley.
8 Using a large, metal spoon, coat the salmon trout with the champagne and cream sauce. Decorate the salmon trout with the parslied mushroom slices, laying them diagonally along the length of the fish. Serve the salmon trout immediately.

Lamb's kidneys in champagne

📐 25 minutes

Serves 4
10 lamb's kidneys
225 g /8 oz button mushrooms
50 g /2 oz butter
salt and freshly ground black pepper
¼ bottle champagne
10 ml /2 tsp cornflour
15 ml /1 tbls lemon juice
30 ml /2 tbls finely chopped fresh parsley,
  plus extra for garnishing
lemon wedges, to garnish

1 Skin the kidneys and cut them in half. With scissors, cut out the centre core from each half and cut the kidneys into quarters.
2 Wipe the mushrooms with a damp cloth and slice them thinly.
3 Melt the butter in a large frying-pan. When it is hot, add the kidneys. Tossing with a spatula, cook over a high heat for 1 minute, or until the kidneys have stiffened and are tinged with brown.
4 Add the mushrooms and cook for 1 minute. Season the mixture to taste.
5 Reduce the heat to moderate and pour in the champagne. Stirring frequently, simmer for about 5 minutes, or until the sauce has reduced and the kidneys are cooked.
6 In a small bowl, mix the cornflour with a little of the sauce and stir it into the pan. Bring it to a simmer to thicken it slightly, add the lemon juice and adjust the seasoning. Stir in the parsley and transfer the contents of the pan to a serving dish. Garnish the dish with lemon wedges and parsley. Serve.

Rump steaks with champagne sauce

🔪🔪 freezing the marrowbone, then thawing, plus about 30 minutes

Serves 4
1 marrowbone about 15 cm /6 in long, sawn
  across into 4 pieces
4 × 175 g /6 oz rump steaks
4 small shallots
100 g /4 oz butter
¼ bottle of champagne or 200 ml /7 fl oz dry
  sparkling wine
1.5 ml /¼ tsp dried marjoram
salt and freshly ground black pepper
For the garnish
1 large carrot, thinly sliced and simmered, or
  steamed until just tender
melted butter

1 Freeze the pieces of marrowbone until the marrow is solid, then carefully push the marrow out from one end of the bone to the other. Let the marrow thaw.
2 Poach the pieces of marrow in boiling, salted water for 3 minutes. Remove them with a slotted spoon and cut each piece into 4 thin slices. Keep them warm.
3 Heat the grill to high. When hot, grill the steaks 4 cm /1½ in from the heat for 2 minutes each side for blue, 3 minutes for rare, 4 minutes for medium and 5 minutes for well done.
4 Meanwhile, peel the shallots but leave them whole. Melt half the butter in a saucepan over a low heat, then cook the shallots until they are soft but not brown. Add the champagne and marjoram, stir until boiling and reduce the liquid to one quarter the original quantity.
5 Remove from the heat and gradually add the remaining butter in small pieces, stirring briskly all the time. Season to taste.
6 For the garnish, cut flower shapes from the slices of cooked carrot, using a small aspic cutter. Brush the carrot shapes very lightly with melted butter.
7 Arrange the steaks on a hot serving dish and top each one with slices of marrow. Spoon the sauce over and garnish with carrot shapes. Serve immediately.

Rump steaks with Champagne sauce

LOIRE

The Loire is the longest river in France and much of it is flanked by vineyards. It is best known for its dry white wine, but the area is large and productive, and a great diversity of wines is to be found there.

Loire wines

The best known of the Loire valley dry white wines comes from two distinct areas, the region of Sèvre-et-Maine, near Nantes, and the area to the east of Orléans, around the towns of Sancerre and Pouilly. The district of Touraine also produces some dry and some sweet white wine.

Sèvre-et-Maine

The best wine from the Sèvre-et-Maine district is Muscadet, named after the grape from which it is made. Pale gold, very dry and slightly acidic, it is traditionally a 'fish' wine, although its refreshing qualities make it ideal for hot summer days and it can be a pleasant aperitif. In some hot years, however, the Muscadet suffers because it loses its acidity.

The reputation of Muscadet outside its own home area is a comparatively recent event. With the greatly increased demand, vineyard area has doubled in recent years and this can mean variable quality. Even the best Muscadet is not expensive by French standards. You would be advised to look for a wine from a single estate or château. Some good names are Château de la Galissonière, Château la Noë and Château de l'Oiselinière.

The qualities which make Muscadet appealing will not improve with keeping and it should be drunk within three years of its being bottled.

Some growers do not filter and bottle all their Muscadet immediately after fermentation, but leave some in the vats for another few weeks in contact with the deposit known as the 'lees'. A wine which has been treated in this way will have the additional description *sur lie*. It is considered to have a little extra body and flavour and will also have picked up a slight tingle resulting from retained carbon dioxide.

Another rather coarser white wine from the same area is Gros Plant. This is again named after its grape and is sold almost exclusively as the local *vin de pays*.

Sancerre and Pouilly

The most distinguished, and expensive, dry white wines of the Loire come from around Sancerre and Pouilly.

The Sauvignon is known locally as Blanc Fumé, and the best wine from Pouilly is called Pouilly Blanc Fumé.

Both Sancerre and Pouilly Fumé are slightly fuller bodied wines than Muscadet. They have a characteristic bouquet usually described as 'gun-flint', because it is reminiscent of the smoke from struck flints. They have been widely adopted as alternatives to Chablis and other very expensive white burgundies.

The production area, however, is small, demand has recently raced ahead of supply, and this state of affairs, particularly in the case of Pouilly Fumé, has been reflected in much higher prices. The district is also very susceptible to poor weather. Both quality and quantity of vintages have been badly affected by frost and hail in the past. Like all dry Loire whites, Sancerre and Pouilly Fumé should be drunk young — the delicate balance of fruitiness and acidity which gives them their charm will be lost after a few years.

The seriousness with which Sancerre and Pouilly Fumé have come to be regarded in recent years is a little inappropriate for wines which used to be considered the white equivalent of beaujolais. There are good Sauvignon wines produced at a more reasonable price in the neighbourhood of Reuilly, Quincy and Ménétou-Salon to the south-west of Sancerre.

Middle Loire

Sauvignon Blanc is also grown widely in the middle Loire district of Touraine — Sauvignon de Touraine is a good bargain, if you can find it. The main white grape of Touraine is the Chenin Blanc, and the best-known dry wines made from this grape come from the towns of Vouvray and Montlouis. Vouvray is generally reckoned to be the better.

The Chenin Blanc is chiefly used for producing sweet wines, so the dry Vouvrays tend to have a distinct fruitiness of flavour, but this is balanced by refreshing acidity. They have all the straightforward, easy appeal which has made Loire wines so popular.

Other dry white wines from the middle

Loire which you may be able to find outside France are Savennières, Touraine-Azay-le-Rideau and Touraine-Amboise.

Rosé

Rosé is one Loire wine that is widely available. The most basic is called simply Rosé de la Loire. More specific, but familiar, names are Rosé d'Anjou and Rosé Cabernet d'Anjou. The latter is generally drier and slightly more scented than plain Rosé d'Anjou but both are ideal for drinking as summer picnic wines.

Rosé wines are also made in the region from the Pinot Noir grapes, especially in the area around Sancerre and Ménétou-Salon. Some of these, especially those from single estates, are worth trying but they do tend to be rather expensive. Good examples are the Gold Medal-winning Ménétou-Salon of Georges Chavet, and Sancerre Clos du Chêne Marchand.

Red wine

The main centre of red wine production is the region of Touraine. The Gamay, the grape of Beaujolais, yields a pleasantly light red wine for early drinking. It has rather less fruitiness and higher acidity than Beaujolais itself; some is even marketed within a few weeks of harvest.

Other red wines are mainly made from Cabernet Franc — known locally as Breton, probably because it was introduced to the region from Bordeaux via the Breton port of Nantes — Cabernet Sauvignon and Malbec, known in the area as Cot. These are all grapes traditionally associated with claret, but in the Loire the wine which results is softer, less tannic and faster maturing, with only a relatively brief spell in the barrel.

The towns chiefly connected with red wine are Chinon, Bourgueil and St Nicolas de Bourgueil. Some growers aim for a more robust and long-lasting wine in the Bordeaux style. These wines will usually be from a single estate, called a *domaine* or *clos*, which, strictly speaking, is a vineyard enclosed by a wall to give added protection from wind and frost. These wines are also frequently bottled by the grower, in which case the words *propriétaire récoltant* will be on the label. They will be a lot more expensive than wines labelled simply 'Chinon' or 'Bourgueil', but will have more body and distinction. A good vintage may develop for up to 20 years.

Sparkling wines

Another increasingly popular Loire wine is the sparkling wine or *vin mousseux*. Made mainly from the Chenin Blanc or Sauvignon Blanc grapes, sometimes with the addition of Pinot Noir, these are true *méthode champenoise* wines and the best have a good, rich flavour. Saumur and Vouvray are the main centres of production. There is also a lighter, less fizzy sparkling wine from the region called Vin Crémant de Loire.

Sweet dessert wines

Through the sales of the sparkling wines of Touraine and the rosés of Anjou the growers are able to continue small-scale production of the wines they consider their greatest

Soupe aux navets

achievement — the fine, but expensive, sweet dessert wines. The Chenin Blanc gives a naturally fruity wine and, if the grapes are allowed to ripen through a long, fine autumn, they will eventually become affected by a fungus called the noble rot, or *pourriture noble*. The fungus attacks the skins, shrivels the fruit and concentrates the natural sugars. It is difficult to make this process sound attractive, but it is responsible for all the world's greatest sweet wines — the Château d'Yquem of Sauternes, the Trockenbeeren-auslen of the Rhine and the Tokay Aszu of Hungary. The grapes for such wines have to be carefully selected when they have reached just the right stage of ripeness, and a large quantity will yield relatively little juice. These factors, and the long storage period needed before the wines reach full maturity, inevitably make them expensive.

Traditionally, these sweet wines are drunk at the end of a meal, though in France it is the current trend to drink them as aperitifs. Ideally, they should be drunk on their own and simply enjoyed for what they are, a glorious mouthful of flavour. The best names to look for are Bonnezeaux, Quarts de Chaumes and Moulin Touchais from the Côteaux du Layon. The vineyard of Moulin Touchais was the only one on the Loire to escape the phylloxera plague of the last century (when virtually every vineyard in France was decimated by the phylloxera louse which attacked and ate the roots of the vines), and until 1959 this extraordinary wine was made only from pre-phylloxera stocks. Look too for the Vouvrays described as *moelleux*, especially those from good growers such as Gaston Huet and Marc Brédif.

Wines from the Loire are known for their appealing qualities of delicacy and freshness, with the additional advantage — in most cases — of being good value for money.

Soupe aux navets

This simple recipe is ideal for baby turnips which are full of flavour and have no coarse fibres. A dry white Loire would make a good, and unusual, partner to the soup.

 15 minutes

Serves 4
500 g /18 oz baby turnips, peeled
salt
freshly ground black pepper
850 ml /1½ pt chicken stock, home-made or from cubes
100 g /4 oz butter
2 garlic cloves, crushed
4 thick slices of bread, crusts removed
100 g /4 oz Gruyère cheese, grated

1 Cut the turnips into sticks, slightly larger than matchsticks. Blanch them in salted boiling water for 2 minutes. Drain them well. Put the stock on to heat through or prepare the stock from cubes and keep it hot.
2 Heat 50 g /2 oz of the butter in a sauce-pan, over a low heat, until it foams. Add the garlic and fry for 1 minute. Put in the turnip and, turning occasionally, cook for 4 minutes, until tender. Reserve and keep hot.
3 Cut the slices of bread into cubes. Melt the remaining butter in a frying-pan, over a low heat, and sauté the cubes until brown on all sides (about 2 minutes). Drain the croûtons thoroughly on absorbent paper.
4 Divide the croûtons among 4 bowls. Season the hot stock with salt and pepper and pour it into the bowls. Spoon the turnip sticks into the bowls and sprinkle with the grated cheese. Serve the soup immediately.

● This soup can equally well be made with tender young carrots.

Baked oysters

🔪 20 minutes

Serves 4 as a starter or 2 as a main dish
24 oysters
about 250 ml /9 fl oz Muscadet or other dry
white wine
beurre manié, made with 15 g /½ oz butter
and 15 g /½ oz flour
30 ml /2 tbls thick cream
1 medium-sized egg yolk
salt
cayenne pepper
butter, for greasing
30 ml /2 tbls finely chopped fresh parsley
lemon twists, to garnish

1 Heat the oven to 220C /425F /gas 7. Open the oysters and, without losing the liquid, remove the flesh and reserve the shells. Carefully strain the liquid through a fine sieve into a measuring jug. Make the liquid up to 275 ml /10 fl oz with the wine.
2 Put the oysters, covered by the wine mixture, into a saucepan over a low heat and cook, just below a simmer, for 1–2 minutes, according to size. Lift out the oysters and reserve them.
3 Reduce the cooking liquid by about one third and then remove the saucepan from the heat. Work the butter and flour together to make a beurre manié and add it to the pan in small pieces, stirring briskly and continuously over medium heat until the sauce is thick and smooth. Gradually stir in the cream but do not allow it to boil. Remove from the heat and beat in the egg yolk. Season with salt and cayenne pepper to taste.
4 Choose the 24 best-shaped oyster shells and wash, dry and butter them. Place one oyster in each and spoon over a little of the sauce. Bake, on a baking sheet, for 10 minutes. Serve at once, sprinkled with parsley and garnished with lemon twists.

Pike steaks with butter sauce

🔪🔪 1 hour

Serves 6
6 × 175 g /6 oz pike steaks
For the beurre blanc
50 g /2 oz shallots, very finely chopped
a pinch of salt
a pinch of freshly ground white pepper
200 ml /7 fl oz Loire or other dry white wine
25 ml /1½ tbls lemon juice
200 g /7 oz butter, cut in walnut-sized pieces
a pinch of cayenne pepper
For the court bouillon
225 g /8 oz fish bones and skin
125 ml /4 fl oz dry white wine
4–5 parsley stalks
salt
freshly ground black pepper
a dash of lemon juice

1 Begin making the beurre blanc by putting the shallots, salt and pepper into the smallest possible saucepan with the wine. Let it reduce, over medium heat, until it becomes a syrupy mixture. This will take 30–35 minutes. Heat the oven to 180C /350F /gas 4.
2 Meanwhile, make a court bouillon by boiling the fish bones and skin in 125 ml / 4 fl oz of water, the dry wine and the parsley stalks, for 20 minutes. Season to taste with salt, pepper and the dash of lemon juice. Reserve and cool the court bouillon.
3 Arrange the pike steaks in a shallow baking dish, strain the court bouillon into the dish and poach the steaks very gently in the oven for 10–12 minutes or until they feel firm but tender. Remove the steaks, discarding the skin, and arrange them in a serving dish. Keep them warm, covered, in a very low oven. Reserve the bouillon.
4 To finish the beurre blanc, remove the reduced shallot-and-wine mixture from the heat, add 25 ml /1½ tbls cold water and some of the lemon juice. Using a fork, whisk in one piece of the butter at a time until the sauce becomes smooth and shiny. Half-way through, incorporate 15 ml /1 tbls of the court bouillon. If the sauce becomes too cool to blend properly, hold it above — but not on — low heat for a few moments, continuing to whisk it all the time. Remove it from the heat and repeat until all the butter is incorporated.
5 Add the cayenne and adjust the seasoning, adding the rest of the lemon juice if necessary. Serve each fish-portion with some of the (barely tepid) sauce on top of it.

Cold sabayon with kümmel

🔪🔪 45 minutes, plus chilling

Serves 4
4 egg yolks
40 g /1½ oz sugar
60 ml /4 tbls dry white Loire wine
7.5 ml /1½ tsp gelatine
ice, for chilling
45–60 ml /3–4 tbls kümmel
1.5 ml /¼ tsp vanilla essence
215 ml /7½ fl oz thick cream, whipped
For the decoration
1 lemon
15 ml /1 tbls toasted, flaked almonds

1 In the top of a double boiler, over simmering water, combine the egg yolks, sugar and wine and whisk until the mixture thickens (10–15 minutes). Remove from the heat.
2 In a small bowl, sprinkle the gelatine over 30 ml /2 tbls cold water and leave for 5 minutes to soften. Place the bowl in a saucepan of simmering water until the gelatine dissolves. Allow it to cool slightly.
3 Stir the gelatine into the egg yolk mixture. Place the top of the double boiler in a bowl of ice and stir the sabayon constantly until it begins to set. Remove from the ice.
4 Using a large metal spoon, fold the kümmel, vanilla essence and whipped cream gently but thoroughly into the sabayon. Pour into 4 individual glasses and chill.
5 Pare the zest of the lemon with a vegetable peeler. Carefully remove any pith with a knife. Cut the zest into very fine julienne strips (the length of a matchstick and 3 mm / ⅛ in wide). Bring a small saucepan of water to the boil, reduce the heat and simmer the julienne strips of lemon for 5–6 minutes. Drain and refresh them under cold, running water. Now drain and dry them.
6 To serve, spoon a few flaked almonds onto each sabayon and sprinkle them with the julienne strips of lemon.

Baked oysters

Cold sabayon with kümmel

Pears baked in cream

Try serving this creamy dessert with a chilled sweet Vouvray or the slightly softer, more gently sweet Montlouis.

 45 minutes

Serves 4
juice of ½ lemon
4 large, firm, ripe dessert pears
275 ml /10 fl oz thick cream
90 ml /6 tbls sugar
5 ml /1 tsp vanilla essence, or 1.5–2.5 ml /
¼–½ tsp almond essence
salt
crystallized violets, to garnish

1 Heat the oven to 180C /350F /gas 4.
2 Add the lemon juice to about 1.5 L /3 pt cold water. (The pears are placed in this to prevent discoloration.) Peel, halve and core the pears. To remove the core use a teaspoon. Insert it on one side of the pear core. Now turn the pear half round in your hand so that the teaspoon cuts in a neat circle.
3 Drain the pears and arrange them, cut side down, in a baking dish.

4 Combine the thick cream, sugar, vanilla or almond essence and a pinch of salt and pour over the pears.
5 Bake in the oven for 25–30 minutes, or until the pears are tender but not mushy. To serve, transfer the pears to a serving dish and spoon over the sauce. If a skin has formed on the surface of the sauce, whisk it in with a fork. Garnish with crystallized violets. Serve hot or cold.

Apple shortcake

Great dessert wines are produced at Coteaux du Layon in the Loire. This shortcake will go well with a Bonnezeaux from this region.

 45 minutes,
plus cooling

Serves 4
45 ml /3 tbls caster sugar
90 g /3½ oz butter
125 g /4½ oz flour, plus extra for dusting
a pinch of salt
2 dessert apples
lemon juice
1 egg yolk
ground cinnamon
45 ml /3 tbls apricot jam
45 ml /3 tbls coarsely chopped walnuts

Apple shortcake

1 Heat the oven to 190C /375F /gas 5.
2 In a bowl, beat the sugar with 75 g /3 oz butter until light and fluffy. Sift together the flour and salt, then stir into the butter mixture. Knead lightly by hand to make a smooth dough.
3 Roll out the dough or pat it gently by hand, to fit a 17.5 cm /7 in square tin. Bake for 20 minutes, or until the shortcake is firm and golden.
4 Meanwhile, core and quarter the apples. Cut the quarters into thin slices. Brush with a little lemon juice to prevent discoloration. Beat the egg yolk lightly.
5 Remove the shortcake from the oven. Brush the surface with the beaten egg yolk. Arrange the apple slices in 3 overlapping rows on top. Melt 15 g /½ oz butter and brush it over the apple slices. Sprinkle all over the top with a little ground cinnamon and return the shortcake to the oven for another 10 minutes.
6 Remove it from the oven and leave it to cool completely. When the shortcake is cold, remove it from the tin. Melt the apricot jam in a small saucepan over a gentle heat. Brush this over the apple slices. Sprinkle fine rows of coarsely chopped walnuts between each row of overlapping apple slices and around the outer edge of the shortcake.

ALSACE WINES

Alsace is the French wine region closest to Germany, geographically and in wine characteristics. A small amount of light red and rosé wines are made here but most of the wine produced is white — fragrant, full-bodied and dry.

Alsace as a producer of quality wines is firmly established, though even now the area has no appellation more specific than 'Alsace', and this was only granted in 1962.

The best vineyards lie in a narrow strip on the lower slopes of the Vosges mountains, looking East towards the River Rhine. Growers and merchants may sometimes use village or estate names on their wine labels, but these have little significance outside the area, if at all, because the wines are traditionally 'varietal'. This means that they are labelled with the type of grape used, not by the place of origin.

The finest wines, Riesling, Tokay (or Pinot Gris), Gewürztraminer, Muscat and Sylvaner, are made from one of five grape types, known as *cépages nobles*. If these are blended, the result is known as *edelzwicker* (noble mixture). The inferior grape types, *cépages courantes*, are mainly blended to produce a light local carafe wine. Most growers in Alsace belong to co-operatives or sell their grapes to the handful of famous merchants in the area, such as Hugel, Dopff, Trimbach and Schlumberger, whose names on a label should guarantee quality.

The wine most usually associated with Alsace is Gewürztraminer; *gewürtz* means spicy, and Gewürztraminer is known for its remarkably powerful and spicy flavour, coupled with a strong-scented nose. It is a big wine, designed to complement the rich foods of the region such as *choucroute* (sauerkraut) and *foie gras* (goose liver pâté). However, in spite of its fullness, it is a dry wine, as the French winemakers prefer strength and dryness to the delicate sweetness of residual grape sugar which is so characteristic of German wines. Gewürztraminer is memorable and attractive, but it lacks subtlety.

The local growers, like their German neighbours, will usually claim pride of place for the Riesling, a vine which never bears heavy crops and also presents more of a challenge to the winemaker. In a good year it is well worth the extra effort; what it lacks in power it makes up for in elegance and delicacy of flavour. The Tokay, or Pinot Gris, from Alsace is a full-flavoured wine more in the style of the Gewürztraminer but without its pronounced fragrance — do not confuse this with Tokay from Hungary, which is a rich, sweet dessert wine.

The Muscat has a heady aroma usually associated with that grape but without its usual sweetness of taste. The Sylvaner, the least interesting of the five, is a reliable but rather bland medium-dry wine, and is now produced less and less.

In recent years new plantings have been made, particularly with the Pinot Blanc grape, which currently accounts for over 17½ per cent of the total acreage under vines — this should be an interesting wine to watch out for.

Alsace wine

Because the French prefer wines suitable for drinking with food, rather than on their own, many of these wines are purposely made less sweet than their German counterparts. The merchants and co-operatives do sometimes produce rich wines in the style of German *auslese* (selected bunches) or *beerenauslese* (selected grapes). These are made from late-gathered grapes whose juice, even after fermentation, retains a high sugar content. These are described in French as *vendage tardive* and *sélection de grains nobles*. They are full, golden wines with great depth of flavour and repay laying down for a number of years.

Conditions are not suitable for these sweeter wines to be made every year; 1977, for example, was a year of late flowering and a poor, rather chilly summer in which the grapes had no chance to achieve the necessary over-ripeness. The years 1982 and 1983, on the other hand, with their prolonged dry heat, produced record levels of natural sugar in many of the grapes and some outstanding late-harvest wines were made which will have a life of at least 20 years.

In general, like other dry whites, Alsace wines should be drunk fairly young. Compared with other French wines of quality, they still represent good value and also offer a variety of distinct flavours to try.

Honeyed chicken

The stuffing for this bird is a delicious combination of sweet and savoury. Serve it with a chilled Riesling d'Alsace.

🍴 2 hours

Serves 4–6
25 g /1 oz butter
1 small onion, finely chopped
125 g /4 oz bacon, in one piece
30 ml /2 tbls oil
2 firm bananas
50 g /2 oz rice, cooked and cooled
salt and freshly ground black pepper
a pinch of cinnamon
1.8 kg /4 lb chicken, dressed weight
30–45 ml /2–3 tbls honey
sprigs of watercress, to garnish

1 Heat the oven to 190C /375F /gas 5.
2 Melt the butter in a small saucepan, add the finely chopped onion and cook over a medium heat until it is soft and translucent (about 5 minutes). Remove from the pan with a slotted spoon. Dice the bacon and add it to the pan and cook for 5–10 minutes, stirring occasionally. Remove it from the pan and leave it to cool.
3 Meanwhile, in a frying-pan, heat the oil until very hot. Split the bananas lengthways and fry them in the hot oil, turning them once with a spatula, until golden brown. (The oil must be very hot so it seals the outside of the bananas, otherwise they will absorb the oil and be soggy.) Remove them from the pan.
4 Mix the onion and bacon with the cooked rice, chop the bananas and add them to the rice mixture. Season with salt and freshly ground black pepper and a pinch of cinnamon. Leave to cool.
5 Wipe the chicken inside and out with a damp cloth. Spoon the cold rice mixture into the cavity; do not pack it too tightly. Truss the chicken. Spoon the honey over the chicken, using the back of the spoon to spread it evenly.
6 Cook the chicken for about 1 hour 20 minutes or until the juices run clear when the thickest part of the thigh is pierced with a skewer. Cover the chicken with foil if it browns too quickly.
7 Remove the chicken from the oven, transfer to a heated serving dish and serve, garnished with sprigs of watercress.

RHONE

The wines of the Rhône Valley include not only some of the most distinguished in France, but also — from the newer Rhône vineyards — 'cheap and cheerful' wines, ideal for everyday drinking.

Rhône wines fall into two separate regions of north and south. Compared with Beaujolais, just to the north, the same robust characteristics apply to both regions. However, many southern Rhône wines are actually quite light. The only really 'big' wine from the south is Châteauneuf-du-Pape. Rhône wines are usually red, although good whites are made in the north. Rosés are made mainly in the southern region.

Most Rhône wines improve considerably with age. They are produced by over 100 parishes or *domaines* under the general label of *Appellation Contrôlée Côtes du Rhône.*

Wines of the northern Rhône

In the northern Rhône valley the vines are grown on both river banks on almost vertical hillsides. The climate is ideal for vines: the summers are long and hot and, as the weather is consistent, good vintages are quite common. In the north Rhône there have been five good vintages in the last ten years. The cold Mistral wind blows down the valley from the north, usually in the spring and early summer. It often dries the grapes after rain, lessening the chance of any mould developing. The red Syrah grape is predominant in the northern Rhône Valley.

Côte Rôtie is one of the top appellations in the region. This rare red wine contains 80 per cent Syrah, which gives it a deep and powerful flavour, and 20 per cent perfumed Viognier grapes, which softens the flavour. The result is a big, gutsy wine rarely at its best before ten years.

Just south of Côte Rôtie are the wines of Condrieu, a dry white wine made from the Viognier grape. Considered one of the best whites from the Rhône Valley, it is at its peak after five or six years of bottle age. Here, too, is Château Grillet, with its own Appellation Contrôlée; the white wine is full and subtle with great finesse.

Further down the east bank of the river are the Hermitage hillsides on which both red and white wines are grown. The reds are burly and deep; a fine Hermitage is for buying and keeping, as it is rarely drinkable in less than ten years.

The vineyards of Crozes-Hermitage produce wines that are not so concentrated and do not last as long, but — being considerably cheaper — they are often the best buys of the Rhône Valley.

St Peray is the most southerly of the northern Rhône vineyards and it produces a sparkling white wine made by the *méthode champenoise.* It is excellent if it is drunk as an aperitif.

Wines of the southern Rhône

The most famous of these southern Rhône Valley wines is Châteauneuf-du-Pape. This is a dark and glorious red wine. It is strong and fruity and matures faster than the wines of Côte Rôtie to the north. Châteauneuf-du-Pape is usually full-bodied with a powerful bouquet and has a higher alcohol content than any other unfortified wine in France. It is the perfect accompaniment to venison and game. Small quantities of white Châteauneuf-du-Pape are still produced.

To the east of Châteauneuf-du-Pape is Gigondas. A good bottle of Gigondas has a great depth of flavour and a strongly recognizable bouquet that is pleasantly earthy.

Near to Gigondas is the area which produces Beaumes de Venise, a delicious, heavily sweet Muscat wine. It is halfway between a dessert wine and a liqueur.

Across the Rhône from Châteauneuf is Tavel, where the well-known rosé of France is produced. It is made from the Grenache grape and is a clear, reddish-pink wine, drier than most rosés and with more backbone.

Lirac, next door to Tavel, produces a pleasant rosé, which is best drunk young. It is just as versatile but cheaper than its famous neighbour. Lirac also produces some noteworthy red wines, with plenty of fruit in them.

The 'Côtes du Rhône Villages' appellation covers 17 communes or villages. Of these, there are several southern Rhône village wines that are well above average and worth looking out for. Vacqueyras is one of the best, with a fine red wine that achieves both depth and balance.

The hilltop village of Cairanne has a modern co-operative that bottles all the local wine. Half the Cairanne vineyards are planted on clay slopes and the rest on stony slopes. The wines are blended to make a warm, sturdy red.

The pinky-orange Chusclan rosé, made from Grenache and Cinsault, should be drunk young to appreciate its fruitiness and pleasant dry after-taste. The village of Laudun makes red, white and rosé wines. The white is outstanding — fresh and full, a natural partner for a fish dish. At Rochegude, the red produced has a softness not usually associated with Rhônes. The red wine from Vinsobres has a great length of taste and will improve in the bottle for some years but is high in alcohol.

Tricastin, Ventoux and Lubéron

These are the newer Rhône vineyards in the warm south, producing 'cheap and cheerful' wines for everyday drinking.

Tricastin is red wine country, most of the reds being dark in colour, smooth, and eminently drinkable, but by Rhône standards not full-bodied. Worth trying are Domaine de Grangeneuve (fruity and soft); Domaine de St Luc (very fruity and bold); Domaine de Bois Noir (with a velvety smoothness); and Domaine de Serre Rouge (slightly perfumed).

The wines of the Côtes du Ventoux are

Salmis of pheasant

mainly red and rosé, with a little white. They are very different in character from the other Rhône wines, being light and low in alcohol.

Co-operatives process most Ventoux, but there are several private growers making individual wines of higher quality, such as those from the Domaine des Anges and Domaine St Saveur.

The Lubéron wines are not Appellation Contrôlée, which accounts for their comparatively low cost. The co-operatives send their wines to the Union des Vignerons de Lubéron for final bottling and packaging. Vin de Pays de Vaucluse, both red and white, is pleasantly dry and unassuming, with an aromatic bouquet. Ruby red Côtes du Lubéron has a little more weight to it and lasts longer in the mouth. A good co-operative wine is Cellier de Marrenon; the red has an ample bouquet, the white is flowery and subtle.

Salmis of pheasant

A rich red Rhône is the perfect wine to accompany this superb game dish with its rich cream and pheasant liver sauce.

 3¼ hours

Serves 4

*1.1 kg /2½ lb plump, young pheasant, dressed
   weight, with liver reserved*
salt and freshly ground black pepper
*2 thin strips pounded pork fat, or unsmoked
   streaky bacon*
25 g /1 oz butter
15 ml /1 tbls olive oil
2 medium-sized onions, thickly sliced
1 small carrot, thickly sliced
15 ml /1 tbls flour
*600 ml /1 pt chicken stock, home-made or
   from a cube*
90–120 ml /6–8 tbls dry white wine
1 garlic clove, crushed
bouquet garni
15 ml /1 tbls brandy
125 g /4 oz white button mushrooms, trimmed
1 shallot, finely chopped
15 ml /1 tbls thick cream
*beurre manié (made by mashing together
   15 g /½ oz butter and 15 ml /1 tbls flour)*
heart-shaped croûtons

1 Heat the oven to 220C /425F /gas 7.
2 Wipe the pheasant clean both inside and out with a damp cloth. Pick off any stray feathers. Season the bird generously both inside and out with salt and pepper. Cover the breast and the legs of the bird completely with thin strips of pounded pork fat, or unsmoked streaky bacon. Truss the pheasant.
3 Place the pheasant on a rack in a roasting pan. Roast for 30 minutes, basting frequently.
4 Remove the bird from the oven and, when cool enough to handle, divide it into 4 serving pieces, taking the breast meat away from the carcass with the wings and legs so that the main part of the carcass, including the breastbone, remains. Remove the skin and discard. Put the pheasant pieces into a flameproof casserole and cover. Set aside.
5 Chop up the carcass. In a medium-sized saucepan, heat 15 g /½ oz butter and the olive oil. Add the chopped carcass and the thickly sliced onions and carrot and cook over a moderate heat for 10–15 minutes, to brown the vegetables.
6 Add the flour, stir and cook for a further 1–2 minutes. Add the chicken stock, dry white wine, crushed garlic clove and bouquet garni and season with salt and ground black pepper to taste. Bring to the boil, reduce the heat, cover and simmer for 45 minutes.
7 Heat the brandy in a large metal ladle over an open flame, or in a small saucepan. Carefully set the brandy alight with a taper and, when the flames are burning strongly, pour it over the pheasant pieces. Allow the flames to burn themselves out.
8 Add the mushrooms to the casserole and strain the pheasant stock over the pheasant pieces, discarding the carcass and vegetables. Cover the pheasant pieces with stock; if there is not enough, make up the quantity with chicken stock.

9 Set the casserole over a low heat and slowly bring it to simmering point. Reduce the heat to the barest simmer; cover and cook very gently until the pheasant is tender. This will take 15–20 minutes.
10 Cut the pheasant liver into chunks. In a small saucepan, melt the remaining butter. Sauté the finely chopped shallot for 5 minutes, or until soft and golden. Add the liver to the pan and continue to sauté gently for about 3 minutes.
11 Rub the shallots, liver and butter juices through a fine sieve. Blend in the thick cream and season with salt and freshly ground black pepper to taste.
12 When the pheasant is tender, using a slotted spoon, transfer it to a heated serving dish and keep it hot while you finish making the sauce.
13 Add the beurre manié to the juices in the casserole in tiny pieces, stirring constantly until the butter has completely melted. Bring to the boil, stirring, and simmer until the sauce has thickened.
14 Reduce the heat to very low. Blend the liver and cream mixture into the sauce and reheat it gently without letting it come to the boil again. Adjust the seasoning. Pour the sauce over the pheasant and garnish with croûtons. Serve immediately.

● If you buy your pheasant ready cleaned, a good poulterer will supply pheasant livers.

OTHER FRENCH WINES

Lesser-known vineyards are scattered all over France and wines from these vineyards are splendid accompaniments for the local dishes. Here, I give you names to look for and recipes to try.

Good wine is produced from vineyards covering the whole of France — some are less well known than others, but it is worth finding out a bit about their wines. This chapter gives you details of some other areas.

Languedoc-Roussillon
This huge wine-growing area produces almost a billion gallons of wine a year. If the wines from this area are not well known, it is because more than 95 per cent of them are not *Appellation Contrôlée* status. Many are Vins de Pays although some have risen to VDQS status.

The VDQS wine produced in the Corbières district matures quickly. The Château de Montrabech is a fruity wine with a deep colour and powerful bouquet. The Costières du Gard VDQS wines are generally reds, although some white and rosés are produced.

In the Coteaux du Languedoc there are many communes or small vineyard areas entitled to add their names to the overall VDQS title. Faugeres makes a fine wine, while St Chinian's red has a scented bouquet, and St Saturnin produces a delicious rosé.

The reds which form the bulk of the wines from the Minervois region are strong in alcohol, vigorous and sometimes slightly peppery, while the Carmargue produces the Vins des Sables which are good table wines.

Latour de France is a good choice for rich

A selection of lesser-known French wines

meat dishes and the best white of the region is probably the sparkling AC Blanquette de Limoux.

Bergerac and Cahors
Bergerac produces pleasant, fruity red and white wines, best drunk when young. Similar to Sauternes, a Monbazillac is a first-class choice to serve with dessert or fresh fruit and cheese at the end of a meal.

Cahors wine goes well with casseroles and red meat. A big co-operative, Les Caves d'Olt at Parnac, makes a good Vin de Cahors.

Marmande and Buzet
From the Côtes du Marmande come soft red wines; there is also a delicious rosé. Most Marmande wines carry a VDQS rating.

Côtes de Buzet wines are AC. Cuvée Napoleon is the best co-operative wine to come from the area.

Gaillac and Madiran
AC Gaillac district is a good source of bargain-price, sparkling white wines. Red Gaillac's are also very agreeable.

Madiran is a rich, full-bodied wine that rates as one of the best reds from the Pyrenees. Côtes de Frontonnais is a local red wine and Château Bellevue-La Forêt is particularly good.

Jurançon and Béarn
Jurançon white is sweet and spicy, and drinking it is an acquired taste. Little of this wine is made and it is strictly for the connoisseur.

Béarn wines are good enough to gain an AC. Most of it is red and rosé and much of it comes from the co-operative at Bellocq. A few kilometres nearer the sea than Béarn is the tiny Appellation of Irouléguy, which has a light rosé that goes with almost any food.

Provence
Côtes de Provence attained AC status in 1977. St Tropez is the natural centre for many of the best rosés. Just behind St Tropez is Château de Minuty, with its expensive Cuvée de l'Oratoire, sought after by connoisseurs.

Most of the wines of the area barely differ from one year to the next. Wines of note are Châteaux de Selle and de Roseline, Clos du Relais and Domaine de Saint-Martin, Domaine de l'Aumerade, Clos Mirelle, Domaine de Noyer and Domaine de Mauvanne.

Just outside the Côtes de Provence area is Côteaux d'Aix-en-Provence, a wine area promoted to AC in 1984. From here comes a highly palatable red wine which is made from a blend of Cabernet Sauvignon, Grenache and Syrah grapes.

To the south of Aix is the tiny appellation of Palette. The only name of note is Château Simone, famous for red wines that are aged

in wood. The rosés and whites are also of fine quality.

On the coast near Marseilles is the tiny Appellation of Cassis. Its white wine is a perfect partner for *bouillabaisse*, the delicious local fish stew. Names to note are Château de Fontblanche and Domaine du Paternel.

Further along the coast from Cassis is Bandol, the best-known specific AC wine area in the region, making as much red wine as rosé.

In general, when buying Provence rosés avoid those exported in fancy bottles bearing florid labels. They have often been sweetened for easy marketing but in the process may lose much of their original charm and vigour.

Jura
The Jura Mountains are on the Franco-Swiss border in eastern France. Along their western slopes between the small towns of Saint-Amour and Arbois are the vineyards.

The area is divided into three main districts — Arbois, L'Etoile and Côtes du Jura.

All the white wines share a distinctively nutty smell, but differ widely on the palate. More unusual are the *vins jaunes*, or yellow wines. They are made exclusively from the Savagnin grape and it is not unusual to find drinkable bottles of *vin jaune* which are 50 years old.

The tiny Appellation of Château Chalon not only produces some of the best *vins jaunes*, but another typical Jura wine, *vin de paille*, or straw wine.

The grapes are laid on straw mats after picking, and allowed to dry in the sun. This results in a rich, long-lasting wine with the flavour of quinces.

These wines by no means exhaust the versatility of Jura winegrowers. Some experts rate the rosés from here higher than the whites. The best of the rosés come from Arbois in a range of different shades. The darker ones are known as *pelure d'oignon*, or onion skin, and the paler ones as *vin gris*, or grey wine. One very individual *vin gris* is Cendre de Novembre, named for its grey, November tinge.

Among the red wines, Marnebour is a supple, slightly sweet wine. The best Jura red, Frederic Barberousse, is from Henri Maire.

Savoie
The Jura Mountains give way to the Alps and the province of Savoie to the south. There are three separate white wine appellations: Seysell, Roussette and Crépy. In addition, there are 60 red, white and rosé wine communes scattered throughout the mountains. Most Savoie wine is white, with a high level of acidity. The red wine is not of high quality. Crépy makes a dry, light sparkling wine from the Chasselas grape.

Corsica
Enough wine is now made on Corsica to allow its export. Over a million cases of wine a year are made in Corsica and six per cent of it is very worthwhile. It comes from seven main areas: Patrimonio, Sartène, Figari, Porto-Vecchio, Côteaux du Ca Corse, Côteaux d'Ajaccio and Calvi.

Two of the best are the strongly alcoholic rosé of Patrimonio and a red from Sartène.

Ratatouille

Conjure up a little Mediterranean sun by serving this classic dish with a chilled rosé from Provence.

 1 hour salting the vegetables, then 1½ hours

Serves 8
3 large aubergines, halved lengthways
3 large courgettes, halved lengthways
salt and freshly ground black pepper
150 ml /5 fl oz olive oil
3 large onions, sliced into thin rings
60 ml /4 tbls tomato purée
3 large green or red peppers, seeded
4 garlic cloves, chopped
5 large tomatoes, blanched, skinned and chopped
a pinch of freshly ground coriander
a small pinch of cinnamon
a pinch of dried basil

1 Cut the aubergines and courgettes across into slices about 20 mm /¾ in thick. Place them in layers in a colander, sprinkling each layer with salt. Top them with a weighted plate and drain the vegetables for 1 hour.
2 Gently heat the olive oil in a broad, heavy pan over a low heat and cook the onions in it until they are transparent. Stir in the tomato purée and cook for 3–4 minutes, stirring occasionally.
3 Dry the aubergines and courgettes; stir them into the pan. Cut the peppers into thin strips and add them and the garlic to the pan. Shake, cover and simmer for about 20 minutes.
4 Add the tomatoes and the rest of the herbs and spices, stir and leave to cook for a further 40–45 minutes. If the dish seems too liquid, remove the lid for the final few minutes to let the sauce reduce.

Wood pigeons with mint

Wild herbs abound on Corsica and they are combined in interesting and unusual ways. Try this one which uses juniper and mint to give a piquant taste to game. Serve with a red Corsican wine.

 1½–2 hours

Serves 4
45 ml /3 tbls olive oil
2 large onions, coarsely chopped
2 large garlic cloves, chopped
4 wood pigeons
15 ml /1 tbls juniper berries
15 ml /1 tbls coriander seeds
400 g /14 oz canned tomatoes
150 ml /5 fl oz strong red wine
125 g /4 oz large green olives
45 ml /3 tbls chopped fresh mint
coarse or sea salt
freshly ground black pepper
sprigs of mint, to garnish

Wood pigeons with mint

1 Heat the oven to 180C /350F /gas 4.
2 Meanwhile, heat the olive oil in a large frying-pan over a medium heat, add the onions and garlic and sauté for about 8–10 minutes until golden brown, then transfer to a casserole dish.
3 Add the wood pigeons to the pan and brown them on all sides over a high heat. Transfer them to the casserole, placing them on top of the layer of onions.
4 Crush the juniper berries and the coriander seeds, add them to the pan and quickly sauté them for 2 minutes before adding them to the casserole.
5 Pour the tomatoes into a large bowl and mash them roughly with a wooden spoon before pouring them over the pigeons. Add the wine, olives and fresh mint. Season generously with salt and freshly ground black pepper, stirring everything to mix it well.
6 Cover the casserole with a tightly-fitting lid and cook it in the oven for 1–1¼ hours until the pigeons are tender (the length of time will vary on the age of the pigeons).
7 With a slotted spoon, transfer the pigeons to a large serving platter and keep them warm while you finish the sauce.
8 Put half the sauce into a liquidizer and blend it to a smooth purée. Return this to the remaining sauce and stir it well in — this has the effect of thickening the sauce and amalgamating the flavours deliciously. Pour the sauce over the pigeons, garnish them with sprigs of fresh mint and serve at once.

ITALIAN WINES

Italy is a wonderful country for wine, since it offers a vast range of different types — from full-bodied reds to delicate, sparkling whites. They are also extremely good value for money.

Most areas of Italy produce wine. In fact, Italy now produces more wine annually than any other country in the world. Her finest wines are powerful reds, but Italy is also the source of lighter, fresh reds and clean, young whites. These lighter wines make fine every-day drinking.

The great benefit of drinking Italian wine is that it is still possible to taste widely and compare different wines without spending extravagantly. Italian wines, except the very finest, remain comparatively inexpensive.

This is partly because of their abundance, and partly because of the Italian attitude to wine as a happy drink, to be drunk and enjoyed with food and then be thought about no more.

Also, it must be said, some wine produced used to be of poor quality because the grapes were picked too early before they had a chance to ripen, so the wine tended to be acid.

Today, production standards have improved to the extent that almost any bottle of Italian wine will be acceptable. It might not be to your taste, but don't be put off and do try something else next time.

Italian wine is always at its best when served with a meal. To bring out the full flavour of Italy, serve a suitable Italian wine to accompany my tantalizing recipes (see page 90).

Try the wines I have suggested, or experiment and discover other good Italian wines for yourself. After dinner, enjoy a glass of Marsala (see page 105), the celebrated, rich-tasting dessert wine from Sicily.

WINES OF THE NORTH-EAST

The north-eastern corner of Italy produces a huge volume of wine in varying degrees of quality. Three of Italy's most famous wines come from the Veneto region: Soave, Bardolino and Valpolicella.

Soave is the archetypal Italian white; if it is

UNDERSTANDING ITALIAN WINES

For a quick guide to the bottle of Italian wine you are buying, here are a few of the words most likely to be found on the label.

Vino da tavola (table wine) is the lowest category of wine.

DOC (*Denominazione di Origine Controllata*) is the official quality guarantee, but there is a considerable overlap between the best and the worst DOC wines, and since they can be named after the grapes, or a place name, or any combination of the two, or even an invented name (like Lacrima Christi), then it is better to read the label on the bottle to get some idea of what you are buying (see the translations further on in this box).

DOCG (*Denominazione di Origine Controllata e Garantita*) is a new classification which so far has only been applied to a very few of the finest Italian wines. Extremely strict conditions are laid down by the Italian Government for wines in this category.

Some fine red wines may be labelled *vecchio, riserva, riserva speciale* or *stravecchio*. These terms are legally controlled and relate to specific lengths of time that the wine has been aged in barrel.

Superiore on a label means that the wine conforms to certain production methods and standards, has a high alcohol level and has been aged for a required amount of time.

If a wine is described as **classico**, it comes from the central area of that region.

Useful wine terms to bear in mind when buying Italian wines are:

Bianco: white
Rosso: red
Rosato: pink
Spumante: sparkling
Secco: very dry
Asciutto: dry
Amaro: bitter
Abboccato: semi-sweet
Amabile: sweeter than **abboccato**
Dolce: sweet
Liquorosco: strong, and usually very sweet
Gradi: degrees of alcohol
Frizzante: half-sparkling
Nero: very dark red

Chiaretto: very light red
Stravecchio: very old, ripe and mellow
Imbottigliato nello stabilimento della ditta: bottled on the premises of the firm
Imbottigliato (or **Messo in bottigliato**) **nel'origine** (or **del produttore all'origine**): estate bottled

Another factor to consider is the vintage date — the *vendemmia*. It is difficult to be specific when discussing such a variety of wines, but if you follow the golden rule of choosing the 'youngest white and oldest (within reason) red' available, you should not go far wrong — remember, however, that the light red wines such as Valpolicella and Bardolino are exceptions to this rule as they are best enjoyed young.

drunk young enough (anything more than two years old is too old), it is almost always fresh and crisp with a hint of almonds.

Bardolino is mainly red, although some rosé is also produced. It should be drunk young, and served cool at cellar temperature (10C / 50F). *Superiore* means that the wine is aged longer and has a higher alcoholic strength, but *classico* is not necessarily any better than straight Bardolino.

Valpolicella is a light, fresh red wine made from a mixture of local grapes in vineyards between Verona and Lake Garda.

Two white wines from the Veneto region are Gambellara and Bianca di Custoza.

The Friuli-Venezia Giulia region, containing six DOC zones, is gaining a reputation for producing interesting and reliable wines. Among these are Picolit, a fine dessert wine, and other wines labelled by the grape variety — Cabernet, Merlot, Pinot Bianco, Sauvignon, and Tocai — rather than the actual locality.

The northern position of another region, Trentino-Alto Adige, is reflected in the German names on the wine labels. The same wine may be labelled in either German or Italian, according to the maker's choice. For instance, a widely exported fruity red may appear either as Kalteresee or as Lago di Caldaro.

Santa Maddalena is a fragrant and supple wine that is frequently undervalued. White wines make up only a quarter of the Alto Adige output, and those that do appear are most likely to have German names like Sylvaner or Weissburgunder.

The Emilia Romagna region is best known for Lambrusco, a red sparkling wine which varies from being rather dry to quite sweet.

WINES OF THE NORTH-WEST

North-west Italy is best known for its powerful red wines. Piedmont is the largest wine region, producing the notable reds, Barolo and Barbaresco. Made from the intense purplish Nebbiolo grape, Barolo may need as much as ten years ageing to make it mellow and inviting. A good Barolo is an unforgettable wine. Barbaresco is smoother and more delicate than Barolo.

Both Barolo and Barbaresco should be brought gently to room temperature before serving. The cork should be removed at least a couple of hours beforehand, to allow the wine to breathe, and the wine may even be gently decanted.

The everyday drinking wine for the Piedmontese is Barbera, named after the widely planted grape variety. The trend now is to make Barbera dry, light and fresh, definitely for drinking young.

Other worthwhile red wines from this north-western corner are Dolcetto (dry, with a touch of bitterness); Carema (a softer version of Barolo); and Gattinara and Ghemme, both made from the Nebbiolo grape.

The white wines in this area are far less numerous, but they include one of Italy's most famous wines, Asti Spumante. In the past it has been regarded as a sweet, cheaper alternative to champagne, but this is no longer so. Although it is not usually made by the classic *méthode champenoise*, its successful production calls for expensive technology

and a great deal of care is taken to preserve the elusive quality of the Moscato bianco grape. Also, the almost universal demand for drier wines has meant that its makers have turned their attention to creating a more elegant, fresh wine with a sweet tinge to satisfy customers.

CENTRAL & SOUTHERN WINES

The area from Florence down to the toe of Italy produces some excellent wines, both red and white.

Chianti, designated DOCG (see the box on the opposite page), is one of the most well-known Italian red wines. It is traditionally contained in straw-covered flasks, although as these are labour-intensive and costly to make, some producers are nowadays opting for high-shouldered claret-style bottles instead.

Perhaps the most famous name is Chianti Classico from the heart of the beautiful Chianti countryside. The black cockerel on the neck label is the trademark of the several hundred members of the Chianti Classico consortium and is one of the most reliable guarantees of quality in the area, although it is not necessarily superior to every other Chianti. A cherub (*putto*) is the mark of a consortium of growers from outside the central Classico zone who produce Chianti Putto.

Other reputable growers choose not to belong to the consortia at all, yet still produce admirable, individual wines. Encircling the Classico zone are six other Chianti regions, together making up the biggest DOCG group in Italy. The names to look out for are Montalbano, Colli Fiorentini, Colli Aretini, Colli Senesi, Colline Pisane and Rufina.

The main Chianti grape is the red Sangiovese, but since the DOCG ruling was brought in it is softened by up to 25 per cent with other grapes, including some white. The exact blend is up to the individual winemaker. This flexibility in the make-up means that different Chiantis can be surprisingly varied in style. As a mark of this, the colour can vary from a light, bright ruby-red to a rich, deep crimson.

Wine-making methods can be very different, too. To make a broad generalization, there are two main types. One group is fresh and fruity, rather in the style of a young beaujolais. These wines often have a slight refreshing 'prickle' that is the result of a secondary fermentation known as *governo*.

The other type is barrel-aged wines. These are not usually subjected to *governo*, are distinctly perfumed, powerful and subtle. The wines marked *riserva* have been aged for at least three years in oak barrels, while those marked *vecchio* have been aged for at least two years. The best of them benefit from further ageing in the bottle, and a ten-year-old Riserva can be a very fine wine.

Chianti makes an excellent drink for any not-too-elaborate meal or any recipe that requires a vigorous red. It is a reliable wine that is always cheap enough to experiment with, but it is still varied enough to be interesting to drink.

Chianti apart, there are some excellent red wines from the central region, for instance the legendary Brunello di Montalcino from

Siena, a long-lived red made from the Sangiovese grape. Sassicaia is an unusual wine made from 100 per cent Cabernet Sauvignon, and Tignanello is in the Chianti mould, but with more body and flavour. These are all expensive, connoisseurs' wines. For ordinary drinking, Sangiovese di Romagna is often a rewarding buy.

Frascati is a popular white wine which comes from Rome and its environs. It is a pleasantly reliable, golden white wine with a strong taste of the whole grape. The extra grape flavour is achieved by keeping the must (the grape pulp in the process of fermentation) in contact with the skins. Frascati is usually dry, labelled *asciutto* or *secco*, but it may also be found in softer, sweeter styles called *amabile* or *cannellino*. Frascati *superiore* has a higher level of alcohol. It is a wine for drinking young — six months is fine, but two years is the maximum.

Orvieto is the most famous wine of Umbria. Classically, this is a smooth, rich wine, golden in colour with a fragrant delicacy that offsets the natural semisweetness. Because of this lightness Orvieto is not a dessert wine, even in the old *abboccato* versions that are slowly being replaced by the more fashionable *secco*. The dry wine the producers prefer to sell nowadays is crisper and paler than the old country wine. It is still perfectly palatable, but less interesting than it once was.

Verdicchio is another famous wine of the region. It is easily recognizable by the shape of the bottle, a tall vase reminiscent of the two-handled vessel of classical times. Many producers do not state the vintage on the label, since Verdicchio is at its best a year, or at most two years, after the harvest.

Est! Est! Est! Legend has it that a bishop sent his servant ahead to mark the doors of inns serving good wine with the word *Est!* (an abbreviation for *Vinum bonum est* — the wine is good). When he stopped at an inn in Montifiascone, he was so impressed with the wine that he wrote *Est!* three times. It is a soft wine in the Orvieto style, once lush and golden but now, like its more impressive neighbour, fashionably drier and paler in colour.

Other white wines from the central region are Trebbiano di Romagna, a reliable wine made from the Trebbiano grape; Montecarlo, a splendid Tuscan white that is well balanced between dry and fruity; Vernaccia di San Gimignano, a highly flavoured wine which makes an unusual aperitif or a partner for more robust fish dishes; and Lachryma Christi (meaning 'the tears of Christ'), an acceptable wine that is best when dry.

SICILIAN WINES

Sicily, the largest island in the Mediterranean, is one of the most prolific of Italy's wine-growing regions.

Corvo is probably the island's best known brand of table wine. The popular Corvo Bianco is a pale, straw-gold colour with a gently fruity flavour. Colomba Platino is subtle and dry with a gentle bouquet. The crimson-coloured Corvo Rosso has a straightforward fruity dryness.

Etna wines are grown actually on the volcanic slopes, and on the south-eastern slopes the same family has cultivated vines for 200 years. The wines have an ashy or smoky taste. Look for Etna Bianco Villagrande — a straw-gold wine with a dry taste — ideal with smoked fish or spicy hors d'oeuvres. Villagrande Etna Rosso is a mellow red and Gattopardo (The Leopard), is a dry rosé.

Regaleali Bianco and Rosso, Settesoli Bianco and Rosso, Moscato di Noto and Moscato di Siracusa are all good, interesting wines to try.

Pasta with squid

Serve this Italian seafood recipe with either a red Sangiovese di Romagna or a light, well-chilled Frascati.

 1 hour

Serves 6
60 ml /4 tbls olive oil
500 g /1 lb Spanish onions, chopped
1 large garlic clove, crushed
1 kg /2 lb prepared squid, cut into 25 mm /1 in rings
800 g /1 lb 2 oz canned, peeled tomatoes
10 ml /2 tsp paprika
5 ml /1 tsp dried oregano
5 ml /1 tsp sugar
salt and freshly ground black pepper
500 g /1 lb fusilli or other pasta
¼ medium-sized red pepper, cored, seeded and finely chopped
¼ medium-sized green pepper, cored, seeded and finely chopped

1   Heat 45 ml /3 tbls oil in a large frying-pan, then add the onion and garlic and fry until soft.
2   Add the squid rings to the pan and cook them for 5 minutes. Stir in the tomatoes, paprika, oregano, sugar and salt and pepper to taste. Simmer for about 20–30 minutes until the squid is tender.
3   Meanwhile, bring a large pan of salted water to the boil, add the pasta and cook for 15–20 minutes, or until it is *al dente*.
4   Lightly fry the chopped peppers in the remaining oil to soften them slightly.
5   Drain the pasta and turn it onto a warmed serving dish. Make a well in the middle and pour the squid sauce into the well. Sprinkle the lightly fried peppers over the centre of the dish and serve.

Neapolitan pizza

Accompany this classic Italian dish with a tossed green or mixed salad and a bottle of vigorous red Chianti.

 45 minutes, plus rising and resting

Serves 4
15 g /½ oz fresh yeast, or 7.5 ml /1½ tsp dried yeast and 2.5 ml /½ tsp sugar
250 g /8 oz flour
5 ml /1 tsp salt
60 ml /4 tbls olive oil

For the filling
400 g /14 oz canned tomatoes
5 ml /1 tsp dried oregano
salt
freshly ground black pepper
175 g /6 oz Mozzarella cheese, sliced
50 g /2 oz canned anchovy fillets, drained and cut into strips
black olives

1   To make the pizza base, dissolve the fresh yeast in 175 ml /6 fl oz warm water. If you are using dried yeast, dissolve the sugar in 175 ml /6 fl oz warm water — 37C /98F — add the dried yeast and leave it in a warm place for 10–15 minutes until the liquid becomes frothy.
2   Put the flour onto a board, make a well in the centre and pour in the yeast mixture, salt and 15 ml /1 tbls oil. Work with your fingers to form a pliable dough, then turn it onto a floured surface. Knead for 5–10 minutes until the dough is smooth and elastic. Transfer it to a large bowl, cover it with a cloth and leave it in a warm place for about 1 hour, until the dough has doubled in size.
3   Heat the oven to 220C /425F /gas 7 and grease a baking sheet with oil. Knock back the risen dough, then roll it out to a 30 cm / 12 in round, 6 mm /¼ in thick. Place the round on the greased baking sheet and brush it with oil.
4   Drain the tomatoes, break them up and spoon them onto the pizza base. Season with oregano and salt and pepper to taste. Cover the tomatoes with the Mozzarella slices, then top them with the anchovy strips, arranged in a lattice pattern. Put one olive in each square. Spoon over the remaining oil and bake for 20 minutes.

Pigeons with peas

Replace the sage with sprigs of rosemary or thyme, if you prefer. Serve this dish with a rich red Barolo.

 1½–1¾ hours

Serves 4
4 young pigeons, oven-ready
salt
freshly ground black pepper
fresh sage leaves
flour, for dusting
25 g /1 oz butter
30 ml /2 tbls oil
1 medium-sized onion, finely chopped
4 thick, unsmoked, streaky bacon slices, rinded and cut across in strips
150 ml /5 fl oz dry white wine
150 ml /5 fl oz chicken stock, home-made or from a cube
500 g /1 lb shelled peas, defrosted if frozen
500 g /1 lb small whole carrots, cooked

1   Season the pigeons inside and out with salt and pepper. Insert one or two sage leaves into the body cavities. Dust the birds all over with flour.
2   Heat the butter and oil in a heavy-based frying-pan or wide flameproof casserole large enough to hold the birds side by side. When

Neapolitan pizza

the oil is hot, fry them briefly, turning them to brown them lightly all over. Lift them out and reserve.
3   Stirring frequently, fry the chopped onion and strips of bacon in the fat remaining in the pan or casserole for 5 minutes.
4   Add the wine and stock, bring to the boil and allow to bubble briskly for a minute. Replace the birds, cover them tightly and simmer them over a very low heat for 1–1¼ hours, or until the birds are tender. Check the liquid from time to time, and top up with a little extra stock if necessary.
5   Add the peas and simmer for 15 minutes or until the peas are cooked and flavoured with the juices.
6   Remove the birds. With a slotted spoon, transfer the peas, bacon and onion and use them to line a hot serving dish. Arrange the pigeons on top.
7   Meanwhile, boil the remaining cooking juices rapidly until well reduced and then spoon them over the birds. Arrange the carrots on the dish and serve very hot.

Chicken in sparkling wine

This makes a delicious supper dish — try partnering it with a dry Asti Spumante or a Sicilian wine.

 1¼ hours

Serves 4
1.1 kg /2½ lb chicken, cut into 4
15 ml /1 tbls oil
50 g /2 oz butter
1 small onion, finely chopped
275 ml /10 fl oz dry sparkling wine (preferably a dry Asti Spumante)
225 g /8 oz canned tomatoes
salt and freshly ground black pepper
beurre manié, made with 15 g /½ oz butter and 15 g /½ oz flour (see step 5 below)

1   Pat the chicken dry with absorbent paper. Heat the oil and butter in a large frying-pan over a medium heat. Add the chicken pieces and brown them on all sides (about 10 minutes). Remove the chicken with a slotted spoon and set it aside.
2   Lower the heat, add the finely chopped onion to the pan and fry it until soft. Return the chicken pieces to the pan in a single layer and stir in the wine and the tomatoes, together with their juices.
3   Season to taste with salt and pepper, stir to roughly break up the tomatoes, then cover the pan and cook over a moderate heat for 30 minutes or until the chicken is tender.
4   With a slotted spoon, transfer the chicken pieces to a heated platter and keep them warm. Boil the juices in the pan to reduce them by a third, scraping the pan to dislodge any stuck pieces.
5   Make the beurre manié: work the flour well into the butter. Whisk it into the juices and continue to cook for 2 minutes until it is thickened. Pour over the chicken and serve.

GERMAN WINES

The wines from the banks of the rivers Rhein and Mosel are the great, light white wines of Germany. Hock is a general English term for those wines which are produced from the Rhein vineyards.

German white wine is easy to recognize in a shop as it is sold in long, slim bottles. Authentic hock is sold in brown bottles with ornate labels. The other well-known German wine, Mosel, is less fruity than hock and is normally sold in green bottles. The best German wines are produced from the Riesling grape, so look for the word Riesling, which should appear on the labels.

All hock (the name 'hock' is thought to derive from Hochheim, a town by the Rhein), Mosels and similar white wines are best served chilled. Deliciously light, the wines vary from medium-dry to quite sweet.

The drier German-style wines go well with fish, shellfish and cold poultry.

The most important Rhein vineyards are in the Rheingau, Rheinhessen and Rheinpfalz areas; Rheingau is on the north bank of the River Rhein and the other two areas are on the south bank.

From the narrow, winding, steep-sided river valley of the Middle Mosel come some of the finest and most famous Mosel wines. They are paler, and often lighter, than the hocks from the Rhein. In past years German wines were often sweet, but in reply to modern trends the Germans now produce a range of much drier wines in the Saar and Ruwer tributaries which are thought of highly.

UNDERSTANDING GERMAN WINES

signifies top quality German wine

village and vineyard in Rheinhessen

types of grapes used

indicates bottling by vineyard

nominal volume

country of origin

guarantee that wine has been approved

area in Germany that grapes are from

description of the maturity of the grapes

exporter

Quite a lot of information about the contents of a bottle of wine can be found on the label. Here are some of the basic facts you may need to know about German wine.

The wine label

Germany's quality control system is based on the sugar levels in the grapes as well as geography. Since 1971 it has been strictly controlled and the labelling informs purchasers about the quality of each bottle.

Deutscher Tafelwein: all German table wine, Deutscher Tafelwein, must be a blend of wines of German origin only and it is suitable for everyday drinking.

QbA (Qualitätswein bestimmer Anbaugebiete): wine which comes from one of Germany's top 11 wine-growing regions will not necessarily be more expensive than Tafelwein. The wine needs to be given official approval and this involves the scientific testing of the wine to see if the levels of sugar, alcohol and acidity are correct and that there is no foreign matter in the wine indicating improper cellar techniques. The region of origin will be named prominently on the label, together with the registered place of origin, vintage and perhaps the grape type.

QmP (Qualtätswein mit Prädikat) relies on natural sugar levels in the must (grape-juice before fermentation is complete), so that in theory each year every QbA wine could be awarded QmP status.

There are five categories of QmP:

Kabinett: the basic QmP category. The wine is light and dry.

Spätlese: the grapes were late picked and fully ripened, indicating a rich wine which is sweeter than Kabinett.

Auslese: grape bunches were selected as ripe and in perfect condition. The sweetness and quality of the wine will be high.

Beerenauslese: the grapes were picked only after the 'noble rot' (a benign fungus which shrivels the grape) had begun to attack the grapes on the vine. The wine will consequently be more concentrated in flavour.

Trockenbeerenauslese: wine of superlative quality, made from grapes that had begun to dry to sultana form on the vine.

All Qualitätswein is also allocated an official coding — the AP number, which gives, in 11 digits, a full record of what it is and when and where it was tested.

A final category is **Eiswein**, a rare, very sweet and expensive wine which is made

MOSEL WINES

The valley of the Mosel (or Moselle to give it its French spelling) is grouped with its two tributaries, the Saar and the Ruwer, to make up one of the 11 quality wine areas laid down by German wine law. The designation appears on the label as 'Mosel-Saar-Ruwer'. The area included is quite large, stretching north east from Trier near the French border to Koblenz on the Rhein.

Grapes thrive on sun and this far north they need ideal conditions to mature to full ripeness before the onset of frosts in autumn. The vineyards of the Mosel valley are perched on every south-facing slope, so that they receive the maximum amount of sun. The canals which have been built along the river increase the reflection of the sun back onto the vineyard terraces, increasing their warmth. The raised level of moisture in the air is also of value and the mountains to north and south protect the valley against early and late frosts.

As with all great wine-growing sites, climate is a vital factor, but it is the soil that imparts a special flavour to the grapes and ultimately the wine. The Mosel cuts through slate mountains and the best vineyards, in the central portion of the valley, all thrive on the eroded soft slate soils of the valley slopes. It is this which gives the wine its firm and sharp flavour. The slate in the soil also helps the grapes to ripen by holding the sun's warmth for longer.

The final important component, of course, is the grape itself. Almost 60 per cent of the vines in the Mosel area are Rieslings, producing the finest wines. Now 20 per cent are the newer type Müller-Thurgau, produced by crossing Sylvaner and Riesling grapes. However, the Riesling vines are grown along the better slopes.

The Upper Mosel

Wines are produced along the Mosel as it passes through France and Luxembourg on a fairly extensive scale, but these should not be confused with the German Mosels, as they are not in the same league. Realistically, nor are the products of the upper Mosel, which is included in the official German Mosel-Saar-Ruwer area. Here the soil is chalky and the wine produced is of modest quality, often thin and acid, and it is used in the manufacture of Sekt sparkling wine.

The Saar and Ruwer

The river Saar, which enters the Mosel just above Trier, is surrounded by more open countryside than the Mittel-Mosel (see below), and the wines are consequently more subject to frost. Saar wines only achieve the highest standards in less than one year in four — but when they do, they are undoubtedly superb. The best villages are Ayl, Oberemmel, Ockfen and Wiltingen.

The Ruwer, which joins the Mosel below Trier, is little more than a stream. For a few kilometres, however, fine vineyards cluster in its valley. Like Saar wines, the best vintages are quite rare but when they occur, the wine is unique, for Ruwer wines are the lightest of all great white wines with a really exquisite fragrance. Best villages are Eitelsbach, Casel and Mertesdorf.

The Middle Mosel

Here the river cuts between the Hunsrück and Eiffel mountains and begins its meandering course to the east of the ancient wine town of Trier. The area known as the Mittel-Mosel (Middle Mosel) ends at the village of Zell. In between Trier and Zell is a valley of incomparable loveliness, centring on the small town of Bernkastel.

The great wines from the Middle Mosel are exquisite and expensive and should be reserved to enjoy on special occasions. However, there are wines from this area to suit all tastes and from every price level. Many are cheap enough for everyday drinking, but still suitable for more formal entertaining.

The first stretch of the Middle Mosel consists of a broad valley as far as the town of Klüsserath. Here the vineyards are set well back from the river. The wines are worthwhile but undistinguished. Longuich is the main village and Probstberg is the designated name of the collective. Longuicher Probstberg is a wine you will often find.

After Klüsserath, the valley begins to narrow and the slopes overlooking the river produce better wines. Klüsserath, Trittenheim and Neumagen-Dhron are the main village names and the collective vineyards enjoy considerable reputations, especially in their good years. Look for the names of Klüsserather Bruderschaft, Trittenheimer Apotheke or Altärchen and also Neumagen-Dhroner Hofberger.

Next, the river takes a long bend, with steep, south-facing slopes above the village of Piesport. This is one of the main centres and wines from here are sought after. Goldtröpfchen, then Falkenberg and Günterslay are the best vineyards and the collective vineyard is Michelsberg. The wine from Michelsberg will be from a wide area and will not have the outstanding quality of the great vineyards, although it may be good.

After a sharp bend at Minheim, the river flows down to Bernkastel. On the way are Wintrich and Kesten, Brauneberg and Lieser. These villages all make good wine, but it is not in the highest class. These wines are softer than other good Mosels and do not have their piquancy.

At the next large bend of the river is the town of Bernkastel-Kues. Here in a single seven-kilometre slope the greatest Mosels of all are produced. Bernkastel-Kues, Graach, Wehlen and Zeltingen-Rachtig are the village names to remember and all produce fine wines. Bernkastel is the name given to the whole of the Middle Mosel, so Bereich Bernkastel means wine blended from any part of the area. Wine labelled Bernkastler Kurfürstlay signifies wine from the Bernkastel region rather than from a particular vineyard. The wines are perfectly acceptable and should not be too expensive.

Just above the town of Bernkastel-Kues are the slopes of the most famous Bernkastel vineyards: Doktor and Graben. Other vineyards in the area with good reputations are Johannisbrünnchen, Bratenhöfchen, Mattheisbildchen and Lay. Further downstream are names just as well known: Gracher Domprobst or Himmelreich, Wehlener Sonnenuhr and Zeltingen-Rachtiger Sonnenuhr or Himmelreich. On the opposite bank is the lesser quality, but still worthwhile, vineyard of Nonneberg. Gracher Munzlay on a label generally indicates a cheaper wine from this stretch of the river. Beyond Zeltingen the river turns east and another series of south-facing slopes producing good wines begins. These wines are highly recommended and less expensive but often as good as their Bernkastel counterparts. The villages are Ürzig, Kröv, Erden, Lösnich and Kinheim. The name given to wine from the area is Ürziger Schwarzlay. Beyond here there are good wines from Traven-Trarbach and Enkirch.

The Lower Mosel

The Lower Mosel, from Zell to the junction with the Rhein at Koblenz, produces wine from vineyards scattered along its whole length. Most are used in the blending of Moselblümchen or other lesser wines made in the region.

Similarly, the area of the lower Mosel from Bullay to the junction with the Rhein, is also undistinguished, with the hard slate soil of this part of the valley often giving the wine a hard taste. The best villages are Cochem, Pommern, Valwig and Winningen.

RHEIN WINES

The most northerly of the world's great vineyards lie in Germany — in the complex of valleys made up by the Rhein river and its tributary the Mosel.

The Rheinhessen produces some of the most famous wines in the world, as well as very large quantities of pleasant but undistinguished table wines. Bingen and the Rheinfront villages export wines of unassailable quality. Three of the roughly square-shaped region's corners are marked by towns on the river: Bingen, Mainz, Worms.

The most productive area, making almost 30 per cent of German wine, is the Rheinpfalz — the Palatinate.

The Rheingau is the outstanding wine-producing area of the Rhein valley. On the right bank, between the bridges across to Mainz and Bingen, the vineyards produce the rich dessert wines for which Germany has no rival.

Situated on a tributary of the Rhein, the Nahe region is less well-known than other famous Rhein-wine regions of Germany, but it ranks very highly since it produces some good dessert wines as well as good quality wines for everyday drinking. The region is small and consequently only provides about five per cent of the total amount of German wine produced each year.

Rheinhessen

Rheinhessen is neatly situated in the bend in the River Rhein known as the Rheinknie (the Rhine knee), and up to 300 million litres of wine are produced here annually. The Sylvaner grape was for some time the most dominant type in the region but recently it has been pushed into second place by the Müller-Thurgau grape.

Behind the town of Bingen rises the steep slopes of the Scharlachberg or, 'scarlet hill', although it is brick-red rather than scarlet. Here is the famous chapel of St Rochas, from which the collective name for the vineyards of the area comes — Sankt Rochuskapelle. The best wines from this region are strong and full of flavour, with a smoky taste. The famous vineyards are Schlossberg, Schwätzerchen and Scharlachberg.

The town of Mainz is one of the main centres of the wine trade, although little wine is actually grown here. To the south is the Rheinfront. Red sandstone soils cover the east-facing slopes of the river banks which are packed with vineyards. The first Rheinfront village, Bodenheim, produces mild wines, known for their bouquet and quality. Nackenheim does not produce much wine, and is not well known outside Germany, but to wine experts, this is a special place. Its wines are now largely sold under the village name and not used in blends. The best vineyard is Nackenheimer Rothenberg; producers, to look for in the area are Gunderloch-Lange, Gunderloch-Usinger and the state-owned Staatsweingut. South of Mainz is Nierstein, important for the quality and quantity of its wine. Its production is massive, and less than 20 per cent is bottled

as wine of high quality under the name of the place where it is produced. The majority goes into the well-known blended wines. However, if the wine is labelled 'Niersteiner', together with the name of the vineyard, it is a good wine. The most famous vineyards are Floss, Glock, Hipping, Orbel, Pettental and Rehbach. There are also producers of considerable fame whose name will appear on the label, including Anton Balbach, Louis Guntrum, Freiherr Heyl zu Herrnheim, Rheinhold Senfer and Franz Karl Schmitt. Oppenheim, the next village up the river, produces wine almost as good as Nierstein. The best vineyards here include Daubhaus, Herrenberg, Kreuz, Sackträger and Steig.

The Rheinfront ends with the village of Dienheim. The wine is still good, although not of the superlative quality of Nierstein or Oppenheim. Watch for these vineyard names: Goldberg, Guldenmorgen, Kröttenbrunner and Rosswiesse.

One final wine of importance comes from Ingleheim, a village situated between Bingen and Mainz. Made from blue Spätburgunder grapes, this is a red wine — one of the best made in Germany — but little is produced and it is not often found outside the country. Other Rheinhessen reds are made from the Portugieser grape, but these are generally only available for local consumption.

The Worms region

The vineyards around the town of Worms are small and they produce an average quality wine which is sweet and fresh. It is used for Liebfraumilch — for more detailed information see page 98.

The Rheinpfalz

The Rheinpfalz occupies a strip of land some 15 kilometres to the west of the Rhein, running for about 80 kilometres from north to south and is the warmest and driest area in Germany, hence the huge scale of its wine yield. In the central portion, known as the Mittelhaardt, lie some of Germany's most famous vineyards.

The southern area, known as the Oberhaardt, is responsible for the larger quantity, although it is not renowned for great wines like its neighbouring region, the Mittelhaardt, to the north. In the past, almost all the wine produced here was drunk locally, as carafe wine or as the heady, milky *Federweisser* (feather-white). This is drunk when so young that it is still half grape juice. The better wines that were not drunk by the local farmers were often used in blended wine — Liebfraumilch, for example — and this was the only way it was likely to be drunk outside Germany. Now, however, the region is changing and many wines are bottled with the name of their particular place of origin being established. Many quality wines are produced, and *Spätlese* and even *Auslese* can be found proudly inscribed on the label. Pale, fruity and light, they make a better accompaniment to food than the more powerful wines. Names to look for are Rhodter Ordensgut and Bergzaberner Kloster Liebfrauenberg.

The four most distinguished villages in

Rhein wine

the Mittelhaardt are Deidesheim, Forst, Ruppertsberg and Wachenheim. Königsbach, nearby, is also highly thought of, although its output is small. Any wine bearing one of these names will be fine and quite expensive. This area favours the Riesling grape and the wine is much deeper in colour — almost amber — than those from further south.

The wine from Forst is reputedly the sweetest in Germany. Near the village is an outcrop of black basalt, a rock rich in potassium which contributes to the fine character of the wine. In consequence, stone from local quarries is crushed and spread on the vineyards of other districts to impart some of the quality of Forst wine to their products. Next to the church at Forst, almost in the centre of the village, are two of the most famous vineyards in Germany — Jesuitengarten and Kirchenstück. A short distance away, Deidesheim, is a charming little village, surrounded by famous vineyards such as Grainhübel, Hohenmorgen, Leinhöhle and Kalkofen. Wachenheim, too, has its famous names — Böhlig, Gerümpel, Goldbächel and Rechbächel among others.

However, these are great wines, hard to come by and to be reserved for that very special occasion.

To the north is the small town of Bad Dürkheim, Germany's largest wine commune. Here, the famous *Wurstmarkt* (sausage fair) is held annually in September. This fair is a really marvellous celebration of both wine and sausage.

The Rheingau

The site of the Rheingau is unique among the Rhein regions, in that the river, which generally flows from south to north, at this point turns, blocked by the Taunus mountains, and flows slightly to the south. The slopes of the Taunus hills face to the sun, making them ideal for vines. In autumn the damp mists gathering over the river encourage the 'noble rot' which attacks the grapes and helps create the fine Auslese, Beerenauslese and Trockenbeerenauslese wines.

Rheingau produces only two per cent of the total German wine production, but much of this is of the highest quality. The soil is a contributory factor. On the high slopes, there is quartzite and weathered slate and closer to the river there are clays, loess and loam.

Lorchhausen and Lorch, the villages furthest downstream and furthest west, are the least distinguished in the region. Some good wine is made, but it has more in common with the lighter, more commonplace wines of neighbouring Mittelrhein. The next village, Assmannshausen, is an exception. Here, red wines are produced from the blue Spätburgunder (or Pinot Noir) grape, while to the west of it the Rüdesheimer Berg produces much of the best wines — golden in colour, strong in alcohol and in flavour.

East of Rüdesheim on the river is Geisenheim, and the revered Schloss Johannisberg a short distance inland. The official German school of winemaking is at Geisenheim, and the wines of the area are good. Johannisberg, however, is in another class and is perhaps the greatest of the Rheingau, or even of the Rhein, areas. Schloss Johannisberg is incomparable, immensely subtle in flavour — and very expensive.

Next along the river, come Winkel, Mittelheim and Östrich, with Hattenheim and Hallgarten in the hills behind. At Winkel is Schloss Vollrads, rivalling even Schloss Johannisberg. Its wines are said to be beyond praise!

At Hattenheim is another famous estate, Steinberg, with the monastery of Kloster Eberbach, where wines have been made for at least 700 years. Erbach, along the river from Hattenheim, has another famous vineyard. Named Marcobrunn, the vineyard has been the subject of a legendary dispute between the villages, but it is now officially in Erbach.

Eltville, next along the river, is one of the larger vineyard towns of Rheingau, providing a centre for the wine trade and the manufacture of sparkling Sekt. Its wines are good, and may be less expensive than the more famous villages in the hills behind: Kiedrich, Rauenthal and Martinsthal.

On the bend in the river that marks the end of the Rhein part of Rheingau lies the major town of Wiesbaden. Although an attractive old spa resort, its own wines are not up to the high standards of its illustrious neighbours flanking its east and west sides. There are four groups of Wiesbaden vineyards: Wiesbaden itself, Schierstein, Frauenstein and Dotzheim.

About three kilometres up the river Main, which joins the Rhein beyond Wiesbaden, is the town of Hochheim, forming the eastern edge of the Rheingau. Although not on the Rhein itself, Hochheim has given its name to all the wines of the Rhein regions in English usage — 'hock'. Hochheim's wines are certainly Rheingau in character, and are among the first rank in quality. The best ingredients, Kirchenstück and Domdechaney, are close to the centre of the town. The wines are soft and fruity and there is one named Königen Viktoria Berg, after Queen Victoria who in 1850 visited a local vineyard and praised the wines.

The Nahe

Although officially Nahe wines are categorized as Rhein wines (hocks), these wines unjustifiably suffer from the reputation that they fall midway between Mosels and hocks. The truth, however, is that the Nahe region produces wines of character, combining the clarity and liveliness of Mosels with the strength and fruitiness of hocks.

Over 80 per cent of the grapes grown are Müller-Thurgau, Riesling and Sylvaner — Germany's great white wine grapes.

The most famous centre of the Nahe is Bad Kreuznach, a picturesque old spa with a 600-year-old bridge. Roman artifacts and mosaics found in the area support the claim that viniculture was started here by the Romans, although it may go back even earlier. Some vineyards are quite close to the town centre — Rosengarten, Kahlenberg, St Martin and Brückes are names worth looking out for. Bad Kreuznach wines are typical of the Nahe area and are of very good quality. To the north and west, scattered back into the hills, there are a number of well reputed wine villages producing wines with strong character and fruitiness.

The most significant name in Nahe wine production is Schloss Böchelheim, which lies further upstream from Bad Kreuznach. Schloss Böchelheim wine has a strong flavour, compared by some to blackcurrants.

Between the two centres are a number of villages on the left bank of the river. Just south of Bad Kreuznach is the huge red rock of the Rotenfels, with the village of Bad Münster below. Vineyards clustering at the foot of this giant sun trap (such as Rotenfelser im Winkel, Höll, Steigerdell and Bastei) are also on ideal soil. They produce some of the best Nahe wine, especially Bastei. Opposite Bad Münster, the Alsenz, a tributary of the Nahe, enters the river. Several good wines come from this valley, particularly from the villages of Ebernburg and Altenbamberg.

A little further along the Nahe is Norheim, again producing wine of the first rank. Vineyards include Dellchen, Kafels and Kirschheck, all close to the river, with Klosterberg and Sonnenberg behind. There are scattered vineyard areas further up the Nahe valley and, in the hinterland, many producing notable wines. Village names to look out for include: Waldböckelheim, Monzingen, Martinstein and Merxheim. All these produce above-average wines that are well worth trying.

Terrine of hare

Use an older hare for this recipe; the terrine will keep for a month if refrigerated. Try serving it with a red wine from the Ahr valley or Mittelrhein.

 2¾ hours

Serves 8
450 g /1 lb cooked hare meat, finely minced
5 ml /1 tsp freshly grated nutmeg
5 ml /1 tsp ground ginger
salt
freshly ground black pepper
275 ml /10 fl oz strong stock, home-made or from a beef stock cube
225 g /8 oz sausage-meat
10 ml /2 tsp freshly chopped parsley
5 ml /1 tsp dried thyme
5 ml /1 tsp dried sage
1 garlic clove, cut in half
50 g /2 oz butter, for greasing
30 ml /2 tbls brandy
8 streaky bacon slices, 6 slices chopped
175 g /6 oz canned chestnuts, drained and chopped
175 g /6 oz clarified butter (see page 24)
hot buttered toast, to serve

1 In a bowl, mix the hare with the nutmeg and ginger. Season well with salt and pepper, then moisten with the stock to make the mixture wet without being slushy.
2 In another bowl, mix the sausage-meat with the parsley, thyme and sage. Season with salt and black pepper. Heat the oven to 180C /350F /gas 4.
3 Rub a 2 L /3½ pt mould with the cut sides of the garlic and then grease well with 40 g /1½ oz butter. Spread half the minced hare mixture on the bottom, pressing it well down, and sprinkle it with 10 ml /2 tsp brandy. Cover with half the chopped bacon, then half the chestnuts. Put all the sausage-meat mixture over the chestnuts, pressing well down, and sprinkle with 10 ml /2 tsp brandy. Cover with the remaining chestnuts, then the bacon. Finish with a layer of hare. Sprinkle with the rest of the brandy. Lay 2 whole bacon slices on top and cover the tin with foil buttered with the remaining butter.
4 Place the mould in a roasting tin half filled with boiling water and bake it for 1¾ hours or until the mixture has shrunk away from the sides of the tin. Remove the terrine from the oven and cool.
5 When cool, remove the bacon slices from the top and pour the clarified butter over. Refrigerate the terrine, then serve it chilled with hot buttered toast.

firmly. Chill them in the refrigerator for at least 15 minutes to set the coating.

6 To cook the veal, heat the remaining butter and olive oil in a frying-pan large enough to take the escalopes in one layer. Lay them in the hot fat side by side. Cook over low heat for 5 minutes. Turn the veal over and cook for a further 5 minutes, or until golden brown.

7 Arrange the escalopes on a heated serving platter or place them on individual plates and serve immediately with thick soured cream.

Peppered monkfish

 1 hour

Serves 4

4 × 175 g /5 oz monkfish fillets
salt
15 ml /1 tbls black peppercorns, lightly crushed
150 g /5 oz butter
125 ml /4 fl oz white wine
175 ml /6 fl oz veal or chicken stock,
   home-made or from a cube
25 g /1 oz flour
150 ml /5 fl oz thick cream

For the garnish
green bean and pimento bundles
sprigs of fresh parsley

1 Rinse the monkfish fillets under cold water and pat them dry. Rub them with salt and sprinkle one side of each with half the crushed peppercorns.

2 Melt 125 g /4 oz butter in a frying-pan large enough to take the fillets in one layer. Place the fish in the pan, peppered-side down, and sprinkle with the remaining peppercorns. Sauté the fillets for 15 minutes, turning them once.

3 Stir in the wine and stock and simmer for 25–30 minutes or until the fish is cooked through. Remove the fish with a fish slice, place on a serving platter and keep warm.

4 Mix the remaining butter with the flour to form a *beurre manié*. Bring the sauce in the pan to a simmer and add the beurre manié. Bring it to the boil and stir constantly until the sauce thickens. Add the cream and simmer for 1 minute, stirring well. Pour the sauce over the fish, garnish with parsley sprigs and green bean and pimento bundles, then serve immediately.

Watermelon dessert

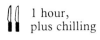 1 hour,
plus chilling

Serves 4

1.5 kg /3 lb watermelon, halved, skinned, cut
   into cubes and seeded
450 ml /16 fl oz sweet white wine
30 ml /2 tbls soft, light brown sugar
5 ml /1 tsp ground allspice
15 ml /1 tbls grated lemon zest
225 ml /8 fl oz soured cream

Peppered monkfish

German veal with almonds

Serve this delicious and unusual dish with a well-chilled Niersteiner Gutes Domtal.

 1 hour

Serves 4

40 g /1½ oz butter
45 ml /3 tbls olive oil
125 g /4 oz button mushrooms, thinly sliced
salt and freshly ground black pepper
25 ml /1½ tbls Madeira
4 × 125–150 g /4–5 oz veal escalopes
125 g /4 oz cooked tongue
2 eggs, beaten
50 g /2 oz fresh white breadcrumbs
40 g /1½ oz flaked almonds, roughly chopped
flour
225 ml /8 fl oz thick soured cream, to serve

1 In a frying-pan, heat one-third each of the butter and oil. Sauté the mushrooms for 5 minutes or until they are golden brown, turning them with a spatula. Season with salt and pepper to taste. Sprinkle the Madeira over the mushrooms.

2 With a meat bat or rolling pin, beat the veal escalopes between sheets of cling film until they are as thin as possible. Season the meat generously with salt and black pepper.

3 Cut the tongue into thin strips. Pile a quarter of the strips in the centre of each escalope and then spoon in the sautéed mushrooms. Fold first the short ends, then the long edges, of each escalope over the filling, to make an envelope-shaped parcel.

4 Pour the beaten eggs into a shallow dish. In another shallow dish, combine the fresh white breadcrumbs and chopped flaked almonds.

5 Coat the veal parcels with flour, shaking off any excess. Dip them into the beaten egg, then coat them with the almond and bread-crumb mixture, patting the mixture on

1 In a medium-sized saucepan, combine the watermelon cubes with the wine, sugar, allspice and lemon zest. Bring gently to the boil over a moderate heat, stirring constantly. Now simmer the 'soup', uncovered, for about 20 minutes.

2 Strain the soup through a fine nylon sieve. Rub the melon through the sieve until only a pulp is left. Discard the pulp.

3 Leave the purée until cold, then stir in the soured cream. Chill it in the refrigerator for 1 hour before serving.

Spiced plum flan

Greengages may be substituted for the golden dessert plums in this unusual wine-glazed flan recipe.

 1 hour

Serves 4–6
125 g /4 oz butter, plus extra for greasing
125 g /4 oz flour
2.5 ml /½ tsp ground mixed spice
grated zest of 1 medium-sized orange
125 g /4 oz caster sugar
2 eggs, beaten
whipped cream, to serve
For the filling
350 g /12 oz golden dessert plums
150 ml /5 fl oz sweet white wine
60 ml /4 tbls redcurrant jelly
juice of ½ medium-sized orange
5 cm /2 in piece of cinnamon stick

1 Butter a 20 cm /8 in sponge flan ring. Heat the oven to 180C /350F /gas 4. Sift the flour with the mixed spice onto a plate.

2 In a mixing bowl, beat the butter until it is soft. Next, beat in the orange zest and the sugar. Beat in the eggs, alternately with the flour. Beat thoroughly.

3 Pour the mixture into the prepared flan ring. Bake for 25 minutes or until the flan is golden and has shrunk slightly from the sides of the ring. Remove it from the oven, cool for 10 minutes in the tin and then turn it onto a wire cake rack to become cold.

4 Meanwhile, halve and stone the plums. Put the wine in a saucepan and boil it until it is reduced by half. Remove the pan from the heat and stir in the redcurrant jelly. Continue to stir until the jelly is dissolved.

5 Add the plums, orange juice and the piece of cinnamon stick to the pan. Poach the plums gently for 10 minutes. Remove them from the heat and leave until they are cold. Discard the cinnamon stick.

6 Arrange the plums, skin side up, symmetrically in the flan. Spoon half the poaching syrup over it, allowing it to sink into the sponge. Just before serving, spoon more of the syrup over the plums. Serve this flan with whipped cream.

OTHER GERMAN WINES

There are two reasons for knowing more about the lesser German wine regions — firstly, because they are recognized by German wine law and their names will appear on bottles, and secondly because they have their own distinctive characteristics and merits. A knowledge of the lesser regions may also provide you with pointers towards good wines that are cheaper than products from the Rhein or Mosel.

There is also a growing realization that there is no point in trying to imitate the great dessert wines of the Rheingau and Rheinpfalz. Indeed, the wines of Franken and, to a lesser extent, those of Baden, are drier than the usual German style and thus may even be preferred by many people.

Franken

The wines of Franconia are dry and full-bodied, but by German standards the dryness of the Franken wines is a failing. They come in the *Bocksbeutel*, a short, flagon-shaped bottle, rather than the normal tall flask.

The area is really that of the River Main, flowing towards the Rhein in a twisting course from the east. This is rich farmland and vineyards are planted only where nothing else will grow. As a result, they are scattered, both along the valley and in the surrounding country. All the sites are more or less exposed and frost damage is frequent. To combat this, the quick-ripening Sylvaner has

traditionally been the preferred grape, although the ubiquitous Müller-Thurgau has now taken over as the most widely planted type. A further consequence of the relatively short growing season is that the Auslesen and Beerenauslesen are very rare and over priced, so stick to the basic QbA and QmP wines (see box on page 92) — when you can find them. The main centre is Würtzburg, with its famous Stein vineyards.

Württemburg

Further south than Franken is the wine area of Württemburg, which centres on the River Neckar and around the city of Stuttgart. It makes eight per cent of German wine, but the locals drink a great deal more than they produce. The area is therefore a net importer of wine, with little allowed for export to the rest of Germany, let alone abroad. Because of the open countryside, the climate is harsh, with extremes of temperature, despite the southern latitude. The vineyards are sited in the most sheltered and sunny positions.

Baden

The most southerly wine-growing districts of Germany fall into the region known as Baden. It is a very large area, stretching some 400 kilometres from Lake Constance on the border with Switzerland, north as far as the River Main.

The area is growing in importance, for 12 per cent of German wine originates here — from scattered vineyards occupying a wide range of localities. Differing soil types and a whole range of grape varieties lead to many dissimilar wines. The Müller-Thurgau grape is proving successful, however, and it now contributes 33 per cent of the total. Small producers work in co-operatives, making many good, if undistinguished, wines.

One of the most famous areas is the shores of Lake Constance — the Bodensee — producing soft whites and *Weissherbst*, a very pale rosé made from red grapes pressed without their skins. These are pleasant

enough, but probably best drunk on a visit to the area. Other Baden areas of note are the Markgräflerland, Ortenau and Kaiserstuhl.

The Ahr

The spectacularly pretty river valley of the Ahr is one of the most northerly of all wine-growing areas and certainly the furthest north producing red wine. Only six per cent of German wine is grown in the Ahr, mostly red from the Spätburgunder, Frühburgunder and Portugeiser grapes, but with the proportion of whites on the increase.

In the steep-sided upper reaches, the visitor can expect to find wines with spicy strength, derived from the partly volcanic and slate soils on the valley terraces. Further down the valley, the wines become fuller and more mellow. They are light in alcohol, colour and flavour.

Mittelrhein

North of Rheingau (see page 95), 100 kilometres of the river is designated the Mittelrhein wine area. For sheer beauty this is the most famous part of the Rhine valley and it is where Wagner set his opera cycle, *Der Ring des Nibelungen*. The wines, however, are of less exalted quality and are almost always drunk locally or used in the manufacture of Sekt sparkling wine.

Almost all the wines from this area are white. The main problem is that the river runs towards the north and the area is subject to frosts and exposed to the wind. This allows the grapes to reach full ripeness only in exceptionally warm autumns.

Hessische Bergstrasse

It is difficult to understand why this small region was designated separately. The level of production is tiny and the wines are similar to the lesser products of Rheinhessen, which is only a short distance to the west. It is a rural area of hills, woods and fruit trees, with a mild climate and light soil. The wine is mostly white, with some rosé.

BLENDED WINES

There are approaching 3,000 registered names that can legally be applied to German wine. This can pose great difficulties when buying, and it is here that branded wines come to the rescue. The key to the consistency of these branded wines — Blue Nun, Green Label and so on — and to the huge quantities that can be produced, is the process of blending. Almost every wine, of course, is to some extent blended. With German wine, the cellar master's role is even more crucial than elsewhere because of the difficulties of obtaining good wine with any regularity at such northern latitudes. As a result, Germany has developed the most sophisticated training system through the Wine Institute at Geisenheim. The result is that German wine is of a generally high standard and relatively cheap.

Liebfraumilch

The internationally familiar wine, Liebfraumilch, is named after the *Liebfrauenkirch*, or 'Church of Our Lady' in the Rheinhessen town of Worms. The name means literally 'Our Lady's milk', although it is believed that the *milch* may be a corruption of *minch*, a medieval word for monk — monks originally tended the vineyard on the site. By

the 19th century the word Liebfraumilch was widely used as a general name for Rhein wines, rather than just that one vineyard. Because of this long tradition and the importance of Liebfraumilch to the export trade, it survived the 1971 tightening up of German wine nomenclature. As a result of 1983 legislation Liebfraumilch must be made of QbA standard wine from more than one Rhein region and must be made of at least 50 per cent Riesling, Sylvaner or Müller-Thurgau grapes. Good examples are Blue Nun, Goldener Oktober and Hans Cristof. The essential character of Liebfraumilch is that it should typify Rhein wine or 'hock'. It should be light and slightly sweet, but also have a hint of strength and body. It should be fragrant and have a good taste of fruit.

Blended Mosels

Blended Mosels do not have a broadly used accepted generic name like Liebfraumilch. Moselblümchen is sometimes applied, but

is really an imitation of the Liebfraumilch name as a way of establishing an internationally recognizable name and has limited meaning. It is only of Tafelwein status. The best blended Mosels try to achieve the typical characteristics of crispness combined with a flowery fragrance and mild sweetness. Deinhard's Green Label is well-known and has a clear, light flavour with the slight crispness.

Sekt

Another important type of blended German wine is Sekt. This sparkling champagne-style wine demonstrates the benefits of the advanced level of cellar technique in Germany. It is blended from all over the German-quality wine-producing areas. Sekt is a cheaper and perfectly pleasant substitute for champagne.

If the Sekt is 100 per cent German it will be called 'Deutsches Sekt' and be classed as a QbA wine.

AUSTRIAN WINES

Until quite recently, Austrian wine was rarely seen outside its native country. However, over the last few years, an appreciable amount of good Austrian wine has become available abroad at reasonable prices.

There are four principal wine regions in Austria — Lower Austria, Styria, Burgenland and Vienna (probably the only capital in the world with its own vineyards). Most of the Austrian wines are sold labelled according to the grape from which they are made. Therefore, it is useful to know the important grape names.

Grüner Veltliner: over 80 per cent of the wine produced in Austria is white and of this the most popular grape is the Grüner Veltliner. It produces a light and spicy wine with an almost 'peppery' taste.

Müller-Thurgau: an early-ripening grape which produces a mild wine with a fruity bouquet and the typical Muscat flavour.

Rheinriesling: wine pressed from this grape matures slowly and reaches its peak after two to four years in storage. It has a delicate bouquet, faintly reminiscent of peaches.

The Neuburger grape is a speciality of Austria and the wines produced from it are full-bodied yet mild, with a fresh aroma.

Weisser Burgunder gives a fragrant bouquet and a flavour of fresh walnuts.

Traminer (or Gewürztraminer) produces a spicy, rich flavour, and a bouquet, likened by some to roses and to violets by others.

Muskat-Ottonel produces a mild, golden wine with a strong bouquet of Muscat which can vary from sprightly to mellow.

Welschriesling does not produce Riesling; 'Welsch' in this case means 'imposter'. It is fresh, spicy, keeps well and can vary in colour from palest yellow to deep gold.

Zierfändler and Rotgipfler are typically Austrian grapes. They produce rich and robust wines with a fine, fruity bouquet, which are often blended together. This wine is excellent if allowed to mature.

Blaufränkische produces the most popular Austrian red wine. Fruity and full-bodied, it has a glowing colour and matures well.

Blauer Portugieser produces a red wine that should be drunk young — it is velvety and mild with a faint spiciness.

St Laurent produces a robust wine, deep red in colour. It has a slight, yet delicious, fragrance of raspberries.

Blauer Burgunder gives an elegant red wine, smooth, velvety and rich.

The Austrian Auslese, Beerenauslese, Ausbruch, Trockenberenauslese and Eiswein are 'special' dessert wines, which have a mellowness about them — like liquid honey spiced with pine and scented with lime blossom.

Baked scallops

Serve these delicate shellfish as the starter for an evening meal. A Gewürztraminer makes a perfect accompaniment.

🔪 30 minutes

Serves 4
8 large scallops
oil, for greasing
2 garlic cloves, finely chopped
25 g /1 oz fresh parsley, finely chopped
2 medium-sized onions, finely chopped
a pinch of ground cloves
1.5 ml /¼ tsp freshly grated nutmeg
salt
freshly ground black pepper
50 g /2 oz fresh white breadcrumbs
olive oil, to sprinkle
sprigs of watercress, to garnish
lemon wedges, to garnish

1 Heat the oven to 220C /400F /gas 6. Prepare the scallops. Clean away the beard, which appears in a black translucent line behind the coral, ease the scallop away from its shell, then wash and dry the scallops and 4 rounded shells. Lightly oil the shells.
2 Chop the scallop meat and corals and place them in a mixing bowl. Add the garlic, parsley and onions. Add the ground cloves and grated nutmeg, season with salt and black pepper and mix the ingredients until they are well blended.
3 Pile the mixture into the 4 oiled scallop shells. Cover with the breadcrumbs and sprinkle a little olive oil over the top.

4 Place the shells on a baking sheet and bake for 20 minutes or until lightly browned on top. Garnish with sprigs of watercress and lemon wedges, then serve.

South Tyrolean wine and beef soup

 25 minutes

Serves 4–6
500 ml /18 fl oz beef stock, home-made or from cubes, or a good quality beef consommé
5 medium-sized egg yolks
250 ml /9 fl oz dry or medium-dry white wine
250 ml /9 fl oz thin cream
ground cinnamon
croûtons fried in butter, to serve

1 Heat the beef stock or consommé to just below boiling point. Meanwhile, in a large bowl, whisk together the egg yolks, white wine, thin cream and a pinch of ground cinnamon.
2 Gradually pour the heated stock or consommé into the bowl, whisking all the time or the mixture will curdle.
3 Put the bowl of soup over a saucepan of gently simmering water and whisk until the soup is well thickened. Serve the soup in warmed soup plates, soup bowls or mugs with croûtons fried in butter and an extra sprinkling of cinnamon.

South Tyrolean wine and beef soup

SPANISH WINES

Spain has the largest area under vines of any country in Europe and though it makes mainly ordinary table wines, the Rioja region can produce wines to compare with château-bottled clarets.

Until recently, Spain was unfairly represented by the worst it had to offer — inky reds of doubtful parentage and imitation French whites such as 'Spanish Sauterne' or 'Spanish Chablis'. As a result, many people think of Spanish wine as a byword for plonk.

The heat of the summer sun produces grapes with high levels of sugar. This ferments out to give wines which are unsubtle in taste. Most of the wine made is *vino corriente*, the equivalent of the French *vin ordinaire*.

This does not mean that Spanish wines of quality do not exist, though with the exception of sherry (see page 105) and Rioja they are not well-known outside Spain. However, the Spanish authorities have taken steps to improve their country's image. A Government Statute of 1970 laid down a strict code of practice for all connected with wine production and distribution. In the statute, 18 limited areas entitled to a *Denominacion de Origen* (similar to the French AC and Italian DOCG) were defined and a network of local authorities — *Cosejos Reguladores* — were set up to enforce standards.

The name Rioja is an abbreviation of Rio Oja, a tributary of the river Ebro, but the Rioja district extends along both banks of the main river for a stretch of almost 100 kilometres. At the end of the last century the vineyards of France were attacked by phylloxera which threatened the whole future of wine production. Many growers from Bordeaux travelled south and settled in Rioja. As a result, Rioja wines are still being made today following the former Bordeaux methods with an ageing in oak.

Unlike France, though, the vines are not trellised but often grown alternating with other crops, and the entire produce of the region is sold to the proprietors of the great wineries, or *bodegas*, who create blended wines. These are then marketed under brand names associated with individual bodegas.

Most of the bodegas are to be found in Rioja Alta, the stretch of country between the traditional wine centre of Haro and the provincial capital of Logrono 40 kilometres down river. The grapes grown in this region for the production of red wine are the Tempranillo, the Graciano, the Mazuelo and the Garnacho. No wine made from one type alone would be satisfactory, so the Riojas are the result of skilful blending, with Temparanillo being the dominant grape. Most red Riojas are given a minimum of two years in oak casks. Reserva or Gran Reserva wines from good vintages are set aside for longer ageing, up to 8 years in the cask. They will then spend an equally long period in the bottle before being ready to drink.

White wines are made in more limited quantities in Rioja from the Malvasia and Viura grapes. Once made by the traditional oak-ageing process, most white Riojas are now made in a light, dry style for drinking young, and spend little or no time in wood.

Panades is a wine region on the north-east coast not far from Barcelona. The wines of Torres of Villafranca have become available outside Spain, and the wine which has brought most prestige is the 1970 Gran Coronas Black Label. White wines are also produced which are fresh and dry by Spanish standards — their Vina Sol is good value.

Spanish wines

Panades is also the centre of production of Spanish sparkling wine.

Still in the North of Spain, but well to the West in the upper valley of the river Douro, is the estate which produces one of Spain's most remarkable and expensive red wines. It is called Vega Sicilia but is almost unobtainable outside Spain.

Other northern Spanish wines of quality are the reds from Navarre and both reds and whites from Galicia in the north-west.

Across the great plateau of central Spain to the wine-growing areas of the south, La Mancha and Valdepeñas, and regions to the east as far as Valencia and the Levante, produce more wine than any other part of Spain. A good deal of it is exported.

In the far south can be found wine from the small region of Montilla-Moriles in Andalucia. Wines sold under the name of Montilla are never fortified but the method of production is quite similar to that of making a sherry (see page 105).

Boeuf St Jean

The full-fat soft cheese in the filling adds a rich creaminess to the succulence of the meat in this rather unusual recipe. A full-bodied red Rioja is a suitable wine to accompany this special dish.

1½ hours

Serves 6
whole-seed mustard (moutarde de meaux)
2 rump steaks, one just over 700 g /1½ lb and one just under
freshly ground black pepper
6 thick bacon slices, rinded
25 ml /5 tsp vegetable oil
60 ml /4 tbls red wine
1 onion, finely chopped
For the filling
175 g /6 oz full-fat soft cheese, flavoured with garlic and herbs
75 g /3 oz full-fat soft cheese
5 ml /1 tsp dried tarragon
1 onion, finely chopped
1 egg, beaten
45 ml /3 tbls dried breadcrumbs
salt and freshly ground black pepper
For the garnish
1 ham slice, cut into strips
stuffed olives, sliced
18 large mushroom caps, sautéed
2 tomatoes, skinned and chopped
parsley sprigs, to garnish

1 Heat the oven to 190C /375F /gas 5. Thoroughly mix together all the filling ingredients. Trim the steaks and season them with black pepper.
2 Spread a thin layer of mustard on one side of each steak and cover the larger piece with half the bacon. Spread the filling over the bacon layer and cover the filling with the remaining bacon.
3 Place the smaller piece of steak, mustard side down, on the bacon and tie securely at 25 mm /1 in intervals along the length, then tie longitudinally. Heat the oil in a frying-pan and quickly brown the meat on both sides to seal in the juices.
4 Place a piece of foil, large enough to enclose the meat, on a baking sheet. Place the meat on the foil and fold up the sides to make a bowl shape.
5 Pour the wine into the frying-pan and stir. Pour the wine over the meat. Sprinkle on the onion.
6 Fold over the foil to make a parcel. Cook in the centre of the oven for about 1 hour until the juices nearly run clear when a skewer is inserted in the centre. Open the foil and continue to cook for 15 minutes.
7 Remove the meat from the oven and let it stand for 2–3 minutes. Place on a serving dish; remove the string. Pour over the juices.
8 Arrange the ham strips in a criss-cross pattern on the meat and dot with sliced olives. Fill the mushroom tops with chopped tomatoes and arrange them around the meat. Garnish with parsley sprigs.

PORTUGUESE WINES

The abundant vineyards of Portugal, which cover much of the country's finest agricultural landscape, produce a variety of wines to suit every palate — from Vinho Verde to the world famous Mateus Rosé.

Portugal has been producing very good wines for many centuries — Louis XIV of France regularly used to serve the Moscatel de Setubal at his state banquets.

Vinho Verde comes from the Minho, the largest of all the country's wine regions, which extends from the northern frontier with Spain and spreads out beyond Oporto. The name literally means 'green wine' — it does not refer to the colour, which is usually almost platinum blonde, but indicates its freshness. Nobody ever drinks a 'mature' Vinho Verde.

Vinho Verde is grown in an area where the vines climb along trellises, on pergolas and up the branches of trees. It must be one of the few places in the wine world where grape pickers can be seen climbing trees to reach the grapes. It is widely exported and if you prefer very dry wines, the Verdes which should appeal are those of 'classic' style. These are usually drunk with rich and spicy food. One of these is the delicious fruity Gatao; others to note are the dry Casalinho and the deeper golden Alvarinho, which comes from the extreme north of the Minho. Look, too, for the more delicate, fruity Verdegar and the not so dry Ribalonga. Aveleda is another name to remember — this is medium dry, and very light on the palate.

While choosing a red wine from Portuguese wine lists, tourists are often baffled to find 'Vinho Verde Tinto' listed — how can green wine be red, they may well ask! In fact it is a glorious light crimson, slightly sparkling like the white, with an astringency which comes as a shock at the first sip! It goes very well with highly spiced meat dishes or even curry.

No contrast could be greater than that between Vinho Verde and the glowing rich reds for which the mountainous region of the Dão in the north has become famous. The vines, which also produce good white grapes, flourish in rocky, granite-studded soil and produce wines of character.

Others to note are Terras Altas — the red is deep ruby and rather earthy, while the white is silky, golden and dry; Dão Ribalonga red is softer and lighter in colour; and Cavas Velhas red is subtle and long maturing. The Cavas Velhas white is dry, greeny gold and rather 'steely'. The 'steely' quality of the whites makes them particularly suitable to serve with all kinds of fish, while the reds go best with roast meat. Like the Vinho Verde, Dão is one of the larger demarcated regions in Portugal.

Although the Douro region in the north is best known as the home of port, its vineyards in the mountains and the foothills produce good, generally full-bodied, red wines, too. It is also the home of the famous, medium-dry, slightly sparkling pink wine, Mateus Rosé.

Another famous medium-sweet rosé is Lancers. This is made by the venerable house of Fonseca, who are also producers of the rich and luscious golden Moscatel de Setubal. This wine's fame goes back many centuries. It is made in an unusual way — after the grapes are picked, they are pressed very quickly and the fermentation is halted by the addition of brandy. Some of the fresh grape skins are added to the must and are left in until the spring following the vintage, which intensifies the perfume.

Bucelas is another notable wine of Portugal. This comes from the area of that name, situated about 30 kilometres north of Lisbon. Sometimes spelt 'Busellas' on antique, English silver wine labels, this used to be called 'Lisbon Hock' and was a favourite of the Duke of Wellington when he fought in the Peninsula Wars. In those days it was much sweeter; now it is a golden, dry wine with a fruity bouquet and a hint of honey.

Sardines in white wine

Use this recipe to cook red mullet as well as sardines. Serve a dry white wine, such as a white Dão or a Bucelas.

 1¼ hours

Serves 4
4 medium-sized potatoes
2 medium-sized onions
105 ml /7 tbls olive oil
salt
freshly ground black pepper
freshly grated nutmeg
8 fresh sardines, gutted
15 ml /1 tbls tomato purée
125 ml /5 fl oz white wine
5 ml /1 tsp dried thyme
For the garnish
black olives
lemon twists

1 Heat the oven to 180C /375F /gas 4. Slice the potatoes and onions on a mandolin or very finely with a sharp knife.
2 Put 45 ml /3 tbls of the olive oil in a casserole dish large enough to hold the fish in one layer. Swirl the oil around so the bottom of the dish is thoroughly coated. Place the potatoes in a thin layer at the bottom of the dish and cover them with the onions. Season with salt, freshly ground black pepper and nutmeg. Pour 30 ml /2 tbls of oil over the vegetables and bake for 40 minutes.
3 Rinse the sardines carefully under cold water and pat them dry. Place the sardines neatly in one layer on top of the cooked potatoes and onions. Set to one side.
4 Mix the tomato purée with the white wine and pour it over the fish. Season with salt and freshly ground black pepper, sprinkle the thyme and 30 ml /2 tbls oil over the fish and bake for 15 minutes, basting if the ingredients become too dry.
5 Garnish with the olives and lemon twists, then serve immediately.

Sardines in white wine

EASTERN EUROPEAN WINES

Wines from the Eastern European countries are overshadowed by those from France and Germany but many excellent red and white table wines are produced in these areas as well as some world-famous specialities.

HUNGARIAN

Hungary is a major wine-producing country, and the Hungarians have known how to make good wine for thousands of years. Many of the old cellars are still there, as is the tradition, passed from father to son, of wine making.

Monimpex, the state export monopoly, keeps some very fine wines for use in the country. These would be well worth searching out during a visit.

White table wines
The Hungarian white wine known best outside Hungary is probably the Riesling, made from the Olasz or Italian Riesling grape. This grape is widely grown, especially in the Great Plain of central Hungary, and produces a pleasant, fragrant, medium-dry wine. A particularly good example is made around the town of Pecs which is in the southwest of the country.

More interesting wines, however, are made from native grape varieties, such as the Furmint, Harslevelu and Keknyelu. These names may be difficult to pronounce but they are worth trying to remember, since many of the wines are identified by the grape types. The wines produced from these native grapes tend to be full-flavoured, aromatic and spicy — the ideal accompaniments for the traditional foods of the country.

Good-quality white wines are produced in the regions of Somlo and Mor and especially around Lake Balaton in western Hungary. On the north side of the lake, a range of hills slopes gently down to the water. Villages and towns on these favoured south-facing slopes have been making wine for hundreds of years. The town of Badacsony has the best reputation, producing fragrant, golden wines of varying sweetness from the Olasz Riesling, Rizlingszilvani (Müller-Thurgau), Keknyelu, Zoldszilvani (Sylvaner) and Szurkebarat (Pinot Gris).

Tokay Aszu
The Hungarians prize above all the sweet white wines. These are served with dessert, or on their own, for they are a delicious drink in their own right. The supreme example of this type of wine is Tokay Aszu.

Tokay is a little town in north-east Hungary on the Bodrog river. The slopes of the nearby hills, with their volcanic soils and favourable exposure to the sun, are ideal sites for vine cultivation. Summers are hot, autumns long, and, in particular, the mists from the nearby river encourage the development on the grapes of a fungus known as the 'noble rot' (*Botrytis cinerea*) which penetrates the skin of the grape, shrivelling it and concentrating the natural sugars. The grapes may not look very attractive, but they produce spectacular results. Similar conditions in France and Germany give us the great dessert wines of Sauternes and the Beerenauslese and Trockenbeerenauslese of the Rhein and Mosel.

The 'noble rot' does not attack the grapes until late in the season and picking is delayed until the end of October, sometimes continuing into December if conditions allow. Grapes which are harvested earlier produce a more conventional white wine, described either by its grape type — usually Furmint or Harslevelu — or, in more general terms, as *Szamorodni* (which means 'as it comes'). Only the wine made from shrivelled grapes is known as Tokay Aszu.

The method of making Tokay Aszu is unique. The grapes are first loaded into tubs where they are allowed to stand while their own weight produces a rich juice known as *Tokay Eszencia*, or essence. This is drawn off from the tubs; it has a very high sugar content and ferments extremely slowly. Today, it is used for blending, but in earlier times it was kept, sometimes for hundreds of years, and was supposed to have miraculous healing powers. The compressed grapes are then added in varying measures to existing one-year-old wine. The measures — 32 litres /7 gallons each — are known as *puttonys* and the quality of the finished wine is assessed by the number of *puttonys* (up to five) which have been used.

This is also an indication of sweetness. Tokay barrels called *Gonci* only hold 35 gallons, so if five *puttonys* are added the wine is entirely Aszu. The Aszu is sweeter than the wines containing less of the shrivelled grape. After a few days this mixture is pressed and allowed to ferment in the usual way. It then matures in oak barrels in the town's ancient rock cellars.

Traditionally, brandy was added to Tokay Aszu to give it added stability; this is now achieved by 'cooking' the wine briefly at a high temperature. This is said to give the wine a slightly caramelized flavour.

Red wine
Hungary does, of course, also produce red wine. Much of this comes from the south of the country where the climate is hottest, but the most famous is made around the town of Eger in the north. Called Egri Bikavér, or Bull's Blood — a name supposedly coined by invading Turks hundreds of years ago — it is a full-bodied rich red. It is made from a blend of Kadarka (Hungary's main red wine grape), Kekfrancos and Medoc Noir (Merlot), sometimes with the additions of Cabernet and Oporto. If allowed to mature and develop, it can be a fine wine.

YUGOSLAVIAN

The wines of Yugoslavia have been known to Europe since the Middle Ages when they were carried there by traders journeying from the Middle East.

White wines
The finest white wines come from Slovenia, the northern province and the best Slovenian wines come mostly from the Drava zone in the north-east, near the borders of Austria and Hungary. Here the beautifully terraced vineyards not only yield excellent grapes from the Laski Riesling vine, but also from Rhine Riesling (known locally as Renski Riesling), Sylvaner, Traminer, Sauvignon and Pinot Blanc. The finer, mature wines are often molten gold, voluptuous but never cloying.

The most notable of the white wines of Slovenia is the medium dry Lutomer Laski Riesling. The most popular of all dryish table wines exported, it is light, pale golden and fragrant, with a slightly flowery bouquet. One of the finer versions is called Slamnak. It is intensely fruity yet dry, with a pretty greeny-gold colour. While Lutomer Laski Riesling is equally good as an aperitif, party or picnic drink, Slamnak goes well with fish, chicken or veal, especially in rich sauces.

Amongst the other Slovian wines, the very pale-blonde, dry Lutomer Sauvignon makes a delicious aperitif, as well as being most suitable to serve with all kinds of fish. The Rhine Rieslings are more golden, dry and fruity. In total contrast, there is the pale topaz, very flowery medium dry Gewürztraminer. This is made from the grape so famous in Alsace, but is much cheaper.

Some delightful white wines come from the Fruska Gora zone in the Vojvodina region. The platinum-blonde Sauvignon is worth seeking out. They also produce a medium dry Traminer with a distinctive bouquet.

One of Yugoslavia's most distinctive white wines is Zilavka. It has a rather 'leafy' subtle taste, is greeny-gold and dry. This makes it a good aperitif and compatible with smoked fish, poultry or the more delicate cheeses.

Red wines
The delightful Milion Cabernet Sauvignon is a dry, deep garnet-coloured wine made in the fine cellars at Oplenac. The southern region of Kosovo also makes good Cabernet Sauvignon wines. Many vineyards, however, are planted with a native vine called Burgundac Crni — the resultant wine is a deep, rich dry red.

The smallest Yugoslav region, Montenegro, produces a very different red wine called Vranac. This is fresh and crisp and is best served slightly chilled. Nothing could be more different from the long established Dalmation favourite, Dingac, from vineyards on the mountainous Peljesac peninsula. It is a powerful robust red wine which tends towards the sweet side.

ROMANIAN & BULGARIAN

A scientific approach combined with modern production methods have put the wines from Bulgaria and Romania into the fore-front of the wine world.

Romanian wine

Romania has an ancient wine-growing tradition. One light dessert wine, Cotnari, used to be famous world over. It comes from Moldavia in the north-east, but much of this land was ceded to Russia after the Second World War and the wine is now rarely seen. Although Cotnari is fairly obscure, the possibility of earning foreign exchange from wine exports has meant more varied and better Romanian wines are appearing in our shops. The whites are well worth trying, especially the Perla from the Tîrnave region of Transylvania, which you will find labelled *Tarnave*. It is light and slightly sweet wine, with just a hint of the German style, although really quite distinctive — a most pleasant wine for warm summer days and by no means expensive. Other cheaper whites are available but tend to be sweet. Murfatler, near the coast on the plateau of Dobrogea, produces a sweet, pale golden-brown muscat. A powerful red made from the Merlot grape is on sale from the Dealul Mare region. This is a hefty, slightly sweet wine for drinking with roast meat or spicy casseroles. Again, it has more body and character than its price suggests, and should certainly be tried.

Bulgarian wine

Bulgaria, just south of the Danube from Romania, has a very different wine past — and present. Five hundred years of Muslim law, when Bulgaria was dominated by the Turks, has had a large effect. During this period wine was outlawed and production survived only on a small and local scale. Since the Second World War, however, enormous strides have been made. Now the state monopoly, called Vinimpex, enjoys total domination and has brought the benefits of modern technology to bear in a big way.

Of the wines likely to be encountered, Cabernet Sauvignon is best known and often the best in quality. The great Bordeaux grape seems to do well in Bulgaria, producing mellow wine with considerable body. For a really reliable introduction, look out for the Cabernet which comes from the northern Sukhindol region.

Another Bulgarian red, in a more expensive category but with individuality, is Mavrud. It comes from the south and is darker, heavier and richer than the Cabernet. It should be drunk in small quantities with a good meal — the Cabernet is for drinking at any time that wine appeals. Why not try a Bulgarian Cabernet with my Hearty hot-pot (see recipe below)?

Bulgarian whites, although good, are less impressive than the reds. A Pinot Chardonnay using the white Burgundy grape is a worthy example, it is strong and fruity. The Misket is worth a try. It is a lively Muscat and not particularly sweet. A medium-sweet white wine which is very popular is Hemus and a very sweet dessert wine is Tamianka.

Hearty hot-pot

2½ hours

Serves 4
1 kg /2¼ lb middle neck of lamb, chined
30 ml /2 tbls flour
salt
freshly ground black pepper
25 g /1 oz dripping or lard
3–4 lamb's kidneys, thickly sliced
100 g /4 oz mushrooms, wiped and quartered,
 if large
1 large onion, finely sliced
450 ml /15 fl oz beef stock, home-made or
 from a cube
750 g /1½ lb potatoes, sliced

1 Heat the oven to 170C /325F /gas 3 and wipe the chined neck of lamb with absorbent paper. Season the flour with salt and pepper, then coat the meat in the seasoned flour. Reserve the left-over flour.
2 Heat the fat in a large saucepan and fry the neck of lamb, in batches, until lightly browned and sealed. Transfer the meat to a hot-pot or deep casserole. Scatter the kidney and mushrooms over the meat.
3 Fry the sliced onion gently in the fat left in the saucepan for a few minutes, then transfer to the hot-pot with a slotted spoon. Add the remaining seasoned flour to the pan and stir until it is lightly browned. Stir in the stock and bring to the boil. Check the seasoning and simmer for a few minutes, until it is slightly thickened.
4 Cover the meat with overlapping potato slices. Pour the sauce over the potatoes, cover the hot-pot and cook it in the oven for 1½ hours. Uncover the pot and cook for a further 30 minutes to brown the potatoes. Serve from the pot.

Hearty hot-pot

ENGLISH WINES

For many people England seems too far north, too cool and too wet to produce wine. There are now over 300 commercial vineyards, producing a distinctive type of wine, to prove these opinions wrong.

Wine was introduced to England by the Romans who established a small number of vineyards. In the Middle Ages the vine became more widespread, especially at monasteries. The decline of English wine production began in the 12th century, when the English crown came into possession of large parts of south-west France, including Bordeaux, and wine began to appear in quantity across the Channel. The dissolution of the monasteries by Henry VIII brought to an end large scale production, although some small vineyards still continued.

After the Second World War, a number of experimental vineyards sprang up. The first was in Hampshire in 1951, and then there was a period of great expansion in the 1970's, powered by a growing enthusiasm and encouraged by the hot summers of 1975 and 1976.

With a few exceptions, English wines are white. The most common style is like light German wine, although English wine is usually more like a light Alsace wine. There is often a flowery bouquet with a fresh, lively flavour, but rarely much body. The difficulties experienced in producing these wines mean that they are relatively expensive (English growers are also taxed more heavily than Continental producers). Whatever you buy, choose carefully and make the distinction between English and British wine. The latter is made from imported grape juice and should be avoided. Some English vineyards make the error of marketing British wine as well as their home-grown product. English wines are not widely marketed, as the overall level of production is not large.

The vineyards are mostly in the south of England, but are widely scattered. They are, however, not restricted to the south; look for a label marked Graiselound from a village near Doncaster. This is the most northerly vineyard in England.

Watch, also, for Schonburger from Wootton vines in Somerset. This won a medal for the best English wine, 1981 vintage. From Kent try wines from Lamberhurst Priory, the biggest wine producer in the country. Generally, the grapes they use, as do a lot of English vineyards, are Müller-Thurgau but they grow a wide range of varieties, including some experimental types. Müller-Thurgau grapes do well on less than perfect sites in Germany and with a protected site flourish in English vineyards. Other Kentish wines of particular note are Biddenden Müller-Thurgau (Biddenden Ortega was an English medal-winner in 1983) and Penshurst, which is a blend of Müller-Thurgau, Seyval and other varieties.

A major Gloucestershire producer is Three Choirs. They use the Müller-Thurgau grape but also the Reichensteiner grape. Westbury in Berkshire is an exceptionally successful producer. Try their Reichensteiner and their red wine made from Pinot Noir.

East Anglia has a number of successful vineyards. The main ones are at Bruisyard St Peter in Suffolk and Magdalen in Norfolk. Both rely heavily on Müller-Thurgau. Elmham Park in Norfolk makes an attractive dry white.

The firm of Carr Taylor from Westfield, Sussex, has the second largest vineyard in the country and produces Guttenborner Medium Dry, a reliable, pleasantly perfumed German-style wine. They have just made an English 'first'. A sparkling wine is now on the market, produced in this vineyard. It has been made by the *méthode champenoise*, although EEC regulations restrict it from being called champagne.

Do make a point of trying a bottle of English wine if you have never tasted it before — a treat awaits you!

Winter fruit compote

A light but fruity, well chilled, English wine with a flowery bouquet makes a perfect accompaniment for this dessert.

soaking the fruit overnight, then 25 minutes, plus chilling

Serves 4–6
250 g /8 oz prunes, stoned
600 ml /1 pt hot, strong tea
250 g /8 oz dried apricots
45–60 ml /3–4 tbls sugar
30 ml /2 tbls port or dry sherry
To garnish
½ orange, thinly sliced
seedless white grapes
30 ml /2 tbls flaked almonds, toasted

1 Place the prunes in a bowl and pour the tea over them. Place the apricots in a separate bowl and cover them with 425 ml /15 fl oz hot water. Cover and leave them to soak for 8 hours or overnight.
2 Pour the prunes and their soaking liquid into a saucepan. Add sugar to taste. Set the pan over a medium heat and simmer for 10 minutes or until the prunes are tender and the syrup has thickened slightly. At the same time, turn the apricots and their soaking liquid into another saucepan and simmer for 15–20 minutes until tender.
3 Using a slotted spoon, transfer the prunes and apricots to a serving bowl. Sprinkle the port or dry sherry over the fruit, then spoon over a little of the cooking liquids. Cover and leave until cold, then chill in the refrigerator for at least 1 hour or until required.
4 Just before serving, cut the orange slices in half and use them to decorate the inside of the bowl. Sprinkle the white grapes on the apricots and prunes and then scatter the toasted, flaked almonds over the top.

Winter fruit compote

FORTIFIED WINES

Fortified wines are wines that have been made stronger by the addition of extra alcohol. They have a more concentrated flavour than ordinary table wines and are usually drunk in smaller quantities before or after a meal.

In Portugal and Spain these wines are called *vinhos generosos* — noble wines. Sip them and savour their warmth and flavour.

Sherry

The name 'sherry' is a corruption of Jerez, (pronounced Hereth), the town in south-western Spain which is the centre of sherry production. Sherry has been drunk for centuries, though originally in Britain it was grouped with other fortified wines from the Mediterranean area under the general name of 'sack'.

Not only is sherry an ideal aperitif, but it can also be drunk with, or added to, soup, and the sweeter varieties are a good alternative to port or liqueurs.

Grades of sherry

Descriptions of sherry (see picture below), as dry, medium or sweet are widely, if vaguely, used. The following definitions are broadly accurate:
1 Fino — dry, or very dry, and pale.
2 Amontillado — medium dry, marginally darker and stronger than fino.
3 Manzanilla — a distinctive, very dry fino from the bodegas of Sanlucar de Barremeda on the coast, which imparts a magically delicate, salty tang to this special sherry.
4 Oloroso — though really a dry sherry, outside Spain this denotes a sweetish one.
5 Amoroso — extra sweet; a rather old-fashioned description for what is also called 'brown sherry'.
6 Cream — a sweet dessert sherry; formerly dark, but today it also comes excellently in pale style.
Vino de pasto — a term very rarely used in Spain for sherry, it is a fairly dry fino type below top quality but can be good value.

It is the Spanish shippers of Jerez, with famous names such as Domecq and Gonzalez Byass, who control the nature and quality of the sherry which reaches the shops. In their wineries, known as *bodegas*, are many vats of wine of different types and ages and it is the blending of these, with the addition of varying amounts of pure alcohol and sweetenings, which produces the many varieties of sherry which are available.

Other countries such as South Africa and Cyprus now produce sherry-style wines, but real sherry can only come from Spain. Spanish sherry is labelled simply 'sherry', while the rest of the world have to label their bottles with the country of origin, for example 'Cyprus sherry'. Prices vary quite considerably, but bearing in mind the high alcohol content, compared with wine, a good bottle can generally be bought at a moderate price.

Port

Although there is a white port, which is a relatively dry drink made from white grapes, most port is a strong, sweet, deep-red wine.

The chief distinction in port is between vintage and non-vintage. The shippers who control the production of port only declare a vintage in an outstanding year. This vintage wine is then aged in wood for two years and then bottled. As a result of this, most of the maturing process takes place in the bottle, during which time a heavy deposit or 'crust' develops which must be removed by decanting before it is drunk. The combination of brandy and wine takes a long time to blend satisfactorily, so a vintage port is not ready to drink for at least 15 years; it is consequently very expensive.

The maturing process can be speeded up if the wine is left in the barrel and not bottled until it is considered drinkable. Non-vintage port is treated in this way and is sold either as 'ruby' if it is still fairly young or 'tawny' if it is older. Since any deposit thrown by the wine is left in the barrel, no decanting is necessary and the wine is also a lot cheaper.

Madeira

The fortified wine Madeira comes only from the island of Madeira. It has an interesting and very distinctive flavour, rather like caramel, which results from the technique of 'baking' the wine at a high temperature before the end of fermentation. The amount of grape sugar still present at this stage determines whether the finished wine will be dry or sweet. Many people think of Madeira as only a sweet wine, and this is true of the varieties called Malmsey and Bual, but there are dry Madeiras known as Verdelho and Sercial which can be drunk as aperitifs.

Marsala

Marsala is based on the strong white wine of western Sicily, which is fortified with grape brandy and then blended with unfermented grape juice. The best variety is called Marsala Vergine and it has a pleasantly nutty flavour and stands comparison with a good medium sherry. Also, for careful savouring are the Marsala Soleras which are dry with a tremendous depth of flavour.

Marsala is excellent served as an unusual aperitif, it can be added to soups and is used in the delicious Sicilian dessert, Zabaione — in a bowl over simmering water, combine 4 egg yolks with 50 g /2 oz sugar and 90 ml / 6 tbls Marsala. Whisk until it is thick and fluffy and serve immediately.

Vermouth

This term covers a multitude of wine-based drinks both red and white, to which sugar, alcohol and various flavourings have been added. Most of the better-known vermouths are from France or Italy; they may be dry like Noilly-Prat or sweet like Dubonnet, bland like Cinzano or bitter like Campari. They can be drunk straight, with soda or mixed with spirits to make a cocktail. Why not devise your own recipes?

1   2   3   4   5   6

Poached sole fillets in vermouth

 35 minutes

Serves 4
8 fillets of sole, skinned
salt and freshly ground black pepper
50 g /2 oz butter, melted, plus extra for
  greasing
120 ml /8 tbls dry vermouth
5–10 ml /1–2 tsp tomato purée
90–120 ml /6–8 tbls thick cream
1 bunch of watercress, to garnish

1 Season the sole fillets with salt and freshly ground black pepper, then roll them up from the wide end and fasten with wooden cocktail sticks. Brush melted butter inside a shallow flameproof dish or frying pan and arrange the fillets in it.
2 In a bowl, blend together 50 g /2 oz butter, the vermouth and the tomato purée and pour the mixture over the rolled fillets. Cut a piece of greaseproof paper the same size as the cooking pan and cut a small hole in the centre. Grease the paper with the rest of the melted butter and lay it, buttered side down, over the fish.
3 Stand the pan over a medium heat and bring it to the boil, then reduce the heat, cover the pan and poach very gently for 10–12 minutes, until the fish is just cooked.
4 Remove the cooked sole from the dish with a fish slice, discard the cocktail sticks and arrange the rolled fillets on a heated serving dish. Keep them warm.
5 Add the thick cream to the sauce in the pan and, without boiling, heat it through, stirring, until the sauce has thickened. Strain the sauce, then spoon it over the fish rolls. Garnish with 'bouquets' of watercress.

Soy-glazed fillet of beef

 marinating the meat,
then ½–¾ hour roasting

Serves 6
1.1–1.4 kg /2½–3 lb fillet of beef, stripped of
  all fat
freshly ground black pepper
For the soy marinade
75 ml /3 fl oz soy sauce
45 ml /3 tbls olive oil
2 garlic cloves, finely chopped
45 ml /3 tbls dry sherry
For the garnish
cartwheel lemon slices (see note)
spring onion tassles (see note)
flat-leaved parsley

1 Season the fillet all over with generous amounts of freshly ground black pepper.
2 Combine the ingredients for the marinade in an oval or rectangular baking dish large enough to hold the fillet. Tie the fillet neatly with string and place it in the marinade; spoon the marinade all over the

Soy-glazed fillet of beef

meat then leave the fillet to marinate for at least 4 hours. Turn the meat several times during the marinating period, carefully spooning over the marinade to ensure that the fillet is impregnated with its flavours.
3 If using the refrigerator to marinate, 2 hours before roasting, remove the fillet to allow it to come up to room temperature. Heat the oven to 220C /425F /gas 7. Place the fillet on a rack in a roasting pan. Spoon over some of the marinade and roast, occasionally basting with the marinade, for 18–22 minutes per kg /10–12 minutes per lb for rare and 30 minutes per kg /14–16 minutes per lb for medium rare.
4 To serve, remove the string and place the fillet on a warmed serving dish. Garnish with cartwheel lemon slices, spring onion tassles and flat-leaved parsley.

● To make cartwheel lemon slices, use a cannelle knife and groove the lemon lengthways, at intervals, before slicing.
● To make spring onion tassels, cut the green part of the onion into strips towards the base; leave the base intact. Soak in chilled water for an hour.

Chicken with port

 2½ hours

Serves 4
1.4 kg /3 lb oven-ready chicken
salt
freshly ground black pepper
65 g /2½ oz softened butter
15 ml /1 tbls chopped mixed herbs
2.5 ml /½ tsp lemon juice
500 g /1 lb button mushrooms, cleaned and
  halved
10 ml /2 tsp cornflour
275 ml /10 fl oz thick cream
1 shallot, finely chopped
75 ml /3 fl oz port
50 ml /2 fl oz brandy

1 Heat the oven to 180C /350F /gas 4. Rub the chicken with salt and pepper. Blend 40 g / 1½ oz butter with the herbs and spread this over the chicken. Roast the chicken for 1¼–1½ hours, basting frequently.
2 Meanwhile, put 50 ml /2 fl oz water in a saucepan. Bring to the boil, then add 15 g / ½ oz butter, lemon juice and salt to taste.

Add the mushrooms. Cover with a tightly-fitting lid and cook gently for 10 minutes.

3   Pour the cooking liquid from the saucepan and reserve. Blend the cornflour with 15 ml /1 tbls of the cream, then stir this cornflour mixture and the rest of the cream into the mushrooms. Simmer for 2 minutes, then set it aside.

4   Transfer the cooked chicken to a wooden board and pour away most of the fat from the roasting tin. Divide the chicken into serving portions and set aside.

5   Add the shallot to the fat remaining in the pan and cook it over a gentle heat for 5 minutes. Add the port and reserved cooking liquid and boil rapidly, until it is reduced to about 75 ml /3 fl oz.

6   Add the mushroom mixture to the pan and simmer for 3 minutes, until the liquid is slightly thickened. Season to taste.

7   Rub the inside of a flameproof casserole with the remaining butter and arrange the chicken pieces in the casserole. Place over a moderate heat and when the chicken begins to sizzle, pour the brandy over it. Ignite and slowly shake the casserole until the flames have subsided. Next, pour in the mushroom mixture, cover and heat it through without boiling for 5 minutes. Serve immediately.

Braised gammon with Madeira sauce

 2½–3 hours

Serves 6–9

1.1–1.5 kg /2½–3 lb smoked corner gammon
25 g /1 oz butter
15 ml /1 tbls oil
1 large onion, sliced
2 large carrots, sliced
3 celery sticks, sliced
1 bay leaf
1 sprig of thyme
freshly ground black pepper
50 g /2 oz mushrooms
10 ml /2 tsp tomato purée
275 ml /10 fl oz beef stock, home-made or
  from a cube
275 ml /10 fl oz Madeira
25 g /1 oz butter blended with 20 g /¾ oz flour

1   Weigh the joint and calculate the cooking time, allowing 77 minutes per kg /35 minutes per lb, plus 35 minutes.

2   Put the joint in a large saucepan, cover it with cold water, bring it slowly to the boil and then drain. Meanwhile, heat the oven to 180C /350F /gas 4.

3   In a deep flameproof casserole, heat the butter and oil and gently fry the onion, carrot, celery, bay leaf and thyme, stirring occasionally, until lightly browned.

4   Season with pepper, and add the mushrooms, the tomato purée dissolved in the stock, and two-thirds of the Madeira. Set the gammon joint, rind uppermost, on top, and bring to simmering point.

5   Cover the casserole, transfer to the centre of the oven and cook for the calculated time.

6   Lift out the gammon and peel off the rind. Carve and arrange the slices on a heated serving dish. Keep them warm.

7   Strain the cooking liquid into a saucepan, pressing the vegetables to extract their juices. Add enough Madeira to flavour the sauce, and bring it to simmering point.

8   Over a low heat, whisk in the blended butter and flour, a tiny piece at a time, and stir until the sauce is lightly thickened and glossy. Adjust the seasoning.

9   Spoon some of the sauce over the meat, and serve the rest in a sauce-boat.

Chicken with pork

HOME-MADE WINES

Delicious wines have been made at home for centuries, and from a variety of ingredients other than grapes. Here, gooseberries, oranges, blackberries and elderberries are used to make unusual and potent wines.

Today's home wine-makers can use sophisticated techniques and equipment to make wine. The basic principle is the same as for commercial wine — the fermentation of a sugar-rich, flavoured liquid. The sugar in the fruit, vegetable or flowers is converted into an alcohol and carbon dioxide, leaving an alcoholic, flavoured liquid from which the solids must be strained.

Although the initial outlay on equipment may be high, the equipment should last for many years, and you will be producing wine at a fraction of the retail price, and deriving great fun from making it at home.

Always keep a complete record of each wine made, so that excellent results may be repeated.

What you need:
● polythene bucket 10–12.5 L /2–3 gal capacity, made from non-toxic polythene;
● straining bag, made from nylon, cotton or calico. Or you can use a nylon sieve and muslin (for straining the pulp);
● funnels, 1 large and 1 small;
● spoon, with a long handle, not metal;
● large 5 L /1 gal glass jars (demi-johns);
● fermentation locks and bungs, to prevent infection of the wine and to indicate when the fermentation has stopped;
● hydrometer and jar, used to measure specific gravity, which helps you control the sweetness and alcohol content of the wine;
● plastic tubing (1 m /3 ft), and glass U-bend, for transferring the wine without the sediment;
● Campden tablets or sodium metabisulphate, used as sterilizing agents;
● wine bottles, corks, polythene stoppers and labels, to finish;
● pectin enzyme (Pectolase), to stop haze;
● nutrients in tablet or granule form — preferably use Tronozymol;
● vitamin B_1 tablets (3 mg): yeast energizers;
● tannin — an aid to clearing and maturation — is necessary for the wine not to be insipid, and it is available in liquid or powdered form;
● yeast — dried yeast but not fresh baker's yeast — to make a yeast starter;
● clearing agents — Bentonite or any other wine finings, ie wine fining gel;
● litmus test papers, to test the acidity;
● citric, malic and tartaric acids, to adjust the acidity;
● record cards or a notebook.

Sterilization
It is essential for all equipment to be sterilized before use, to prevent unwanted bacterial growth. Make a stock solution from 20 g /¾ oz crystals of sodium metabisulphate dissolved in 750 ml /1¼ pt warm water. Take 50 ml /2 fl oz and add a pinch of citric acid. Place this in a wine bottle and top it up with cold water. Use until the smell goes, then replace it from the stock solution. Or, more simply, dissolve 6 Campden tablets in 600 ml /1 pt water. Swirl either of these solutions around in the demi-johns or other equipment to sterilize them. Afterwards store the liquid for future use, tightly covered.

Yeast starter
An active starter is needed to get fermentation going. Prepare this 24 hours before you begin making the wine. Put 15 ml /1 tbls white sugar and one vitamin B_1 tablet into a sterilized bottle. Using a sterilized funnel, add the juice of one orange and top up to just below the shoulder with cooled, boiled water. This should be no more than blood heat (37C /98F). Mix well, then add 5 ml /1 tsp yeast. Plug the bottle with cotton wool and leave it to stand where there is a temperature of 21C /70F. The yeast should be active — bubbly and creamy — within 24 hours.

The must
Sterilize a 10 L /2 gal bucket and all equipment to be used. Crush the fresh fruit, or cut and simmer or boil the vegetables, then strain to extract their juices. Next, add sugar according to the recipe and level of sweetness required. Make up to the required volume with cooled, boiled water. This mixture of fruit juice and water is called the 'must', which is left to ferment.

The specific gravity registered on the hydrometer will determine if more sugar is required. The starting gravity should be about 1.900. As fermentation proceeds, it will fall and at 0.900–0.996 indicates 12 per cent alcohol in the liquid, which is equivalent to that of commercial wine. This is called 'fermenting out to dryness'.

Next, test for acid balance with litmus paper; follow the manufacturer's instructions for this test. A pH figure of 3.2 is desirable for most wines. If it is above, add acids to it. Add the nutrient and tannin, which also helps to mature the wine. To clear the wine, add the Pectolase and Bentonite. Put in the yeast starter and cover the bucket with a lid or piece of cloth secured with string.

Stir the must twice daily. After 2–4 days, depending on the recipe, strain off the wine through a straining bag into the demi-john. When the level of the liquid is just below the shoulder of the jar, fit the fermentation lock and put a few drops of sterilizing solution in the cup of the lock. Place the demi-john in a dark place, one where you can maintain an even temperature of 15–21C /60–70F. Pour any surplus wine into a sterilized bottle, plug it with cotton wool and secure a small plastic bag over the top with an elastic band. (Use this to top up the demi-john after racking.)

Sweetness
When the bubbling subsides, fermentation has finished. For dry wine this will take 3–4 weeks; for a sweet wine allow a little longer.

If a sweet wine is required, add more sugar than stated in the recipe. Make the additions when the specific gravity is down to 1.010 at a rate of 150 ml /5 fl oz at a time, in syrup form, until fermentation stops. This will take about 3–4 weeks.

To make sugar syrup: use 500 g /1 lb sugar for each 300 ml /10 fl oz water. Put the sugar in a saucepan with the water, bring to the boil, and simmer until the liquid is clear. Do not boil the liquid longer than is necessary as it can quickly caramelize the sugar. This will affect the colour and flavour of the wine. Allow it to cool. Add the syrup to the wine 150 ml /5 fl oz at a time. If you are adding extra sugar to make a sweet wine, balance each addition with 1.5 ml /¼ tsp citric acid or tartaric acid according to the individual recipe.

To rack off
This results in clear, stable wine and it involves siphoning off the wine from the lees (sediment) of yeast and solids. Start when the wine stops fermenting — that is, when bubbling finishes.

First sterilize the plastic tubing, glass U-bend and the other demi-john. Place the full demi-john on a table with the empty one on the floor. Attach a U-bend to the plastic tubing and slowly lower the glass of the U-bend into the wine. Suck on the tube until the wine flows through. Close the end with your finger while you place the tubing into the empty demi-john. Take care not to tilt the full demi-john as this will only disturb the sediment.

If necessary, to fill the demi-john, top up with wine from the reserved bottle. If the wine level still does not reach the shoulder, add cooled, boiled water. Add 1 crushed Campden tablet. Plug the fermentation lock and leave in a cool place, until a sediment of 5–15 mm /¼–½ in deep has formed. This may take 1–3 months according to the type of ingredients used. Rack off again as soon as more sediment has formed.

Rack the wine again, as before, adding one crushed Campden tablet. Leave for 3 months before racking again. The wine should now be clear and ready for drinking, but it will improve if it can be left for a further 3–6 months.

Bottle the wine and try it! You will get 6 × 75 cl bottles from one demi-john of wine, with half a bottle left over which you can use for sampling.

Do's and don'ts:
● do remember to sterilize all equipment, including a cloth for wiping the table and the outside of bottles, after filling;
● do decide on sweet or dry and the colour before you start;
● do try to continue racking the wine until it is crystal clear;
● don't use enamel, copper, brass, bronze or iron utensils;
● don't store the wine in plastic for a long time;
● don't have more than 15 mm /½ in air space between the cork and the wine;
● don't store half or partially filled bottles.

Elderberry wine

⏱🍶 6 days, then at least 11 months

Makes 5 L /1 gal
For the yeast starter
15 ml /1 tbls white sugar
3 mg vitamin B₁ tablet
juice of 1 orange
5 ml /1 tsp yeast
300 ml /10 fl oz cooled, boiled water
For the must
450 g /1 lb over-ripe bananas, peeled
1.8 kg /4 lb red-stalked elderberries, stalks removed
4 Campden tablets
1.4 kg /3 lb sugar
450 g /1 lb raisins, minced
5 ml /1 tsp Pectolase
5 ml /1 tsp Bentonite
5 ml /1 tsp nutrient (Tronozymol)
½ can grape juice concentrate
extra 100 g /4 oz sugar, if necessary

1 Make the yeast starter by mixing together the ingredients, then leave them for 24 hours (see Introduction). Sterilize all equipment.
2 Boil the bananas in 850 ml /1½ pt water for 20 minutes. Wash the elderberries and place in a bucket to ferment. Strain in the liquid from the bananas, add 1 crushed Campden tablet, cover. Leave for 24 hours.
3 Put 900 g /2 lb sugar in a pan, add 600 ml /1 pt water, stir over a low heat until it has dissolved, and boil until the liquid is clear. Add to the bucket.
4 Add the raisins to the bucket and allow to cool to 21C /70F. Stir in the Pectolase, Bentonite, nutrient, grape juice concentrate and the activated yeast. Make up the bulk to 5 L / 1 gal with cooled, boiled water and cover.
5 Leave the wine to ferment for 2 days only. As elderberries are high in tannin, do not ferment the pulp any longer or the wine will take several years to mature.
6 After 2 days, strain into a demi-john; fit an airlock. When the specific gravity (SG) drops to 1.010, add sugar at the rate of 100 g / 4 oz at a time in syrup form (ie 75 ml /2½ fl oz — see Introduction). Repeat when SG drops to 1.010 again, until the fermentation ceases. This takes up the reserve 450 g /1 lb sugar. Ferment to dryness (SG 0.900–0.996). If a sweet wine is required, add sugar to bring the SG up to 1.015 after fermentation has ceased. Rack off.
7 Crush a Campden tablet and add it to the wine. Leave it for 2 months.
8 Rack off the wine, adding a third Campden tablet. Leave a further 3 months and then rack off the wine as before, adding a Campden tablet.
9 Decant the wine into bottles (sampling if you wish). Store the wine for 6 months; it will continue to improve for up to 2 years.

Dry gooseberry and grape wine

⏱🍶 5 days, then at least 9 months

Equipment for wine-making

Makes 5 L /1 gal
For the yeast starter
15 ml /1 tbls white sugar
3 mg vitamin B₁ tablet
juice of 1 orange
5 ml /1 tsp yeast
300 ml /10 fl oz cooled, boiled water
For the must
900 g /2 lb unripe, green gooseberries
225 g /8 oz raisins
4 Campden tablets
900 g /2 lb sugar
900 g /2 lb ripe green grapes
16 g /⅔ oz malic acid
5 ml /1 tsp nutrient (Tronozymol)
2.5 ml /½ tsp tannin
5 ml /1 tsp Bentonite
5 ml /1 tsp Pectolase

1 Make the yeast starter by mixing together the ingredients, and leave them for 24 hours (see Introduction). Sterilize all equipment.
2 Cut the gooseberries in half. Now wash and mince the raisins and place both fruits in the plastic bucket, pouring on 3.4 L /6 pt hot, boiled water. Add 1 crushed Campden tablet, cover the bucket with a clean cloth, secure it with string and leave for 24 hours.
3 Put the sugar in a saucepan, add 600 ml / 1 pt water. Stir over a low heat to dissolve and bring to the boil, then cool the syrup.
4 For the must, extract the juice from the grapes by squeezing or using a juice extractor. Add the juice to the bucket, together with the malic acid, nutrient, tannin and Bentonite. Add the sugar syrup in batches.
5 When the must has cooled to below 21C / 70F, add the Pectolase and the activated yeast. Keep covered. Stir daily for 3 days while the must ferments. Strain off the liquid into a demi-john and fit the airlock.
6 When the bubbling has stopped (after approximately 3–4 weeks), rack off for the first time, and add 1 crushed Campden tablet. Repeat after 3 months or when a sediment has formed, and after a further 3 months, until the wine has cleared.
7 Decant the wine into bottles. Drink the wine now if you wish or lay it down to mature for 3 months, before drinking.

Sweet orange wine

🕐 ⦀ 2 days, plus 9 months, then 9 months maturing

Makes 5 L /1 gal
For the yeast starter
15 ml /1 tbls white sugar
1 vitamin B₁ tablet
juice of 1 orange
5 ml /1 tsp yeast
300 ml /10 fl oz cooled, boiled water
For the must
1.8 kg /4 lb oranges
450 g /1 lb raisins
1.4 kg /3 lb sugar
5 ml /1 tsp nutrient (Tronozymol)
5 ml /1 level tsp tannin
2 Weetabix or Shredded wheat
5 ml /1 tsp Bentonite
3 or 4 Campden tablets
100 g /4 oz additional sugar, in sugar syrup form, if necessary

1 Make the yeast starter by mixing together the ingredients, then leave them for 24 hours (see Introduction). Sterilize all equipment.
2 Wash the oranges, squeeze them and place the juice in the plastic bucket.
3 Heat the oven to 140C /275F /gas 1. Remove the skins from half the oranges used, removing all the white pith. Place the skins

From the left, Dry gooseberry and grape wine (see page 109), Blackberry wine, Sweet orange and Elderberry wine (see page 109)

on a baking sheet in the oven until they are dry and curly. Meanwhile, wash and mince the raisins.
4 Add the orange skins to the bucket with the raisins, sugar, nutrient, tannin, crushed Weetabix or Shredded wheat, Bentonite and the yeast starter. Add cold, boiled water until the volume reaches 5 L /1 gal.
5 Cover the bucket with a cloth, secured with string, and leave the pulp to ferment for 2 days at room temperature (maximum 23C / 75F), stirring twice a day.
6 Strain carefully into a sterilized demi-john and add 1 crushed Campden tablet. Fit the airlock to the demi-john and leave at room temperature for approximately 6–8 weeks for fermentation to complete.
7 When the bubbling stops, rack off the wine and test for sweetness. If the specific gravity is 1.015 on the hydrometer, it will be sweet enough. If lower, add sufficient sugar to bring it back up to 1.015. Top up with cooled, boiled water and add another crushed Campden tablet.
8 Leave until clear, racking again within 4 months and adding a Campden tablet. If a heavy deposit forms at the bottom of the demi-john, rack the wine again.
9 Decant the wine into bottles. Leave it to mature at least 9 months, when the wine will be ready for drinking.

Blackberry wine

🕐 ⦀ 4 days, plus 10 months

Makes 5 L /1 gal
For the yeast starter
15 ml /1 tbls white sugar
3 mg vitamin B₁ tablet
juice of 1 orange
5 ml /1 tsp yeast
300 ml /10 fl oz cooled, boiled water
For the must
1.8 kg /4 lb blackberries
3 or 4 Campden tablets
1.4 kg /3 lb sugar
10 ml /2 tsp tartaric acid
5 ml /1 tsp nutrient (Tronozymol)
5 ml /1 tsp Pectolase
5 ml /1 tsp Bentonite

1 Make the yeast starter by mixing together the ingredients, then leave them for 24 hours (see Introduction). Sterilize all equipment.
2 Wash the berries; discard mouldy ones. Place in the bucket and crush. Add 1 crushed Campden tablet and leave for 24 hours.
3 Add the remaining ingredients (except the Campden tablets) and the yeast starter. Add 3.4 L /6 pt water and stir well. Cover with a cloth, secured with string, and, stirring daily, leave to ferment for 3 days.
4 Strain the liquid into a demi-john and fit an airlock. As the fermentation dies down, top up with cooled, boiled water.
5 When the bubbling stops, after 3–4 weeks, rack off into a clean demi-john. Add 1 crushed Campden tablet and leave for 2 months. Rack off and add 1 Campden tablet. Leave 3 months, then rack again if not clear.
6 Decant into bottles and store it for 3 months before drinking.

Index

111